LEGENDARY LOCALS OF

CABARRUS COUNTY

NORTH CAROLINA

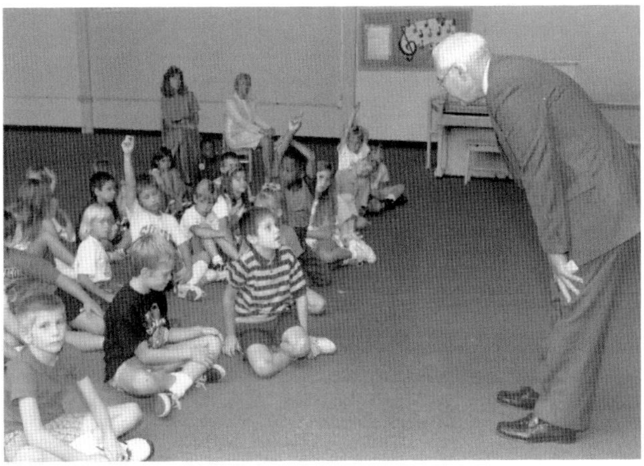

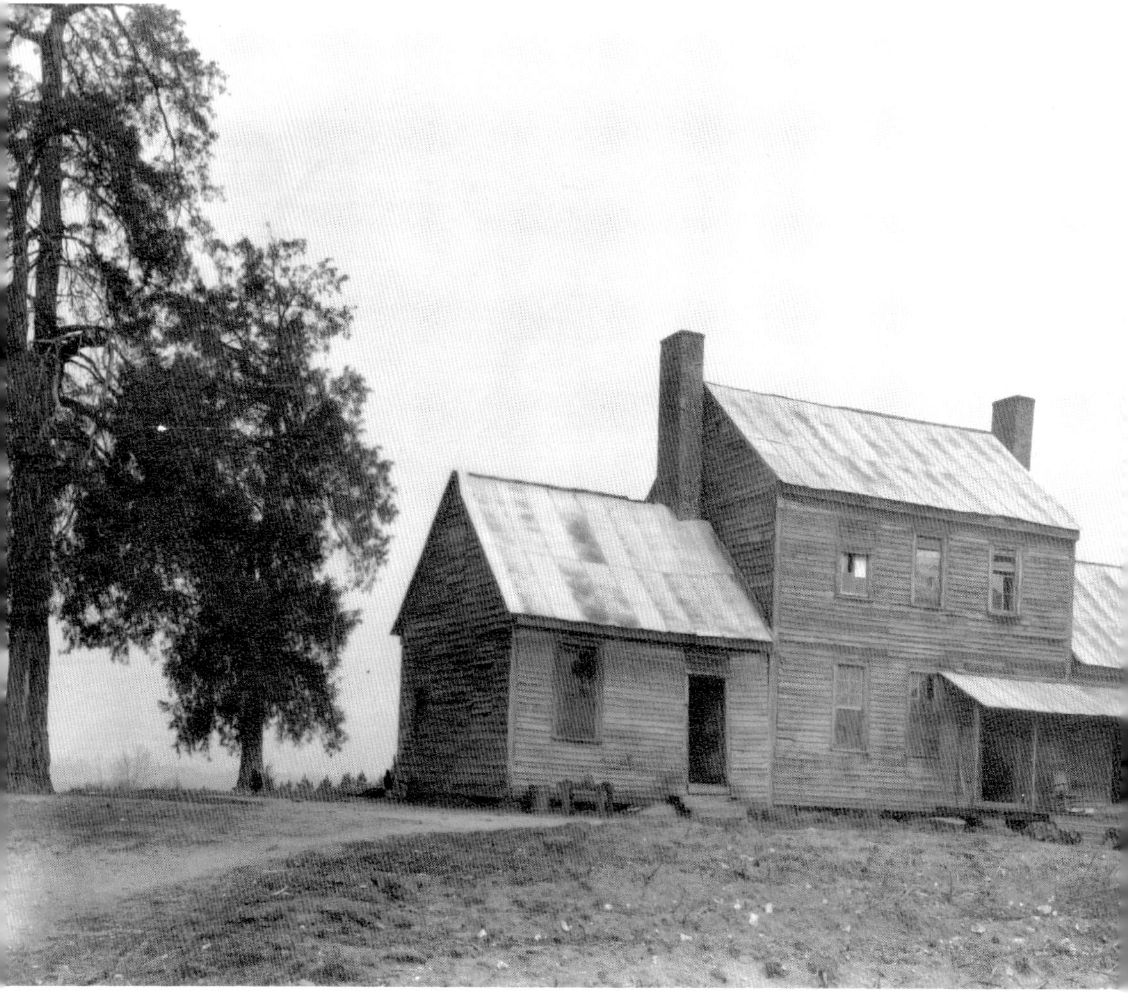

Martin Phifer
The dilapidated dwelling seen here in the 1960s was once a majestic inn on Red Hill, one of a trio of plantations owned by Swiss immigrant Martin Phifer Sr. He was a zealous patriot and prominent North Carolina statesman in the late 1700s. During a 1791 Southern tour, Pres. George Washington stayed at this site by the invitation of his friend, Phifer's son Martin Jr. (Courtesy of Concord Public Library.)

Page 1: Bachman S. Brown Jr.
No citizen's needs—or size—were too small for this caring first mayor of the newly incorporated Kannapolis. Brown (see page 19) practiced law for six decades, doing much pro bono work. An active member of the community, he taught Sunday school for 50 years. (Courtesy of Concord Public Library.)

LEGENDARY LOCALS

OF

CABARRUS COUNTY

NORTH CAROLINA

MICHAEL EURY

LEGENDARY LOCALS

ISBN 978-1-4671-0219-3

Legendary Locals is an imprint of Arcadia Publishing
Charleston, South Carolina

Printed in the United States of America

Library of Congress Control Number: 2015936392

For all general information, please contact Arcadia Publishing:
Telephone 843-853-2070
Fax 843-853-0044
E-mail sales@arcadiapublishing.com
For customer service and orders:
Toll-Free 1-888-313-2665

Visit us on the Internet at www.arcadiapublishing.com

Dedication

To Patricia Chandler, who so ably continues the tradition of Kathryn Bridges and honors the memory of sisters Adelaide and Eugenia Lore

On the Front Cover: Clockwise from top left:
Haskel Stanback, football player (Courtesy of Scott Boggs; see page 118), Anne Hege Wilson, community theater leader (Courtesy of Anne Hege Wilson; see page 45), Eddie Ray, record producer and museum director (Courtesy of North Carolina Music Hall of Fame; see pages 112, 113), Elizabeth Safrit, beauty queen and youth advocate (Courtesy of the *Independent Tribune*; see page 120), John Washington Carriker, businessman and postmaster (Courtesy of the Town of Midland; see page 28), Betsy Carpenter, animal rights activist (Courtesy of Concord Public Library; see page 17), Nikita Koloff, wrestler-turned-evangelist (Courtesy of Nikita Koloff; see page 124), A.L. Brown, business executive and public school champion (Courtesy of Kannapolis History Associates; see page 32), Corine Cannon, civil rights pioneer (Courtesy of Concord Public Library; see page 15).

On the Back Cover: From left to right:
Don Frye, amusement park originator (Courtesy of Tammy Frye Jordan; see pages 70, 71), J.E. Mainer and His Mountaineers, bluegrass musicians (Courtesy of North Carolina Music Hall of Fame; see page 110).

CONTENTS

ACKNOWLEDGMENTS

This volume would not be possible without the foundation of decades of research by Cabarrus County's historians and genealogists. Their dedication to preserving the legacies of our forefathers rivals the tenacity of the Scotch-Irish and Germans who, nearly 300 years ago, settled what would become this county.

Also invaluable was the documentation left behind by newspaper reporters and photographers of yesteryear. Little did they realize that their efforts to capture current events would one day provide a blueprint of the past. Special thanks go to the *Independent Tribune* and its managing editor, Lee Buchanan.

I am indebted to my wife, Rose Rummel-Eury, whose assistance in securing photographs and information was vital to the production of this book. Special thanks also go to Patricia Chandler of the Lore History Room at the Cabarrus County Public Library–Concord Branch (herewith Concord Public Library) for assisting with my research, providing images, and reviewing my manuscript for accuracy and to my Arcadia Publishing editor, Erin L. Vosgien.

The author gratefully acknowledges Shelley McBride and the Kannapolis History Associates (herewith KHA) and Ben Callahan, Vicki Bost Isenhour, and Mount Pleasant's Eastern Cabarrus Historical Society (herewith ECHS) for their aid and for allowing me access to their archives and Janet Morrison and Kathy Kitts for their help in pointing me toward Harrisburg's and Midland's legendary locals.

Lastly, my sincere thanks go to the following, who provided information, access to special collections, permissions, or who helped in some other fashion: Kim Anderson, Frances Bess Brown, Evin Burleson, Sherry Frye Carawan, Veronica Cordle, Cathy Earnhardt, Iris Bost Elliott, Chad Fortner, Frankie Godley, Phil Goodman, Brad Hinson, Sarah Huskey, Dakeita Vanderburg Johnson, Debra Johnson, Sarah M. Jones, Winston Kelley, Kathy Kitts, Michael Knox, Tony McClamrock, Steve Morris, Connie Moss, Emily Patridge, Mark Plemmons, David Pugh, Lloyd Quay Jr., E.Z. Smith III, Dianne O. Snyder, Kitty Taylor, Wayne Troutman, and Tonya Walker.

INTRODUCTION

Of North Carolina's 100 counties, Cabarrus County is its most visited. Chief among its attractions are the expansive Concord Mills shopping mall, motorsports mogul Bruton Smith's Charlotte Motor Speedway and its sister racing arenas, and the family-friendly Great Wolf Lodge. Cabarrus County is the home of David H. Murdock's North Carolina Research Campus, which is rapidly becoming one of the nation's premier health-sciences research centers. Within the county, one can find a flourishing airport, the North Carolina Music Hall of Fame, a minor-league baseball franchise, worldwide corporate headquarters, and cutting-edge technology businesses. With a mushrooming population that has exceeded 192,000, Cabarrus County, North Carolina, has become the center of "high-octane living," as local tourism advertising is prone to say.

Yet, as Cabarrus County has revved forward, it has never lost sight of its past. Throughout its five main municipalities—Concord, Harrisburg, Kannapolis, Midland, and Mount Pleasant—are remnants of the Old South, from lordly plantation-style estates, to repurposed textile mills, to historical sites, including Reed Gold Mine and Bost Grist Mill. Ultramodern industrial complexes are juxtaposed against pastoral farmland and long-standing churches. Cabarrus County adroitly maintains a sure-footed balancing act between a future of progress and a past of tradition.

Once the lushly forested site of a trading path on which colonists traveled to exchange goods with Waxhaw and Catawba Indians, the land that would eventually become Cabarrus County was first settled in the early to mid-1700s, with some local legends crediting a Pennsylvanian named John Rodgers as its premier pioneer. Soon, others of his Scotch-Irish ilk followed, as did Germans, their cabins and farms populating the fertile countryside. Another noteworthy pioneer, Robert Harris, rooted his family into a region that would one day bear his name, Harrisburg. To the east, a wagon stop dubbed "Mount Comfort" attracted settlers whose heirs would later inhabit Mount Pleasant. For these immigrants, their Bibles were as important as their plows and livestock, and St. John's Lutheran Church, established around 1745, initiated a convention of worship that has since remained the bedrock of life for many in Cabarrus County.

The earliest settlers were among the colonies' most fanatical patriots. In May 1771, nine young men (later dubbed the "Cabarrus Black Boys" because of their soot-camouflaged faces) hijacked and detonated a British munitions shipment, executing what many believe to be the first strike against the crown, two years before the Boston Tea Party. The valiant Lt. Col. John Phifer and other heroes of the Revolutionary War blazed a path toward independence.

In this nation's infancy, this region of North Carolina was part of Mecklenburg County, until fiery voices like Martin Phifer's cried out for the formation of a new county in the Rocky River region. John Paul Barringer petitioned the North Carolina House of Commons to form a new county; some believe that a split vote was broken in 1792 when Barringer offered the Speaker of the House, French immigrant Stephen Cabarrus, the right to name the county after him if he voted in its favor. The Speaker once again left his mark upon Cabarrus County after penning a persuasive 1794 letter encouraging its squabbling founders to form a pact—a "concord"—in selecting its county seat. Concord was established on a 26-acre tract two years later.

A stone's throw away, on John Reed's Cabarrus County farm, Reed's 12-year-old son Conrad, while fishing in Little Meadow Creek, stumbled across a 17-pound "rock" in 1799 that would later be identified as the first documented gold discovery in the United States. The resulting gold rush joined agriculture as the county's economic drivers. The disciplined, devout families of early Cabarrus County labored in its soil, while shrewd captains of industry flocked to the area to capitalize on its natural bounty.

Cotton was king among Cabarrus County's crops, providing opportunities for both small farming clans and plantation owners. From this sprouted an industry that would long dominate the county: textile mills. Paul Barringer and John T. Phifer founded the first, the Concord Steam Cotton Factory, in February 1839, with William Jenks as its superintendent. Many mills would follow.

In 1855, a railroad slicing through Cabarrus County was opened, and the region became a gateway for the export of cotton and cloth products. Descendants of Robert Harris had provided access for the railway, and their neck of the woods took the name of its train stop, which doubled as a post office: Harris Depot (it would be renamed Harrisburg in 1879). The former "Mount Comfort" was incorporated as the town of Mount Pleasant in 1859. The Civil War and Reconstruction derailed the county's economy, but once it rebounded, a proliferation of textile mills soon made jobs plentiful.

Like the Phifers and Barringers before them, new family dynasties emerged to propel the county into the 20th century and an era of advancement, including patriarchs John M. Odell, James W. Cannon, Daniel Branson Coltrane, W.R. Kindley, Lawson G. and Alexander Foil, and L.E. Heilig. Warren C. Coleman broke racial barriers by becoming the state's wealthiest African American through his successful mercantile and real estate ventures, and he then made history by starting a cotton mill staffed exclusively with black workers. Cannon expanded his business by literally creating a mill village—Kannapolis—of cloth-production plants with affordable housing for workers.

The textile business withered in the century that followed, but clever visionaries and eager entrepreneurs have anchored the region through challenging transitions and reshaped it for a new millennium. As with the remarkable people chronicled in the author's previous book, *Legendary Locals of Concord*, these amazing citizens have transformed their communities through measures large and small. These are the legendary locals of Cabarrus County, friends and neighbors whose stories are cherished.

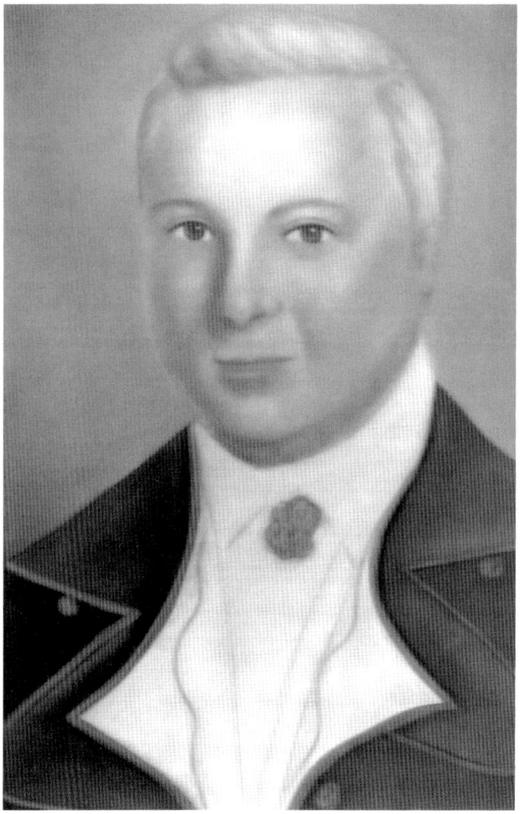

Stephen Cabarrus
Cabarrus, a wealthy sophisticate born in Bayonne, France, was 22 when he arrived in Edenton, North Carolina, to stake his claim in the New World. After serving 25 years in the House of Commons, he retired to his Pembroke plantation, where he died in 1808. Both the county and a portion of Raleigh's Capitol Square are named in his honor. (Courtesy of Historic Cabarrus Association, Inc.)

CHAPTER ONE

Piedmont Pioneers

Imagine stepping into the unknown—a frightening proposition that might intimidate even the heartiest of souls.

For these industrious Cabarrus County citizens, their achievements, today viewed through the lens of history and perhaps even taken for granted, must have given them pause. Was Ralph Earnhardt chasing a dream by auto racing, when common sense suggested he was better off working in the mill? Future mayors Martha Melvin and Bachman S. Brown Jr. took on the monumental tasks of convincing the communities of Harrisburg and Kannapolis that incorporation was in their best interests. Betsy Carpenter would not allow her physical limitations to obstruct her quest to provide humane treatment for the county's four-legged, furry denizens.

Consider the unbearable pressure that weighed upon Corine Cannon, the first woman of color to work at Cannon Mills, or the petite powerhouse Margaret Towell King, the head of the Sun-drop Bottling Company. These women shattered ethnic and gender barriers to establish themselves within their professions. Japanese immigrant Toky Canup settled in Cabarrus County when hostilities stemming from World War II fomented distrust, yet her warm demeanor melted even the iciest reception.

Other Piedmont pioneers were simply living their lives when chance nudged them into the role of trailblazer. Conrad Reed, 12, was fishing one Sunday morning when he found a large stone, unaware that he had literally struck gold. Missy Eury could slug one out of the park better than most boys her age and simply wanted to play Little League Baseball, not knowing at the time that she was also scoring a home run for equality.

Regardless of their circumstances, these legendary locals opened doors through which a future of hope and harmony would emerge.

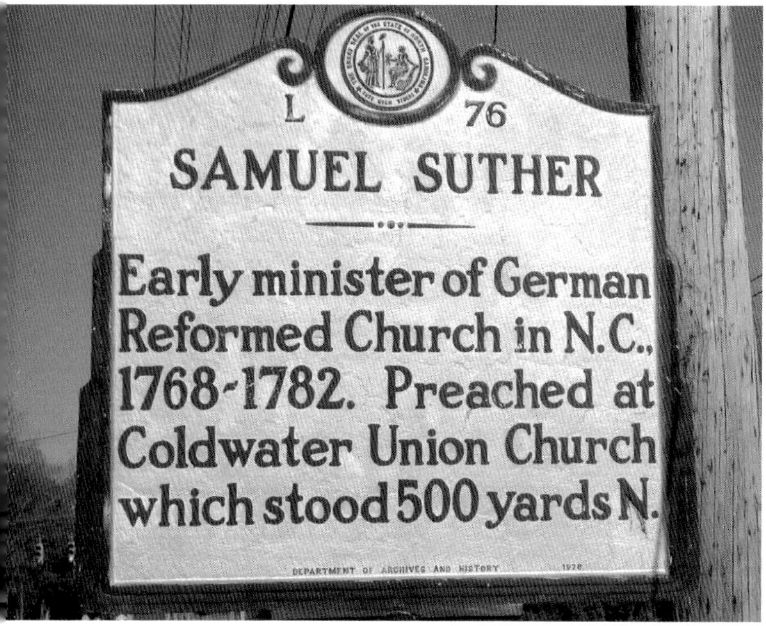

Samuel Suther
Many of the Suthers populating Cabarrus County trace their lineage to this Swiss colonist, the only member of his family to survive a 1738 Virginia shipwreck. Before migrating to the Piedmont, Suther was a German teacher and German Reformed Church minister in Pennsylvania and South Carolina. His Cabarrus claim to fame came from his use of the pulpit at Coldwater Church to incite revolutionary activism. (Photograph by the author.)

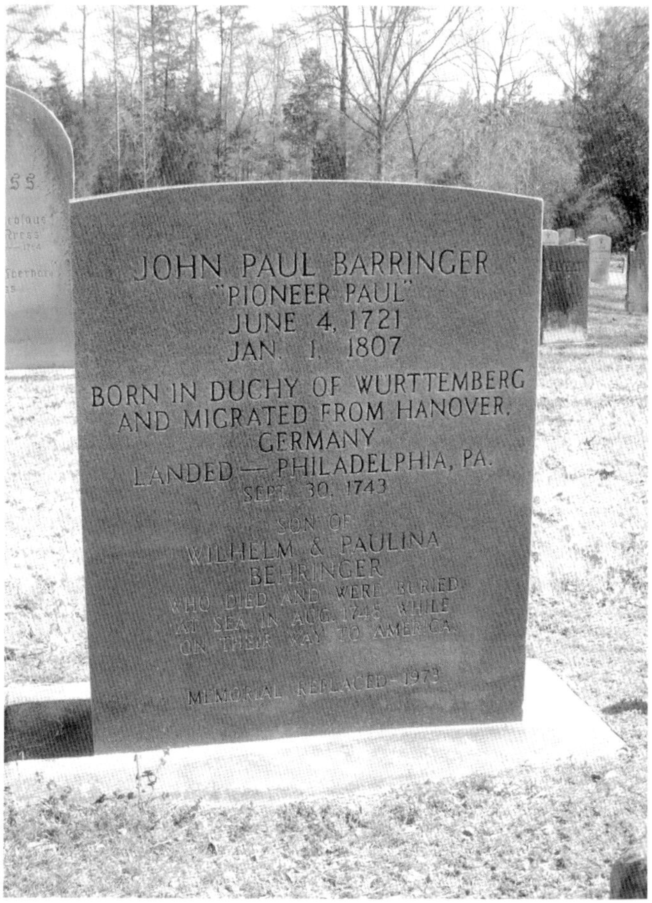

John Paul Barringer
"Pioneer Paul" began purchasing land in the eastern county's predominantly Dutch settlement in the 1750s. Local lore says he named his first home here "Mount Pleasant." Truculent but principled, Barringer was a Revolutionary War militia commander whose patriotic fervor continued into the 1790s, when he famously lobbied the state House of Commons to form Cabarrus from Mecklenburg County. He is buried at St. John's Lutheran Church cemetery. (Photograph by the author.)

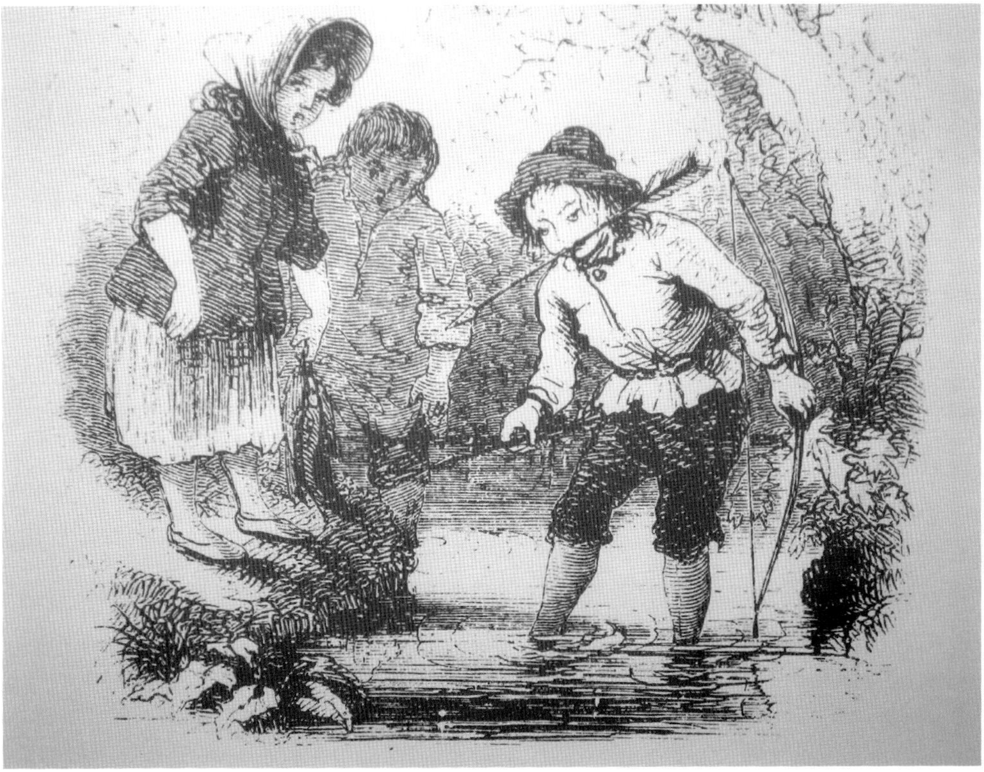

Conrad Reed

Cabarrus was known as "Upper" Mecklenburg County in the 1780s when an uneducated Hessian immigrant named Johannes Rieth (also Ried and Riedt in various documents), who would Anglicize his name to John Reed, settled into the life of a farmer and took Sarah Kiser as his wife. But without the accidental discovery made by his son Conrad, one of his eight children, the senior Reed might have died in obscurity.

Conrad, born in 1787, made history by happenstance after skipping church on a Sunday morning in 1799, presumably in the spring. While fishing in Little Meadow Creek with a few of his siblings, the 12-year-old eyed "a yellow substance shining in the water" and retrieved a large stone. Young Reed's find, weighing a whopping 17 pounds, was used as a doorstop until 1802, when his father suspected that the rock boasted greater value. (An alternate account suggests that the senior Reed, a British army deserter, initially shielded this discovery to maintain his low profile.) Once a Fayetteville jeweler categorized this "doorstop" as a gold nugget, Conrad's fishing expedition became the first documented gold discovery in the United States. The jeweler swindled John, buying the nugget for a mere $3.50, roughly one-thousandth of its value. The senior Reed later realized his error and demanded more money from the jeweler, then began mining his property's creek and later his farmland with slaves, profiting handsomely. A North Carolina gold rush followed, later usurped by the California Gold Rush and ultimately encumbered by the Civil War and fruitless shafts.

Details of Conrad's later life remain sketchy, but it is known that he married Martha Love around 1805 and, by 1830, had six children and owned nine slaves. Reed left behind an estate valued at $4,000 upon his 1834 death, but his greatest legacy remains his boyhood discovery of gold, as depicted in this illustration, produced in August 1857 for *Harper's Weekly.* (Courtesy of Reed Gold Mine.)

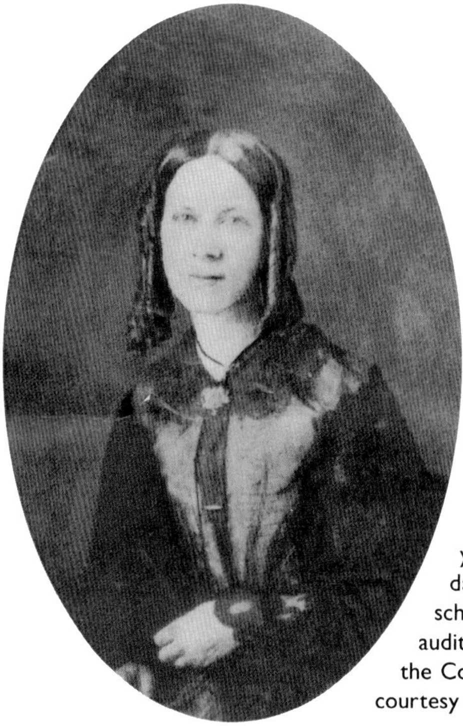

Susan E. Bigelow Bittle

A liberal-arts girls' school in tiny Mount Pleasant was a risky proposition in 1859. Yet, following the lead of the town's Western Carolina Male Academy, Susan Bittle (left), wife of the male academy's president, Rev. D.D. Bittle, designed and originally oversaw a two-story house that would become a Lutheran-based institution. Mount Pleasant Female Academy—later renamed Mont Amoena—was reconfigured after a 1911 fire and remained in operation until 1927. Mount Pleasant Collegiate Institute (MPCI), as the male academy was later known, closed its doors five years later. Below, a 1910s postcard depicts graduation day for both Mont Amoena and MPCI. At this time, the schools held shared graduation ceremonies in the town auditorium, located in downtown Mount Pleasant above the Cook and Foil's Store. (Left, courtesy of ECHS; below, courtesy of Janet Morrison.)

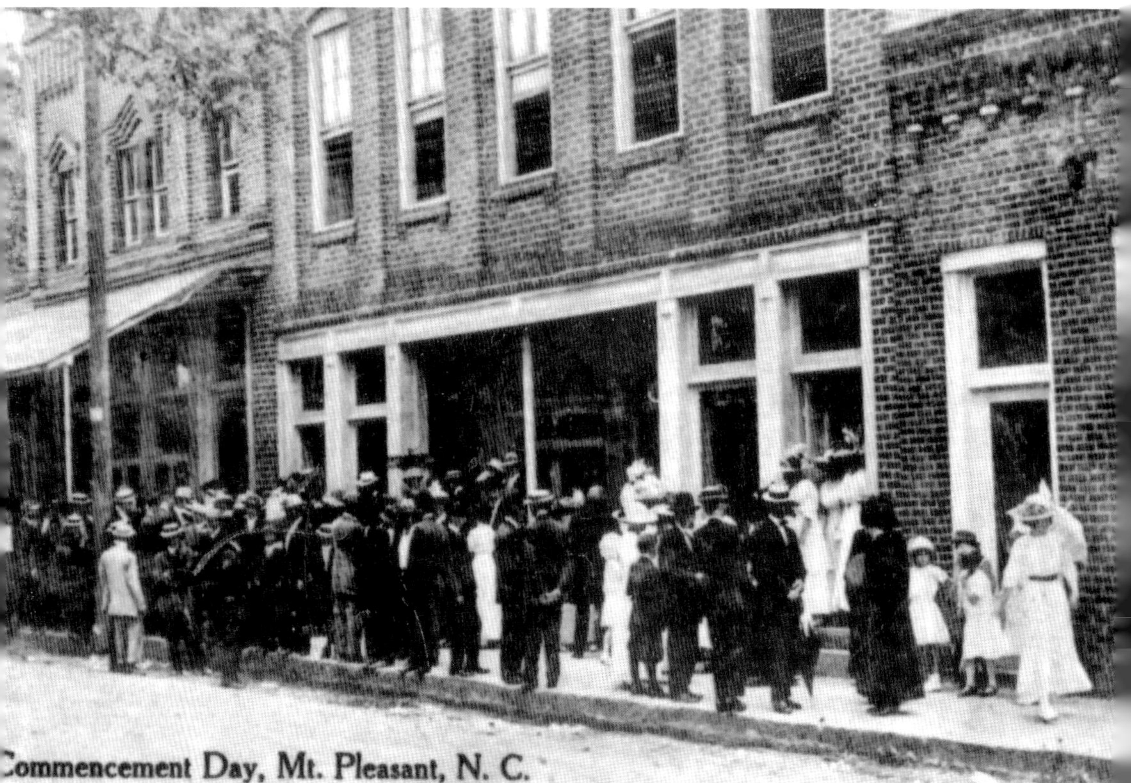

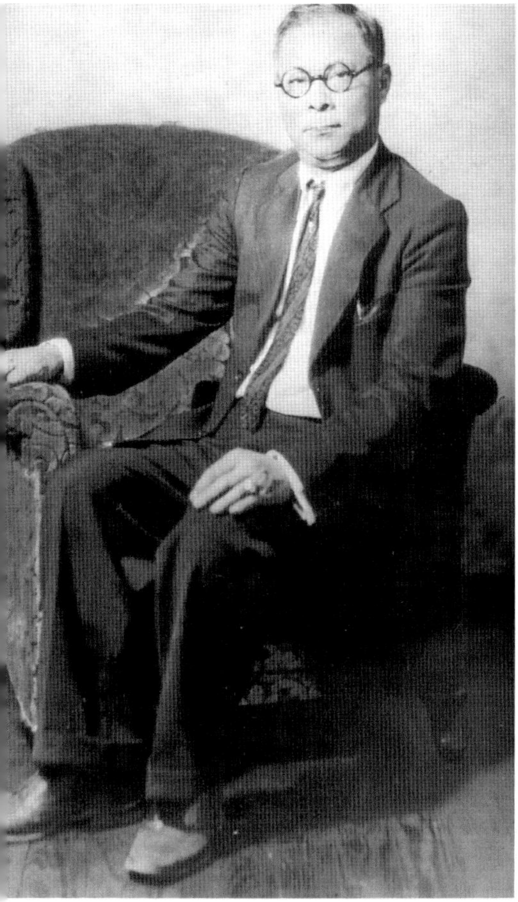

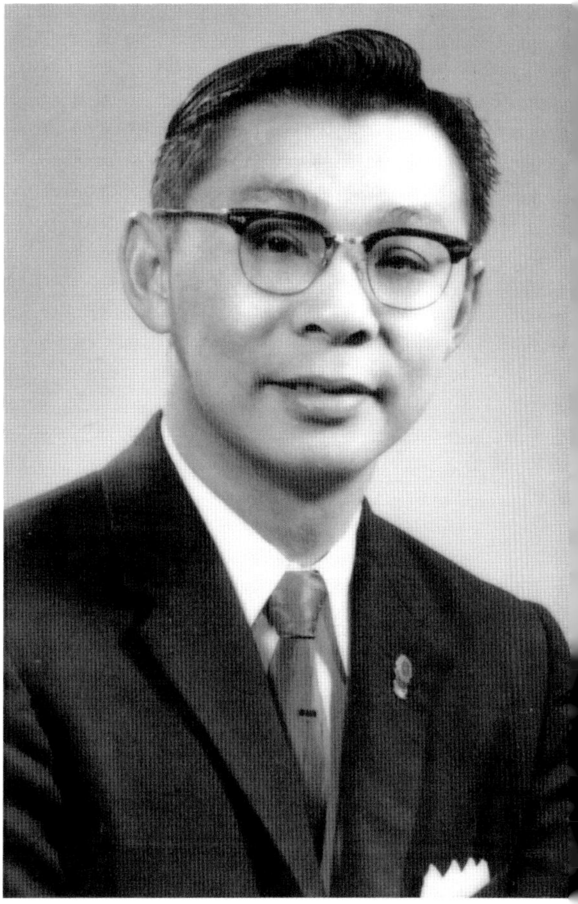

Daniel and Newmoon Jung

At a time when business ownership in Cabarrus County was the domain of white men, or of African American men in segregated neighborhoods, Daniel Jung (left) was an Asian American pioneer of commerce. He emigrated from China in 1913 and settled in Concord, where he operated a laundry. At the behest of James W. Cannon, Jung opened a laundry in Cannon's new mill village of Kannapolis in 1919. Daniel and his wife, Lee Qi, were living in their business when the first of their six children, Newmoon (right), was born. Newmoon took over the operation of the laundry business in the late 1940s and went on to become one of Kannapolis's best-known entrepreneurs, founding the Buyer's Market, Inc., and the Carpet Connection. Newmoon Jung was honored in 1996 as one of the Kannapolis Town Heroes. (Both, courtesy of KHA.)

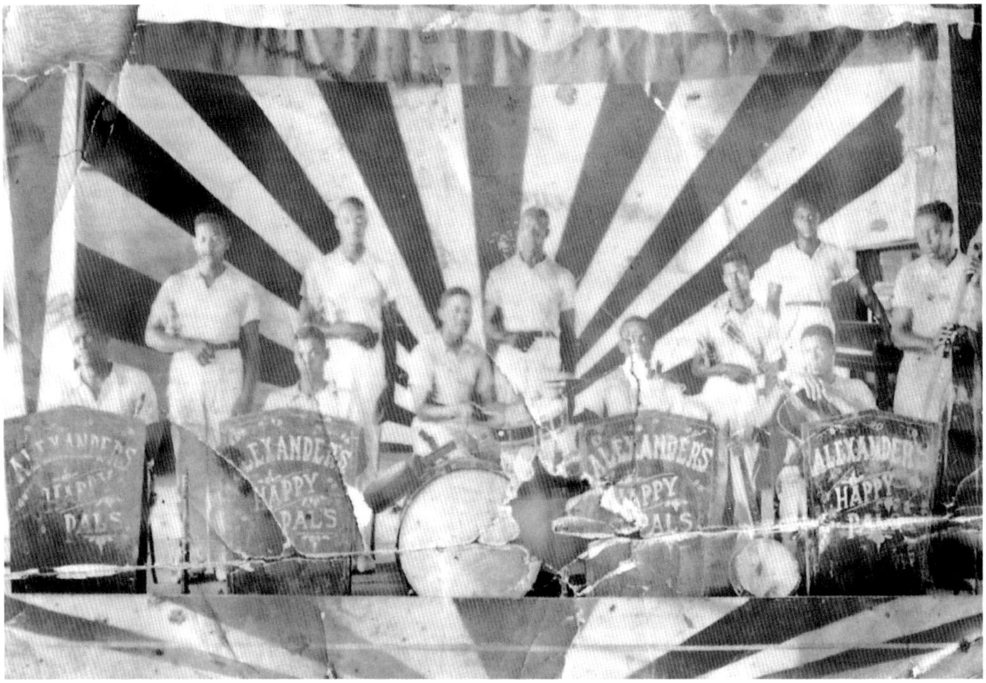

Charles W. Alexander Sr.

Alexander (front row, far left) was tall in height and talent. Born in 1905, "Charlie" was an African American business pioneer, owning a cinder-block plant and rest home in Concord. But his musicianship truly made this versatile instrumentalist a legend. His dance band, Alexander's Happy Pals, toured in the 1920s and 1930s. Around 1939, he formed the first band at Logan High School. (Courtesy of James Alexander Jr.)

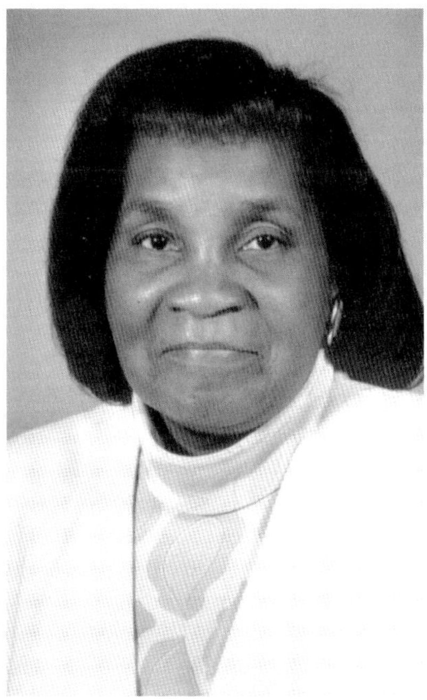

Betty Evans-Eddleman

Eddleman made history in 1969, becoming the first African American elected to the Concord City Board of Education. In 1982, Betty Bruner-Alston was the first black elected to the Cabarrus school board, and when the Concord and Cabarrus school systems merged in 1983, Eddleman was elected to the newly formed Cabarrus Board of Education, joining Bruner-Alston. Eddleman retired in 1990 and died in 2001. (Courtesy of the Concord Public Library.)

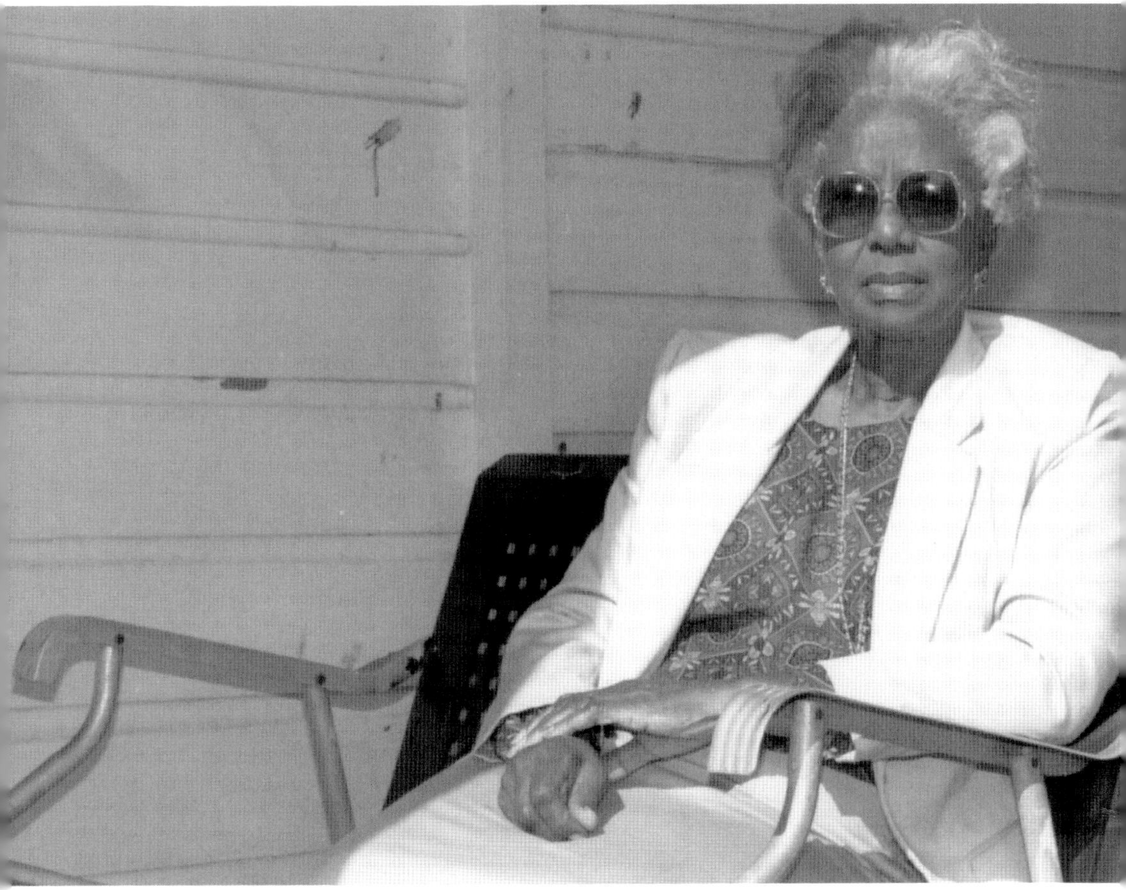

Corine Cannon

The first African American female to be hired for a Cannon Mills production position, Cannon remembered how her 1963 arrival was received by white employees. In the 2012 Leadership Cabarrus–produced documentary *Stitched in Time*, she said, "[I was] looked at like, 'What's happening, what are you doing here?' " Piercing glares of disapproval were often accompanied by whispered remarks or vocal taunts. A white supervisor recommended that Cannon turn the other cheek and not respond, but to privately report abusive whites. Cannon Mills' plants were segregated when she joined the workforce, including the restrooms, but Corine Cannon was soon followed by more women of color and, later, black men in management positions. Today, Cannon, in her 90s, remains active in Cabarrus County as a speaker, sharing stories about the challenges of the civil rights era.

Several members of her family have also achieved acclaim, including daughter Katie Geneva Cannon, the first black woman to be ordained a Presbyterian minister. Hollywood celebrity Nick Cannon is Corine Cannon's grandson. (Courtesy of Concord Public Library.)

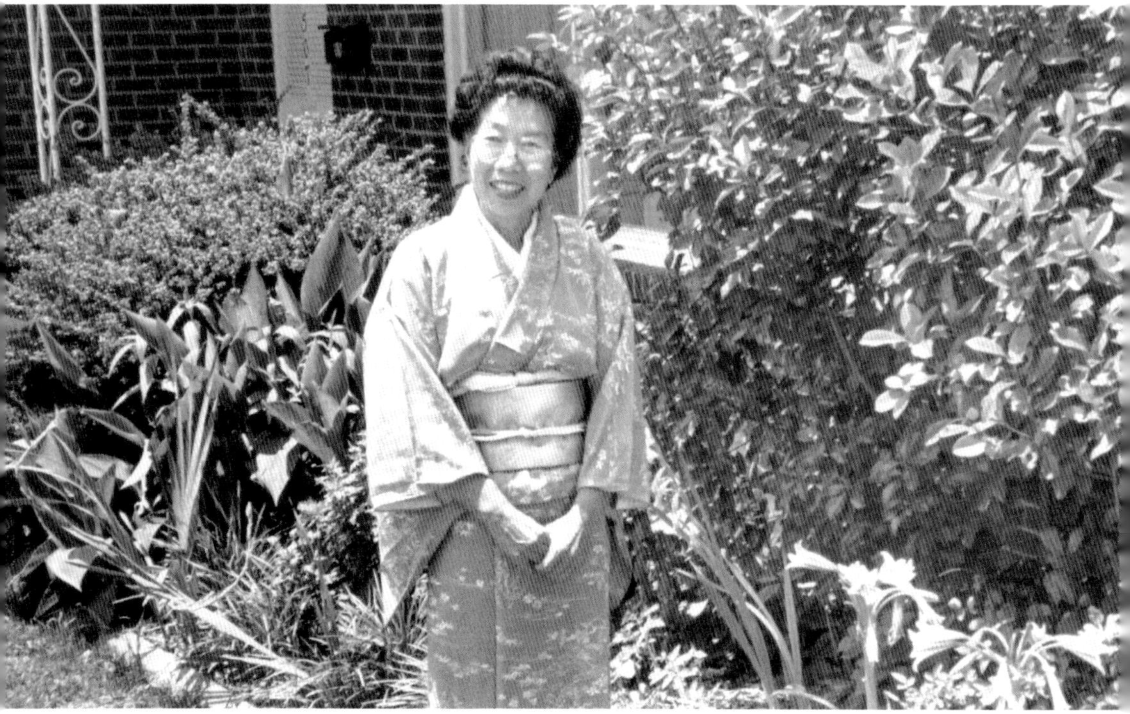

Motoko Canup

When Franklin Harlee "Bill" (or "Billie") Canup Jr. brought his Japanese bride home to Concord after the Korean War, culture shock raised some neighbors' eyebrows. Many who had lived through World War II deeply resented the Japanese. And, at the time, only segregated neighborhoods of blacks and whites comprised Cabarrus County's ethnic population, with rare exceptions. But locals soon fell in love with the kindhearted "Toky," as she called herself, as her name, Motoko, was difficult for many to remember. She met her husband-to-be while Bill was serving in the Army in Korea. He was wounded and shipped to Japan to convalesce and soon was assigned to a military engineering depot's supply office, where he met 19-year-old Motoko Ishiwata, an employee. She was raised in Yokohama, Japan, and was a child during the American bombings of World War II. "We had no freedom," she remembers of the Japan of her youth. Bill and Toky wed, settled in Concord, and adopted a daughter, Emily. But the new family's bliss was shattered in January 1967, when Bill, who had since enlisted in the Navy and was serving in Vietnam, went missing in action, presumably drowned. His body was never recovered, leaving Toky to raise her child alone. Yet she never was truly alone—she was embraced by her friends at Forest Hill United Methodist Church and was bolstered by her faith, having become a Christian years earlier. In the years that followed, Toky was Cabarrus County's unofficial Japanese ambassador, sharing her heritage with area newspapers and friends while becoming so ingrained in her community that she was once given the Concord Business and Professional Women's Woman of the Year Award. (Courtesy of Concord Public Library.)

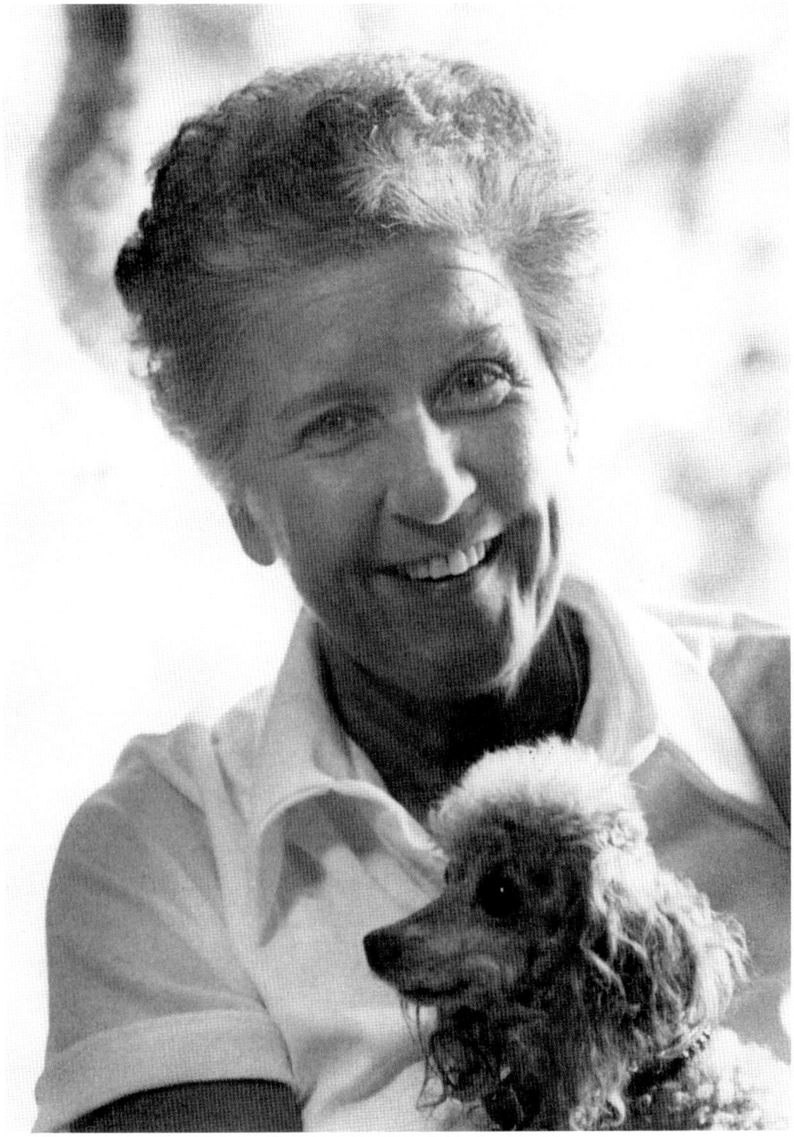

Betsy Carpenter
Cabarrus County's premier animal rights advocate made some enemies during her life. Pet abusers and negligent farmers vehemently disliked her, as she rallied to the aid of the innocent beasts they mistreated or ignored. To most, however, Carpenter was a champion, never refusing to rescue, nurse, feed, or relocate an animal in need. Like many of the creatures she befriended, she was caged, trapped in a wheelchair due to a lifelong medical condition that also slurred her speech. Yet her physical limitations could not quell her resolve. Carpenter was the founder and president of Cabarrus Animal Protection Society, the county's first organization of its type. A talented journalist and poet, she might often be spied wearing a compassionate smile and "Justice for Animals" T-shirt. Upon her death in 2012, Carpenter was eulogized thusly by her friend and protégée, Patsy Beeker: "The pathways to heaven will be lined like a Macy's Christmas parade with throngs of furry and feathered friends she saved, waiting to welcome her. And Betsy will skip like a young pup among them." (Courtesy of Concord Public Library.)

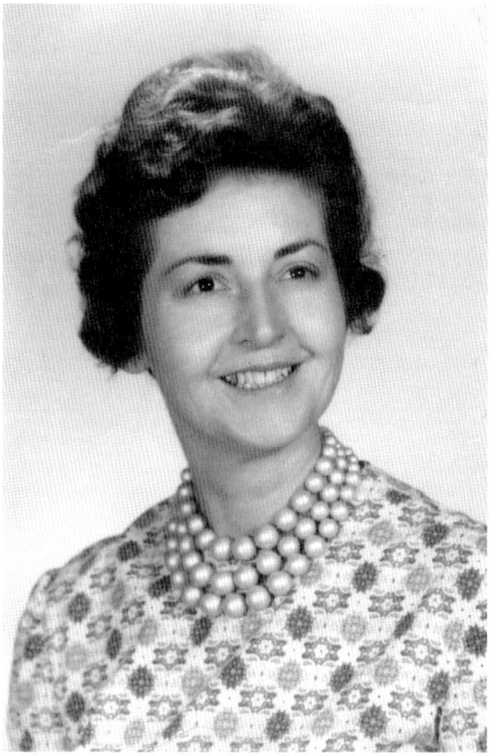

Martha Melvin

The adage "the third time's a charm" might describe the political career of this pioneering mayor of Harrisburg. When Melvin posed for this portrait in 1972, she was well known in the community, a popular, peppy science and home economics teacher at Central Cabarrus High School. This vivacious visionary realized that Harrisburg, the tranquil home of agriculture and a train depot, was rapidly becoming a bedroom community of nearby Charlotte. She wrote in a 1981 *Concord Tribune* editorial that an average of one family per week was moving into Harrisburg. Such expansion would no doubt pose infrastructural challenges to the unincorporated small town. In November 1972, Melvin became the driving force behind a campaign to incorporate Harrisburg. As the sole woman on a steering committee (which met at her house so she would not have to hire a babysitter), the committee gathered data, hosted sometimes-contentious town meetings, drafted a city charter, proposed geographic borders, and appointed Melvin as temporary mayor. On May 29, 1973, a referendum of Harrisburg's registered voters was held, with Melvin loading her car and a truck with polling booths borrowed from the county board of elections office in Concord. Harrisburg incorporated that day, with 361 voting for and 77 voting against. Melvin's whirlwind process toward incorporation was completed in only six months.

For Harrisburg's first election of officials, Melvin believed that her gender was a barrier—women's lib might have been sweeping America's cities, but Harrisburg clung to traditional values—so she ran for and was elected to a town council position instead. She was chosen as mayor pro tem; when the elected mayor resigned at the third council meeting, she became the Honorable Martha Melvin, mayor of Harrisburg. This unusual circumstance happened again, after the town's second election, and Melvin once again became mayor after the elected mayor stepped down. Despite her two terms, she still believed that the town would not directly elect a woman mayor, and she declined to run in Harrisburg's third election. On election night, she returned home from her second job, teaching adult night school, and was stunned to find her house festooned with balloons and congratulatory cards—the townspeople had elected her via a write-in campaign! Melvin later served as a member of the Cabarrus County Board of Commissioners. (Courtesy of Martha Melvin.)

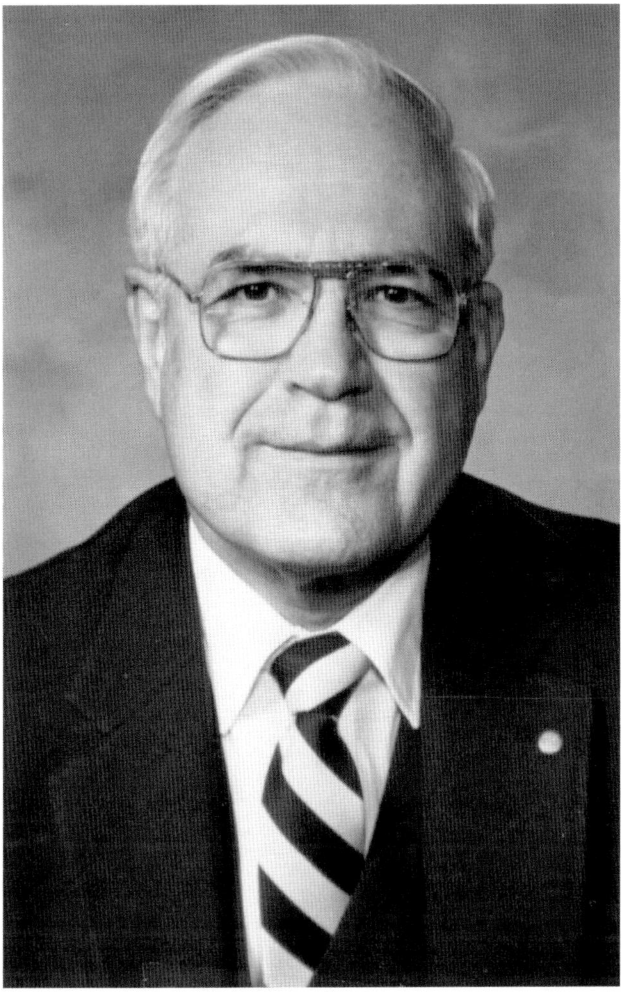

Bachman S. Brown Jr.

While historians regard James W. Cannon as the "father of Kannapolis," many will argue that the distinction belongs to Brown. He was Kannapolis's first mayor, elected in 1984 after steering an 18-member study commission to incorporate the city. Brown helmed Kannapolis through 1993, liberating it from under the thumb of Cannon Mills and transforming it into a municipality that controlled its infrastructural resources, including its water supply, sanitation services, and police department. A noble, humble soul, Brown eschewed accolades for these accomplishments. Yet his contributions to his community were unparalleled and extended well beyond his tenure as mayor.

After being admitted to the state bar in 1950, Brown, a veteran of World War II, practiced law for 61 years. He often represented needy clients for a fraction of what he would normally charge, and he frequently worked pro bono. Brown devoted himself to a variety of organizations, including the American Red Cross, United Way, Kannapolis Rotary Club, Cabarrus County Board of Elections, and city and county chambers of commerce. His father and paternal grandfather were Lutheran ministers, but Brown followed a different spiritual path, teaching Sunday school for 50 years at Kimball Memorial Lutheran Church and serving the statewide synod for nearly three decades. Throughout his life, he was the recipient of numerous awards, chief among them the Order of the Long Leaf Pine, North Carolina's highest civilian honor, presented to him in 2008 by Gov. Mike Easley. Brown died in 2014 at age 88. (Courtesy of Concord Public Library.)

Ralph Earnhardt

He is remembered as the patriarch of NASCAR's "royal family," with son Dale Earnhardt Sr., grandsons Dale Earnhardt Jr. and Kerry Earnhardt, and great-grandson Jeffrey Earnhardt having followed in his skidmarks. Yet Ralph Earnhardt's greatest legacy may be as a motorsports pacesetter. He was one of the sport's earliest superstars, as well as the first stock-car racer to employ driver's door crash bars and to fully grasp the physics of tire stagger.

Like most racers, Earnhardt, born in Kannapolis in 1928, was a risk taker. In his case, he dared to leave his mill job—which did not pay much but offered stability to this young husband and father—in hot pursuit of his dream to drive and build cars. As his wife, Martha, told gatherers at a February 2015 meeting of the Kannapolis History Associates, "he had a unique and natural talent for motors and those kind of things." Earnhardt was hands-on with his cars, building them, souping them up, and repairing them—for himself and for other racers. The sound of revving engines from his home garage was a fond childhood memory of his kids. As a racer, Earnhardt graduated from Cabarrus County dirt tracks to the pros in the early 1950s, when he was in his 20s, roaring on to a 23-year NASCAR career in which he won over 350 races. Nicknamed "Mister Consistency," Earnhardt died of a heart attack in 1973. He is buried at Center Grove Lutheran Cemetery in Kannapolis.

Seen here in the late 1950s or early 1960s, Earnhardt (right), having recently received the Autolite Racing Award, poses with Bob Petty of NAPA Motor Parts in Kannapolis. (Courtesy of KHA.)

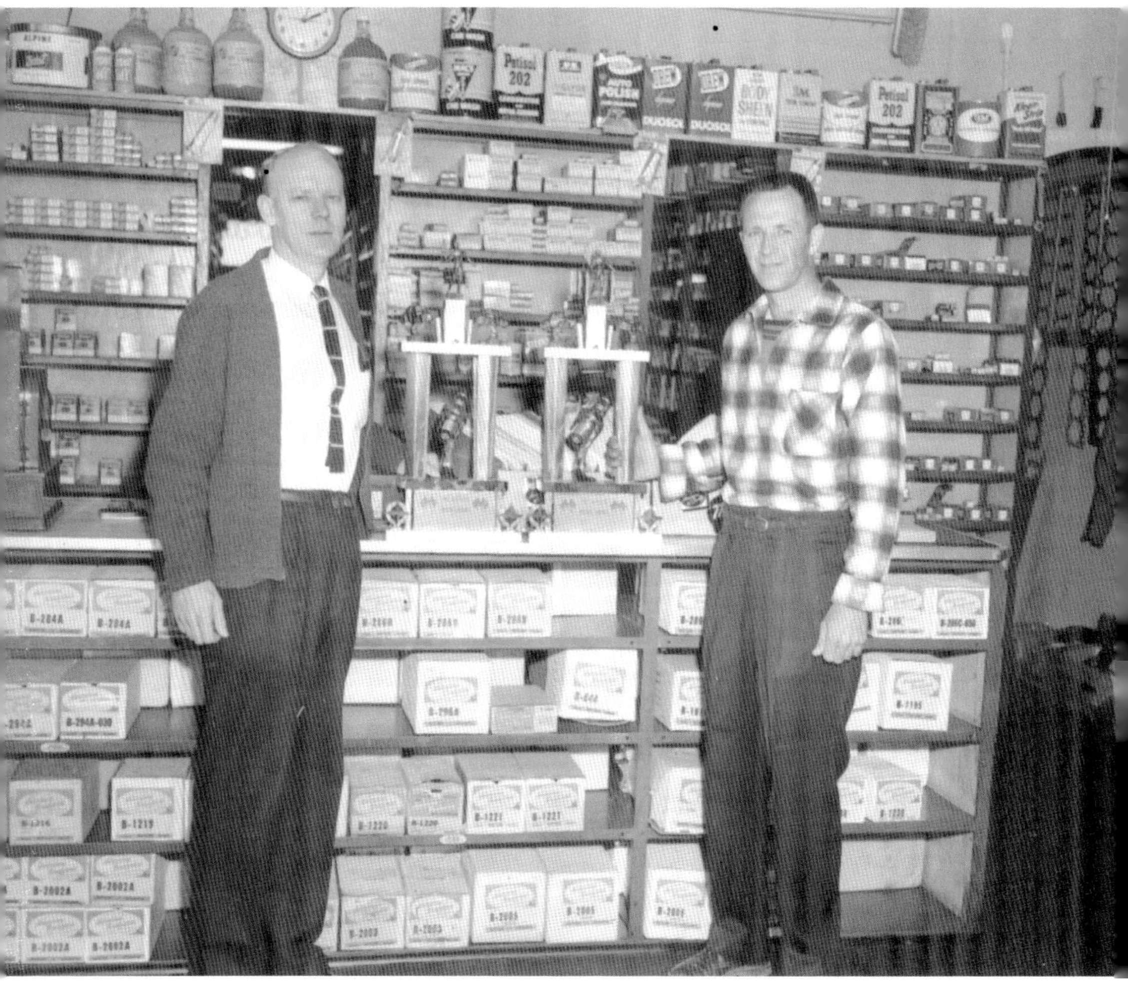

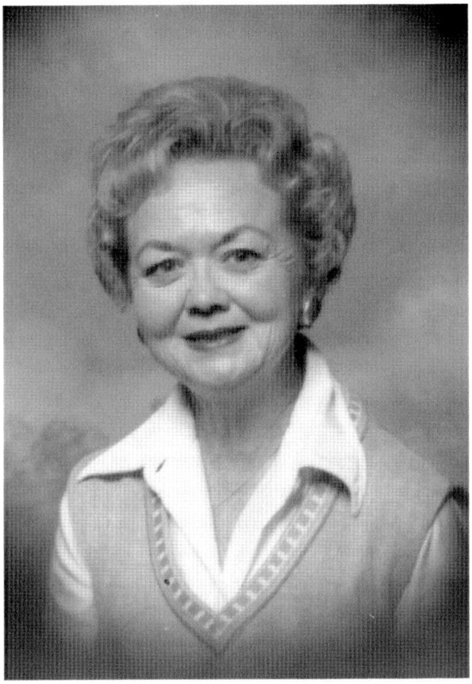

Margaret Towell King (Moses)
This little woman made a big impact as a trailblazing female business leader. King learned the soda business from her uncle, Tommy Honeycutt, and, for the latter half of the 20th century, ran Sun-drop Bottling Company. Cabarrus County's first female chamber of commerce president and charter president of the Cabarrus Arts Council, she was the Concord Business and Professional Women's 1984 Woman of the Year. (Courtesy of Concord Public Library.)

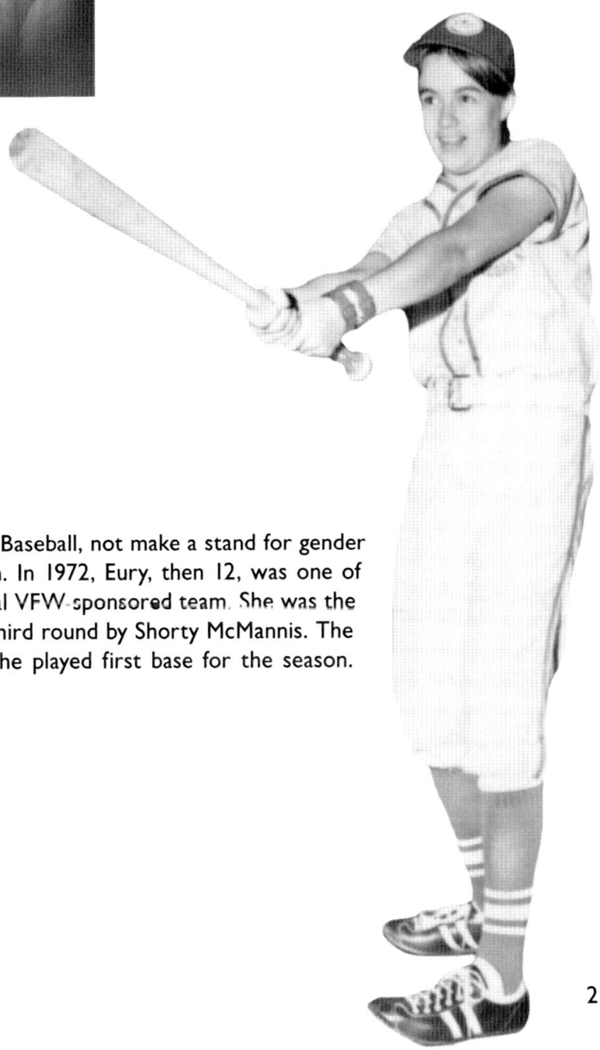

Missy Eury
She only wanted to play Little League Baseball, not make a stand for gender equality—but Eury succeeded at both. In 1972, Eury, then 12, was one of several girls who tried out for the local VFW-sponsored team. She was the only one who made it, picked in the third round by Shorty McMannis. The county's first female Little Leaguer, she played first base for the season. (Courtesy of Missy Eury.)

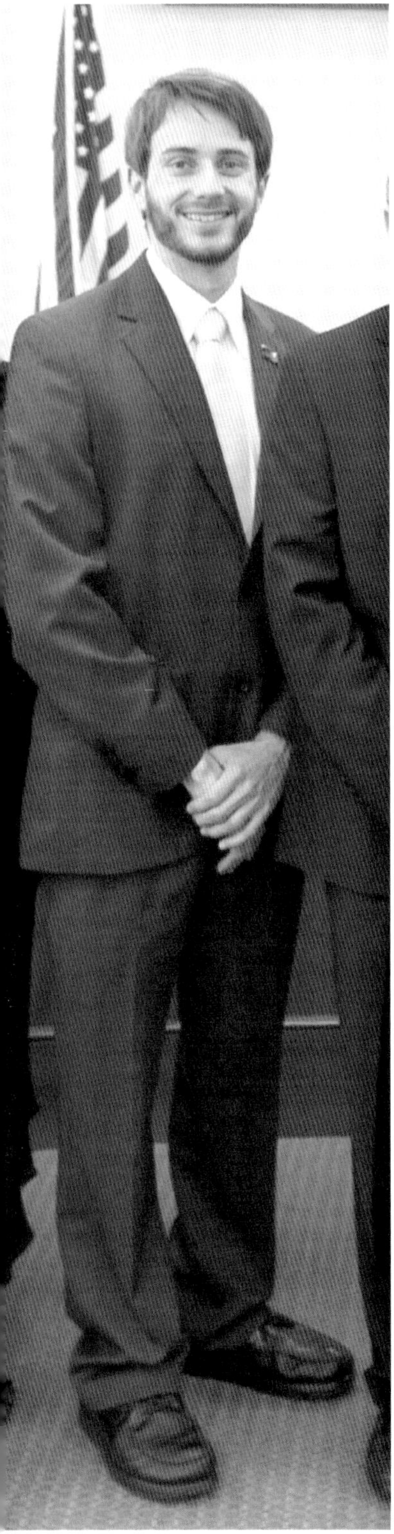

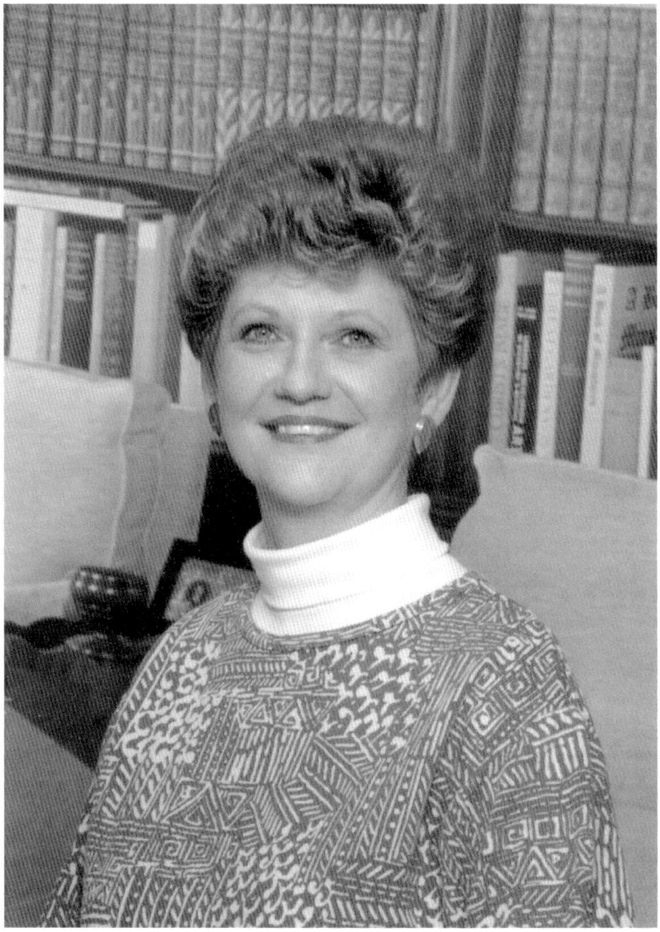

Linda F. McAbee (ABOVE)
McAbee, Cabarrus County's first female register of deeds, had been a linchpin at the register's office since 1973. She was appointed in 1999 to replace the ailing elected register, Bill Ross. She officially ran for and won the office in 2000 and served three consecutive terms, retiring in late 2012. McAbee was fundamental in the digitization of records, some dating back to 1792. (Courtesy of Kara McAbee Widener.)

Ryan Dayvault (LEFT)
A mere seven years after his 2004 graduation from A.L. Brown High School, Dayvault became the youngest person elected to the Kannapolis City Council. While his ancestors played fundamental roles in Kannapolis's past, Dayvault, voted mayor pro tem in 2014, has set his sights on moving his hometown into the future, including his work with the North Carolina Research Campus's Nutrition Research Institute. (Courtesy of Ryan Dayvault.)

CHAPTER TWO

Community Builders

For the burgeoning communities in Cabarrus County, the cotton mills held great promise. Yet that promise could not have been realized if not for the investments and inventiveness of citizens devoted to the common good.

Jonas Cook and H.C. McAllister provided much of the foundation onto which the town of Mount Pleasant would develop. Meanwhile, John Washington Carriker's mercantile venture brought goods—and, soon, mail—to the rural Midland/Bethel region, and Paul M. Dayvault's farmland was sold to become the site of James W. Cannon's ambitious mill village of Kannapolis. Years later, the actions of A.L. Brown, J. Carlyle Rutledge, Samuel B. Stroup Jr., and David H. Murdock steered Kannapolis through its next phases of progress.

As the region grew, dedicated physicians, such as Nicholas E. Lubchenko and Archibald L. Barringer, devoted themselves to the health of their Harrisburg and Mount Pleasant neighbors. George A. Batte Jr. believed that the hardworking folks at Cannon Mills deserved an adequately equipped medical facility. With Cannon Mills president Charles A. Cannon, Batte made Cabarrus Memorial Hospital a reality. Years later, C.C. Griffin, a retired educator, and David Lockhart, a retired physician, helped establish community clinics serving low-income households.

Realizing that an appreciation for the arts and history enriches the soul, cultural patrons, such as Robert F. Phifer, Margaret McConnell Holt, the Eastern Cabarrus Historical Society, and the Kannapolis History Associates, orchestrated efforts to nurture creativity and preserve the past. Ed Hosack and Pat Miller have fed a different type of hunger, fronting charities that provide assistance to those in need.

Whether their efforts were publicly lauded through fanfare and commemorative plaques or occurred quietly with little or no recognition, these community builders laid the groundwork for the lifestyle that residents are privileged to enjoy today.

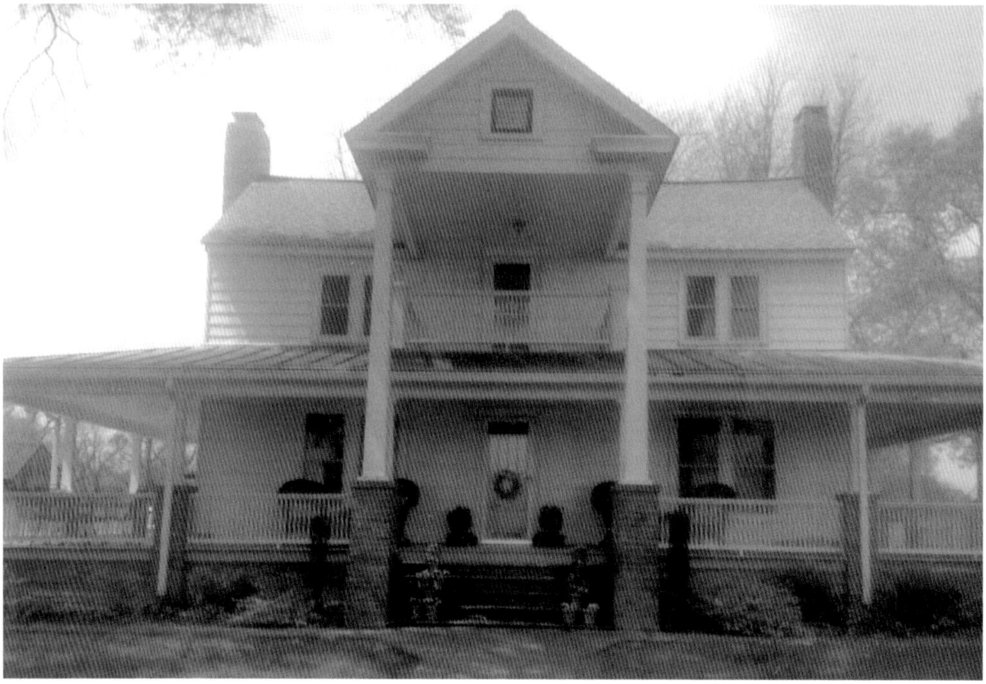

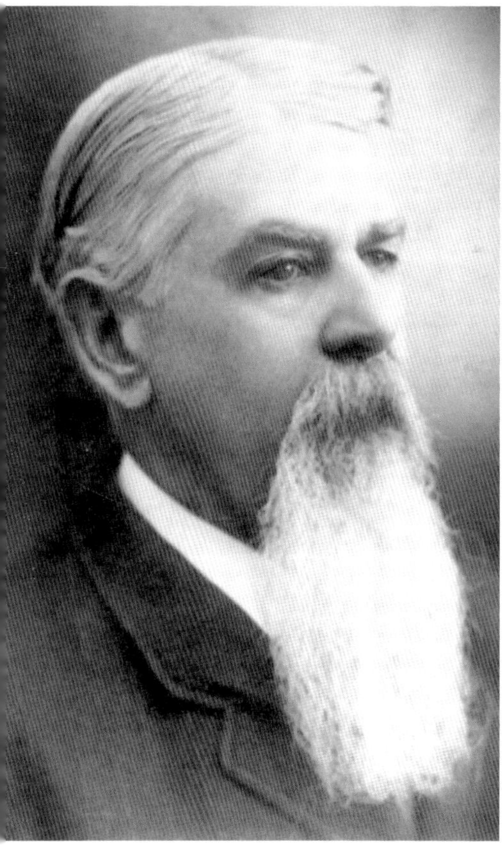

Alexander "Sandy" McKinley

Many longtime Harrisburg families trace their lineage to plantation owner and Harris Depot postmaster Alexander McKinley (1807–1869) and his wife, the former Elizabeth Morrison. McKinley's majestic Colonial Revival home, on Hickory Ridge Road, was built by his father, John McKinley, and has remained in the family for six generations. Sandy's descendant Lloyd Quay Jr. currently resides there. (Photograph by Rose Rummel-Eury.)

Jonas Cook

This Confederate veteran and Alexander Foil (the one-time associate of Jonas's father, Matthew Cook) managed the Cook & Foil general store at the Mount Pleasant town square. Cook's influence was vital to Mount Pleasant's prosperity in the last decades of the 1800s, as he served sometimes-multiple terms as postmaster, justice of the peace, town commissioner, and mayor. He was also a North Carolina College trustee. (Courtesy of ECHS.)

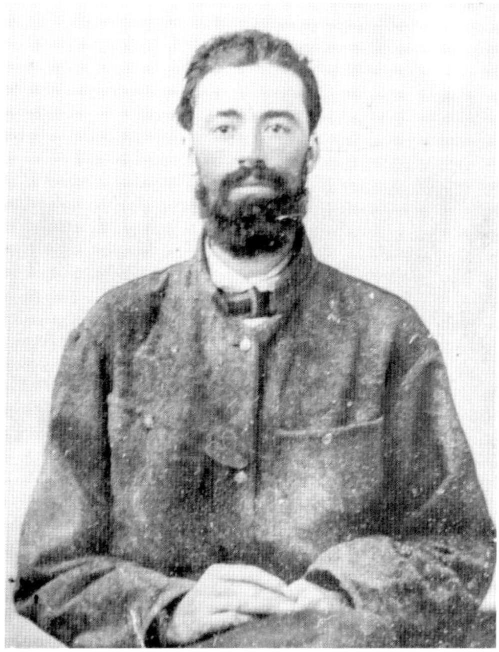

Isaac Newton Pharr
Pharr, at one time Gen. Robert E. Lee's flag bearer during the Civil War, was known throughout Cabarrus County for his family's gristmill. But his enduring endowment is his memoirs, penned on wallpaper scraps, in which he shared observations of the county's development during its post-Reconstruction textile boom. Pharr's letters are archived by Historic Cabarrus Association, Inc., and will eventually be available for online viewing. (Courtesy of the *Independent Tribune*.)

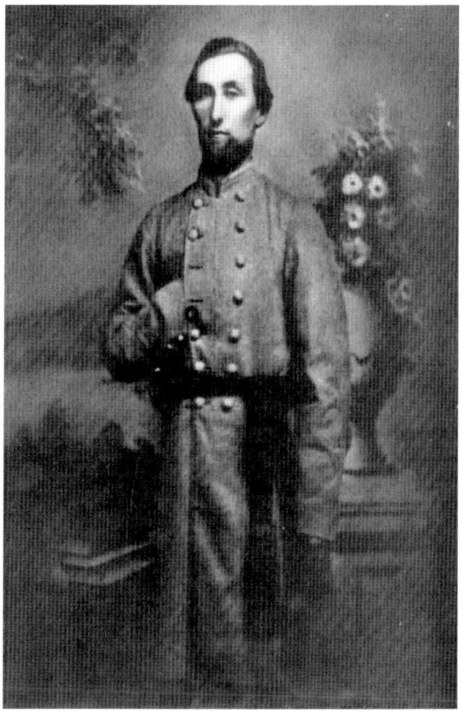

Harvey Caswell McAllister
This pillar of Mount Pleasant was a Gaston County resident who first visited Cabarrus County as a brick mason hired to help build Western Carolina Male Academy. A Confederate officer, after the Civil War, H.C. McAllister married Mount Pleasant's Francis Christine Cook and eventually took up residence in town. He became involved with local politics, with education being his focus. McAllister was voted Mount Pleasant's mayor in 1889. (Courtesy of ECHS.)

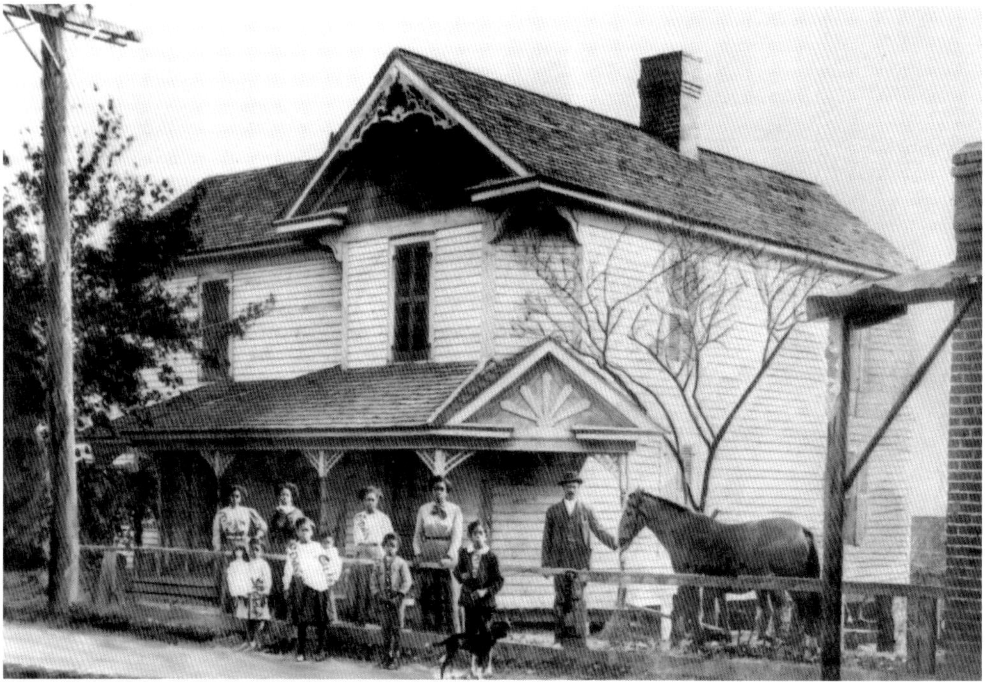

Edward W. Lawing

The roots of Cabarrus County's prodigious Lawing clan were planted with this carpenter and merchant. Born in 1874, Lawing was one of the first African Americans in the community to own a farm. This early-1900s photograph, taken at the Lawings' Rocky River homestead, shows, from left to right, the following: (first row) Stella, Odessa, Elliott (in Odessa's arms), Andrew, and William; (second row) Mamie, Ivey, Edna, wife Julia, and Edward. (Courtesy of Concord Public Library.)

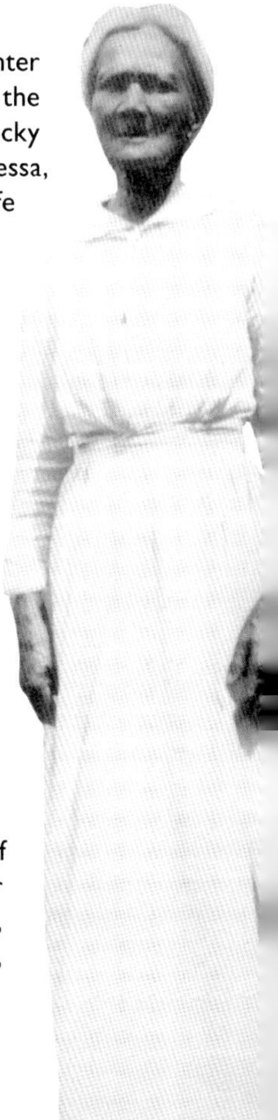

Idella "Aunt Dill" Misenheimer

Eastern Cabarrus County's most famous midwife delivered, by some accounts, "half the babies in Mount Pleasant," both white and black. It is believed that "Dillie" (her slave name) was purchased in 1860 by J.J. Misenheimer as a wedding gift for his wife, Martha. After emancipation, she married Harry Heilig, a former slave from Virginia, and gave birth to several children. She died in 1941. (Courtesy of ECHS.)

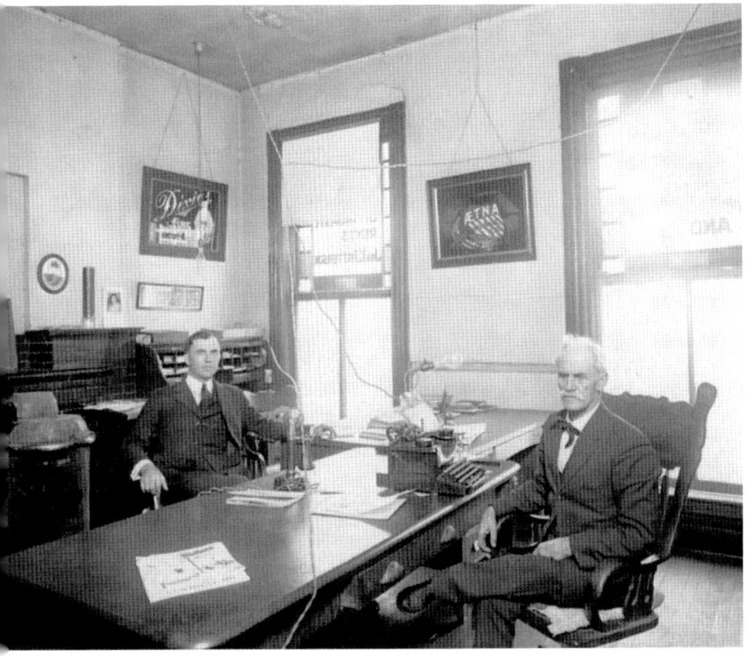

John K. Patterson
In the early 1900s, this Concord insurance and real estate agent was tapped by his friend James W. Cannon to canvas for Cabarrus County properties onto which a mill village could be constructed. Patterson sold land options to Cannon for 600 acres north of Concord, which eventually became the site of Kannapolis. Patterson (right) is shown with son S. Kay Patterson in his Concord insurance office. (Courtesy of Alex Patterson.)

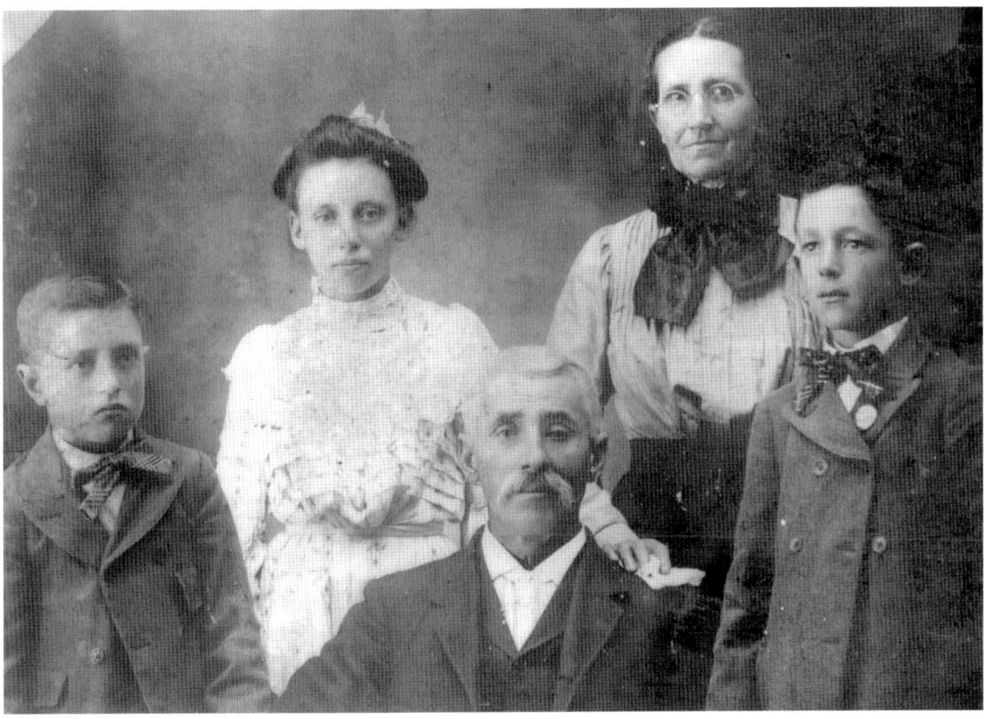

Paul M. Dayvault
Dayvault's 72 acres of farmland were among the land options acquired by John K. Patterson for James W. Cannon's mill village. It was here that the town's "heart," its lake, would be created, alongside Cannon Mills' Plant No. 1 and main office. Shown in this Dayvault family portrait are, from left to right, Dolph, Laura, Dayvault (seated), Hettie, and Mark. (Courtesy of KHA.)

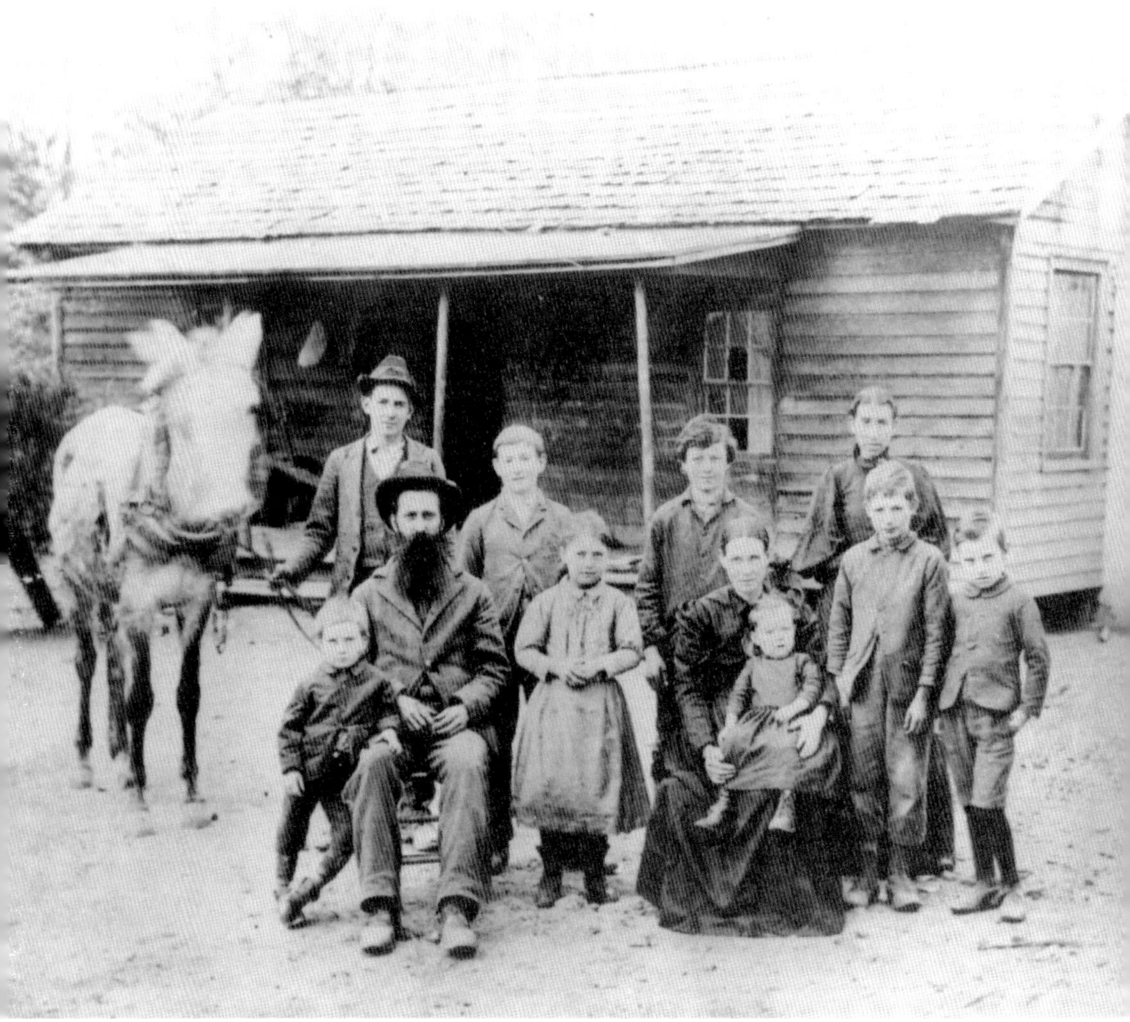

John Washington Carriker

At the turn of the 20th century, Carriker erected a simple wooden structure near Flowes Store Road, Bethel Methodist Church, and the sprawling farmland belonging to Sam Black. This was known as Carriker Store, which served as a general market for rural southeastern Cabarrus County. It soon became the region's post office, one of over two dozen such tiny mail facilities serving the sparsely populated county in the early 1900s. Carriker also constructed a steam-powered sawmill on the site. This photograph, taken around 1900, shows the Carriker family at their homestead. The family members are, from left to right, (first row) Hoyle Dayvault, John, Ada Matilda, Martha Frances (holding Lola Mae), Stacy Clausell, and Walter Atlas; (second row) Charles Levi, Joseph Henry, Arthur Oscar, and Eula. Another child, Margaret, was born to the Carrikers in 1905. (Courtesy of the Town of Midland.)

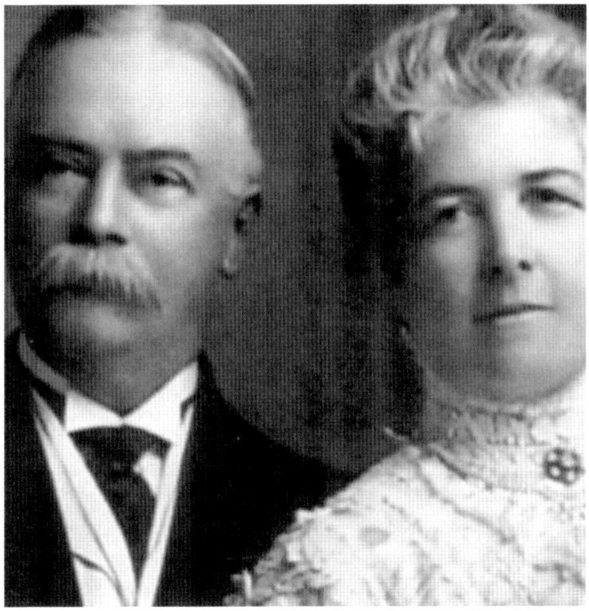

Mary Ella Bost Cannon
Cabarrus County's collective heart stopped in 1921 when Cannon's husband, textile pioneer James W. Cannon (left), passed away. But his widow assisted in Cannon Mills's leadership transition by serving on its board of directors—a rarity for a woman in this era—and by backing her son Charles to succeed his father. Hailing from the prominent Bost Grist Mill family, Mary Ella Cannon generously supported several public institutions. (Courtesy of KHA.)

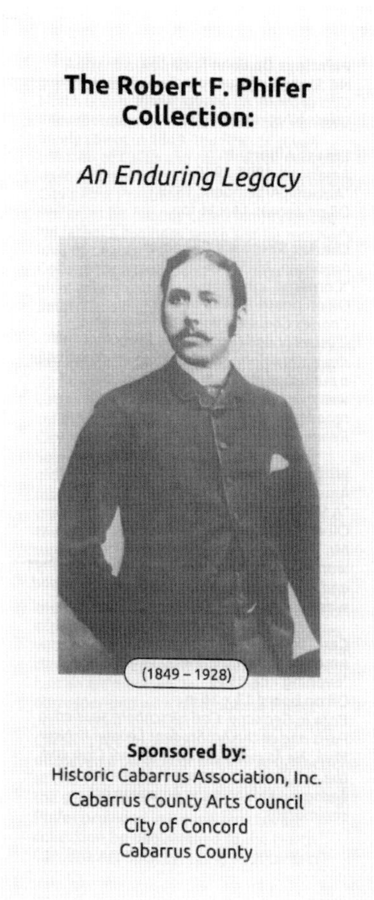

Robert F. Phifer
A member of one of Concord's oldest and most influential families, this prosperous businessman turned his attention in his early 30s toward travel and acquiring oil paintings. Upon his 1928 death, the bequest of Phifer's collection became the cornerstone of Raleigh's North Carolina Museum of Art. A 2015 exhibit in Concord displayed paintings of Phifer's for the first public showing in over 40 years. (Courtesy of Historic Cabarrus Association, Inc.)

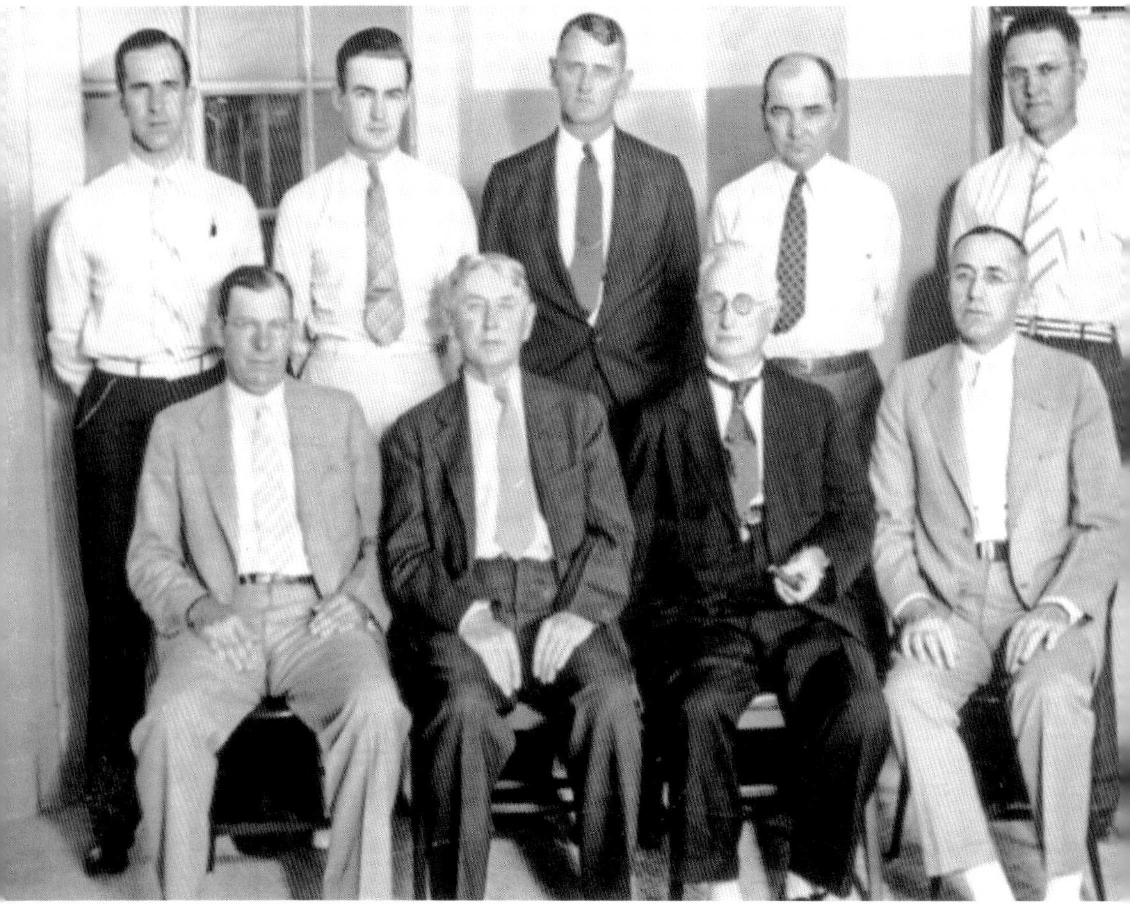

George A. Batte Jr.

The Great Depression detoured Batte, a Davidson College graduate with a chemistry degree, from medical school and into a job at Cannon Mills. There, after working his way up the ladder, his partnership with the mill's owner, Charles A. Cannon, led to the founding of Cabarrus Memorial Hospital (now Carolinas Medical Center–NorthEast), built upon land donated by Mary Ella Bost Cannon. Originally containing 46 beds, the hospital, which opened in 1937, supplanted the small, overburdened "sick house" on Union Street in Concord and better addressed the region's influx of newcomers seeking jobs in the mills. For nearly 60 years, Batte dedicated himself to the welfare of his community via charitable work with the Cannon Foundation and the Cannon Charitable Trust. The current hospital's cancer center, established in 1997, is named in his honor. Also bearing his name is Wingate University's $8.5-million George A. Batte Jr. Fine Arts Center, which opened in 1999.

This photograph depicts the Cabarrus hospital's original board of trustees, selected from the county's different communities. Shown are, from left to right, (first row) Joe D. Glass (Kannapolis), W.W. Flowe (Concord), Col. George F. McAllister (Mount Pleasant), and T.N. Spencer (Concord); (back row) Batte (Concord), Douglas Kincaid (business manager), J.O. Nolan (Kannapolis), Zeb B. Bradford (Kannapolis), and Eric G. Flannagan, the hospital's architect. Cannon, the board's chairman, is not depicted. (Courtesy of the *Independent Tribune*.)

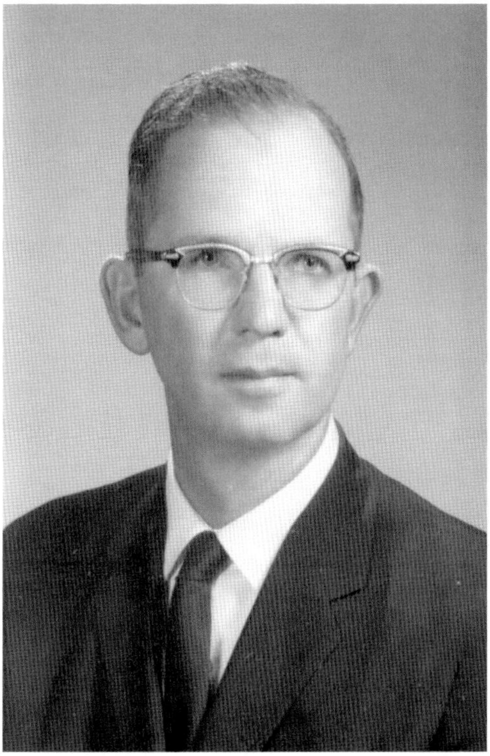

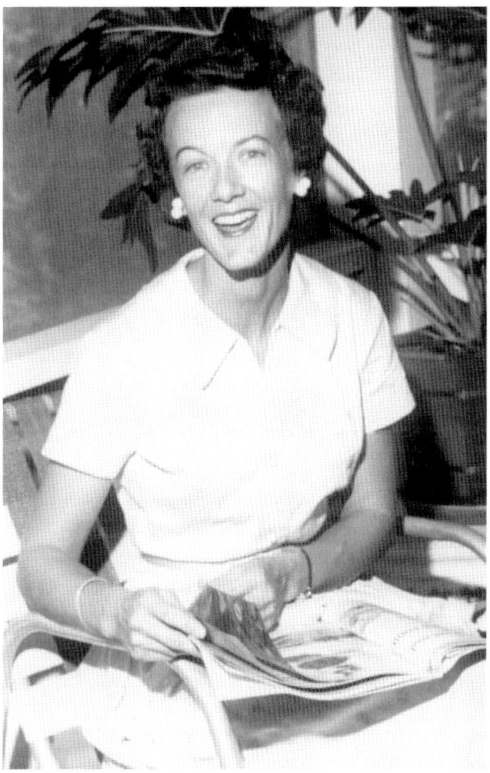

Lester D. and Phyllis Coltrane III
The descendant of Concord business pioneer Daniel Branson Coltrane, "Bub" Coltrane selflessly continued his family's tradition of civic investment. The president of the Concord National Bank for three decades, Coltrane, a World War II veteran, worked with numerous boards and organizations, including the Concord Telephone Company and the chamber of commerce. He died in 2007. His wife, the former Phyllis Crooks, has similarly devoted herself to a variety of causes, with an eye toward health care, including a long history of volunteering with the American Red Cross and the Bloodmobile program. Among the couple's many honors was their becoming the Concord Business and Professional Women's first husband-and-wife team to receive its Man and Woman of the Year Awards, in 1977. The Coltranes have provided long-term endowments to the NorthEast Medical Center. (Both, courtesy of Concord Public Library.)

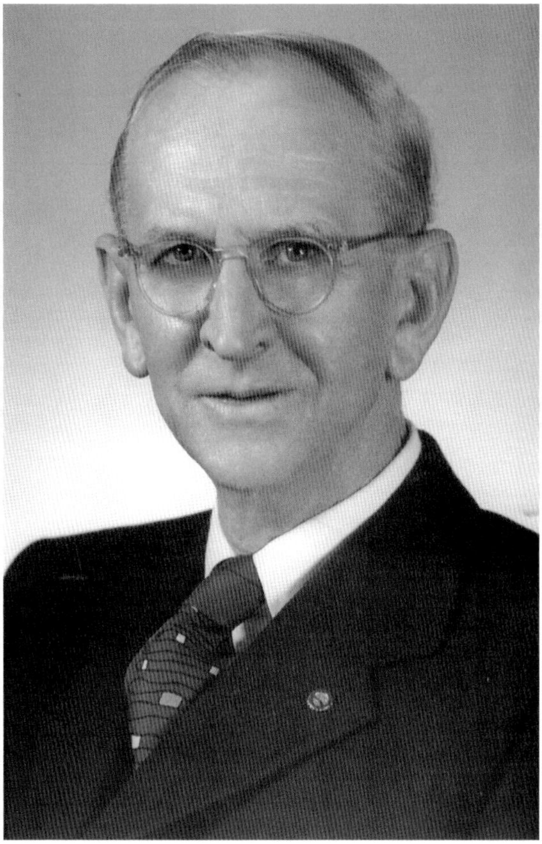

A.L. Brown

The man heralded as Kannapolis's "first citizen" actually had his roots in Concord. As a teenager, Alfred Luther Brown, born in 1870, labored with his father, A. Monroe Brown, at the M.L. Brown & Brother Livery Stable on Depot Street (now Cabarrus Avenue). At age 18, he was hired by James W. Cannon to work 12-hour shifts as a cotton opener in Cannon's first mill, in Concord. Thus began Brown's long and distinguished career with Cannon Mills. After seven years at the Concord plant, he was promoted to manager of Cannon's Cabarrus Mill location and continued a steady rise through the ranks that would ultimately direct him to the roles of vice president and general manager, his headquarters shifting to the operation's Plant No. 1 in the heart of Kannapolis. As one of Cannon Mills' chief executives, Brown was "always direct in his business dealings" and "quiet and unassuming," wrote *Daily Independent* reporter Bill Workman in 1955. Charles A. Cannon, who succeeded his father, James W. Cannon, as the company's president after James's 1921 death, once called Brown "one of the best friends our employees ever had."

While Brown was known to many from his role with Cannon Mills and from his involvement with the development of several subdivisions in Kannapolis, his unremitting public service stamped his name into the annals of Kannapolis history. The well-being of young people was his topmost concern: he was a major benefactor of the YMCA and the city's public school system. His devotion to the latter earned him the 1951 distinction of Kannapolis's new high school being named in his honor. Brown also delighted in dairy farming; he bred blue-ribbon cattle from his Clear Springs Dairy Farm in Cabarrus County.

Brown died unexpectedly—and tragically—on December 19, 1955, when he accidentally drove his vehicle into the frigid depths of Town Park Lake, at Cannon Mills Plant No. 1. The freak accident occurred within view of many witnesses, several of whom plunged into the icy waters for an attempted rescue. Brown is buried at Oakwood Cemetery in Concord. (Courtesy of KHA.)

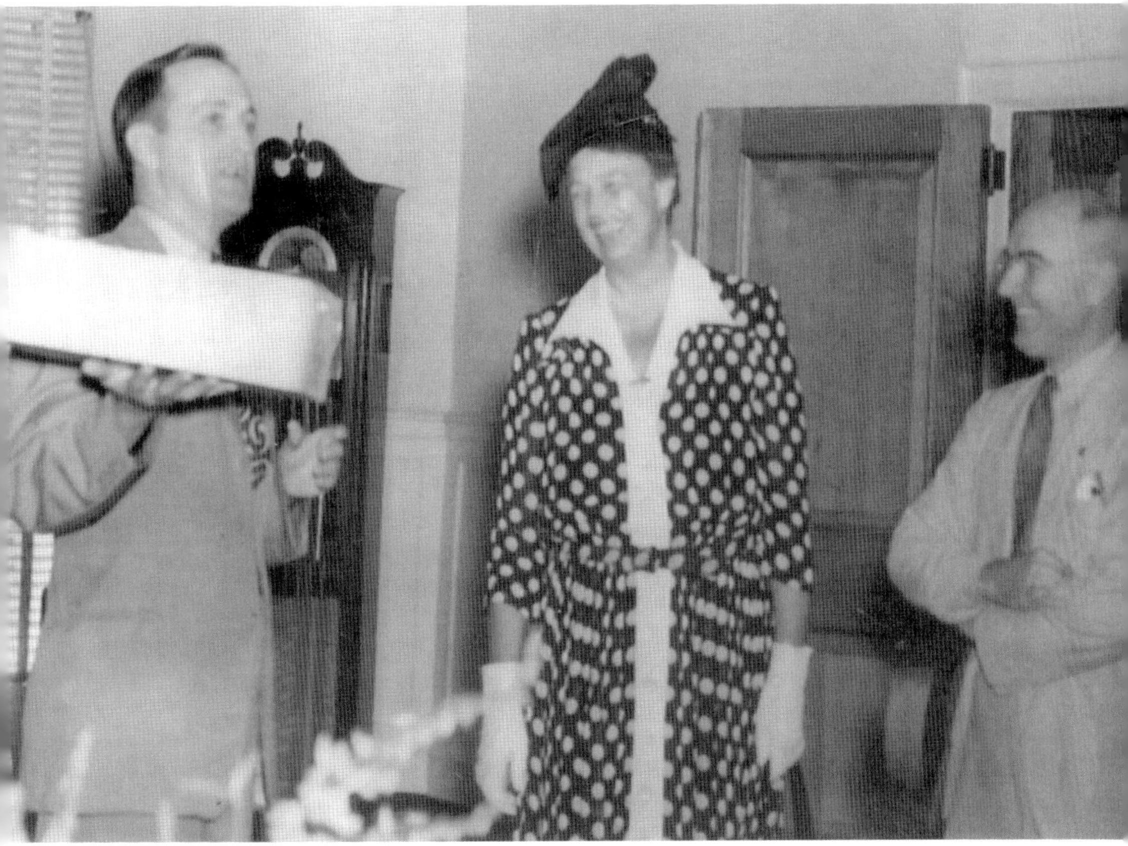

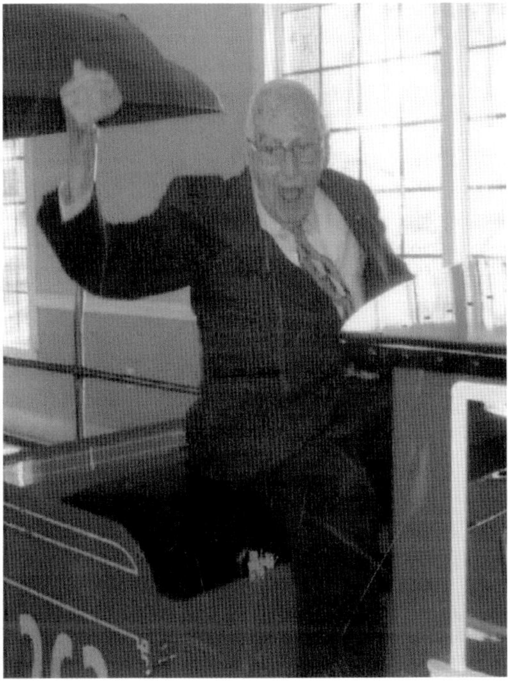

J. Carlyle Rutledge

In the above photograph, Rutledge (left) was an up-and-coming Kannapolis attorney in 1942 when he presented a gift of Cannon towels to visiting First Lady Eleanor Roosevelt, with the glowing approval of Charles A. Cannon (right). Rutledge remained a professional and civic cornerstone of Kannapolis throughout his long and prosperous life, which ended in 2008. While he represented Cabarrus County in both the state house and senate, his heart belonged to the Towel City, where he was acutely involved with the Gem Theatre, real estate, his church, the YMCA, and the Kannapolis Rotary Club. Rutledge so endeared himself to his community that he became the unincorporated city's spokesperson during its transition from Cannon to Murdock ownership. His generous 2006 gift of $50,000 allowed for the construction of Village Park's train ride, which he is shown enjoying in the photograph at left. (Both, courtesy of KHA.)

Mary Ann Black

Mary Ann Black Black (she was a Black who married a Black from another family) does not just tell a story about yesteryear—she acts it out, as if in a one-woman show, gesturing, posturing, inflecting, singing, and bringing to life the voices of those she knew and loved from a bygone era. Her house is a museum, each nook and cranny storing a coveted image or artifact that offers a tangible bridge between the present and the past: her father's handmade sander, a lid from one of her mother's canning jars, and hundreds, possibly thousands, more items. When sharing a story, Black zips with uncanny precision from one relic to another, illustrating her tale with a prop, each item meticulously annotated with her hand-printed description. It is no wonder that this high-spirited octogenarian is famous in Midland as the town's go-to historian. "Everything has its own history," she often says, and Black—who was a mere five years of age when her farmer father died in an automobile accident, leaving her widowed mother to raise eight children—is determined to keep those legends alive.

Mary Ann was only three when the Black family ventured into Concord for this 1936 portrait. Seated are her parents, Emmett Clinton "Clint" Black (with Mary Ann on his knee) and Pernelia Ann "Annie" Pope Black (Vanderburg; she remarried in 1956). The children are, clockwise from bottom left, Joyce, Joseph Benson "Ben," William "Bill" Henry, Smaro Lee, Avous Lusane, Kathleen, and Clinton McCoy "Coy." (Courtesy of Concord Public Library.)

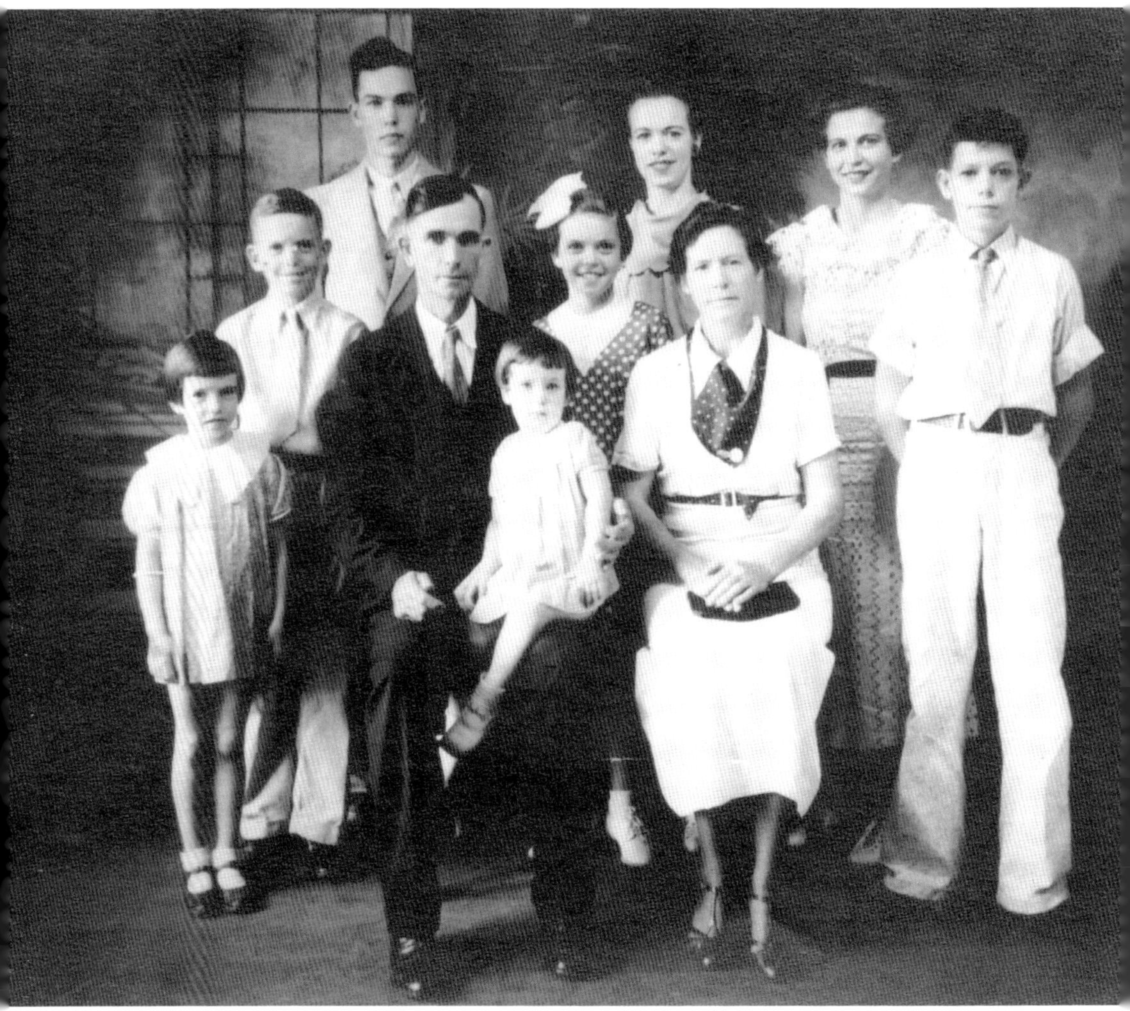

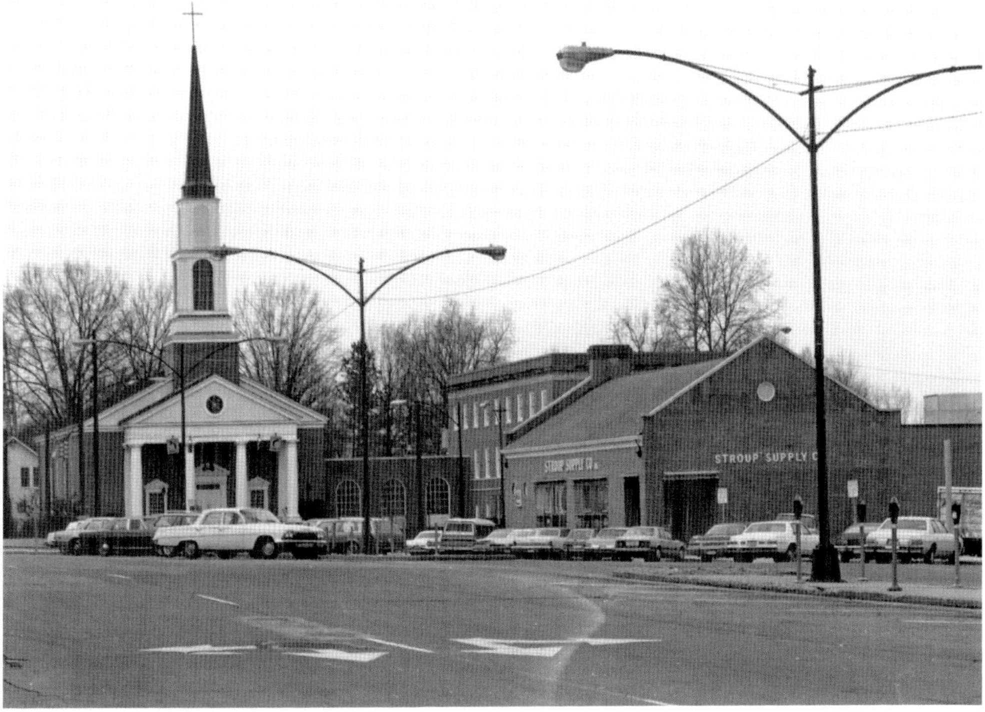

Samuel B. Stroup Jr.

While some Kannapolis customers of Stroup Supply (above) may have been unaware of its owner's civic contributions, their lives were certainly improved by them. Stroup sat on the Kannapolis School Board for 25 years, chairing the group from 1961 through 1969. He was a proponent of vocational education and witnessed the building of A.L. Brown High and several other schools. He played a vital role in Kannapolis's incorporation, serving on its charter commission and on its first city council. Stroup was chairman of the YMCA Building Fund, director of the Kannapolis Chamber of Commerce, a founder of the Kannapolis Community Fund, and he participated in many other organizations. His warm, genuine smile is on view in the photograph at right, taken in 1986, three years before his death. (Above, courtesy of KHA; right, courtesy of Alice Stroup Jackson.)

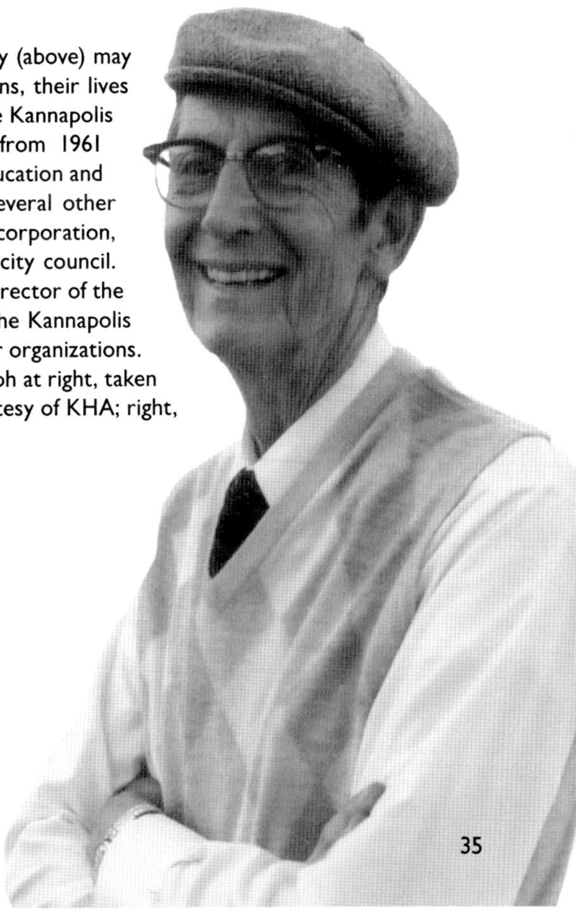

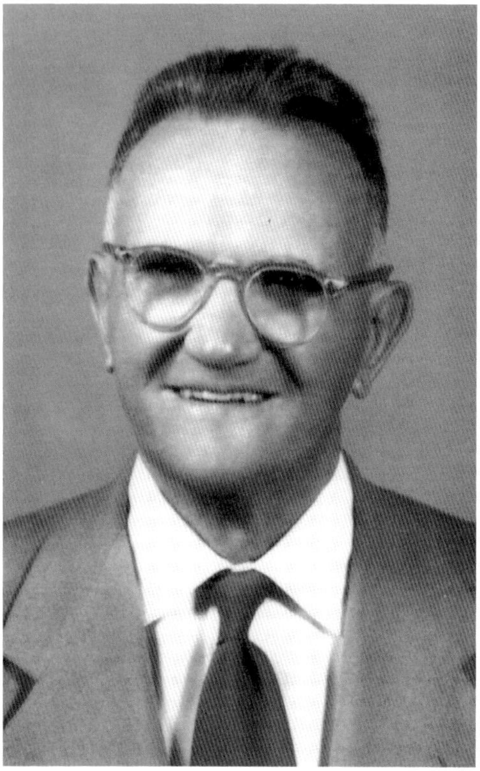

Nicholas E. Lubchenko
Some in Harrisburg know of Lubchenko from his former house on Robinson Church Road, from which he ran his doctor's office with his wife, Ollie, a nurse. Others recall his lead-footed emergency responses in his 1955 Chevy. A Russian expatriate, "Dr. Lube" practiced medicine in Harrisburg from the 1920s through the 1950s, and his donation of land gave birth to the town's volunteer fire department. (Courtesy of Jenna Sue Taylor.)

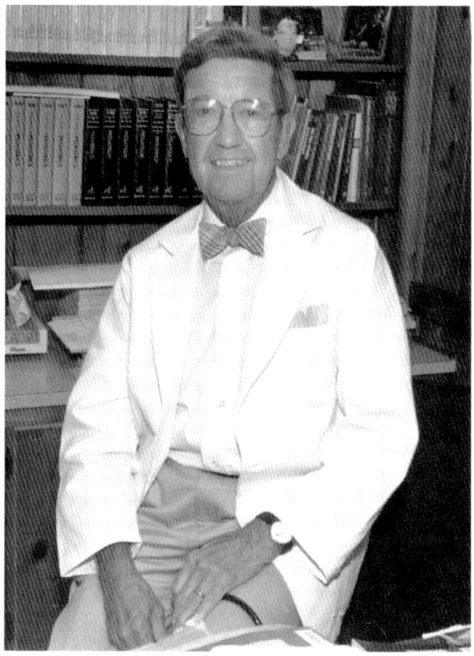

David Lockhart
With a genial smile as wide as his bow tie, this Concord pediatrician cared for families for 40 years. At Lockhart's 2009 passing, his youngest son, Malcolm, remarked of his father, "He wanted to create something for people who fall through the cracks." This was the Community Free Clinic, cofounded by Lockhart and fellow physician George W. Liles Sr. after they both had retired from their practices. (Courtesy of Betty Sue Lockhart.)

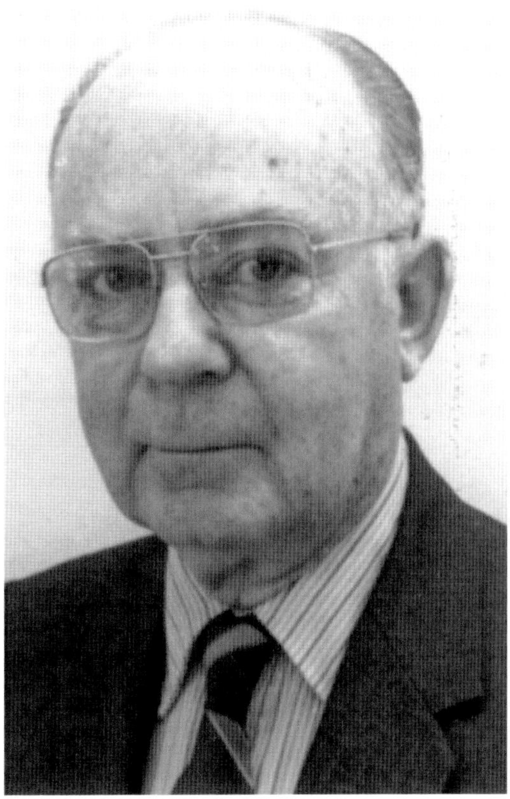

Archibald L. Barringer

After distinguished service in the Navy during World War II, Dr. Barringer, a 1928 graduate of Mount Pleasant High School, treated patients of all ages for decades as his community's primary physician. He even delayed his retirement until a successor could be found. Archie Barringer was honored in 1983 when the high school football field was named after him. He died in 1998. (Courtesy of Concord Public Library.)

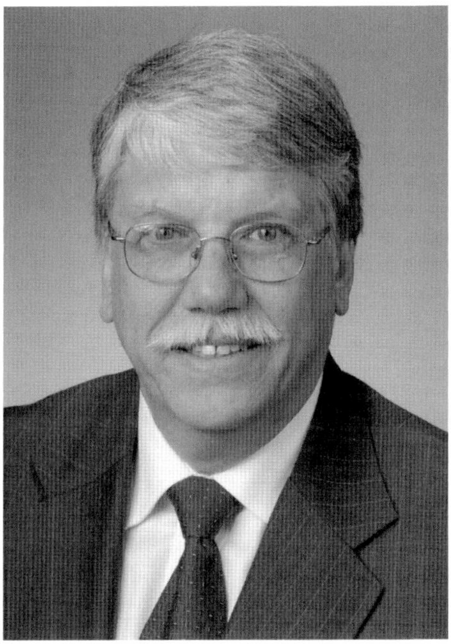

Allen Dobson

Following in the footsteps of Mount Pleasant's longtime physician Archie Barringer, Dobson has been fundamental in expanding health care services throughout the region, state, and nation. The founding chair of family medicine at Cabarrus Memorial Hospital (now Carolinas Medical Center–NorthEast), Dobson opened Mount Pleasant Family Physicians, developing it into the area's largest primary-care practice, and Cabarrus Family Medicine residency for new family practitioners. (Courtesy of Paul Mahoney.)

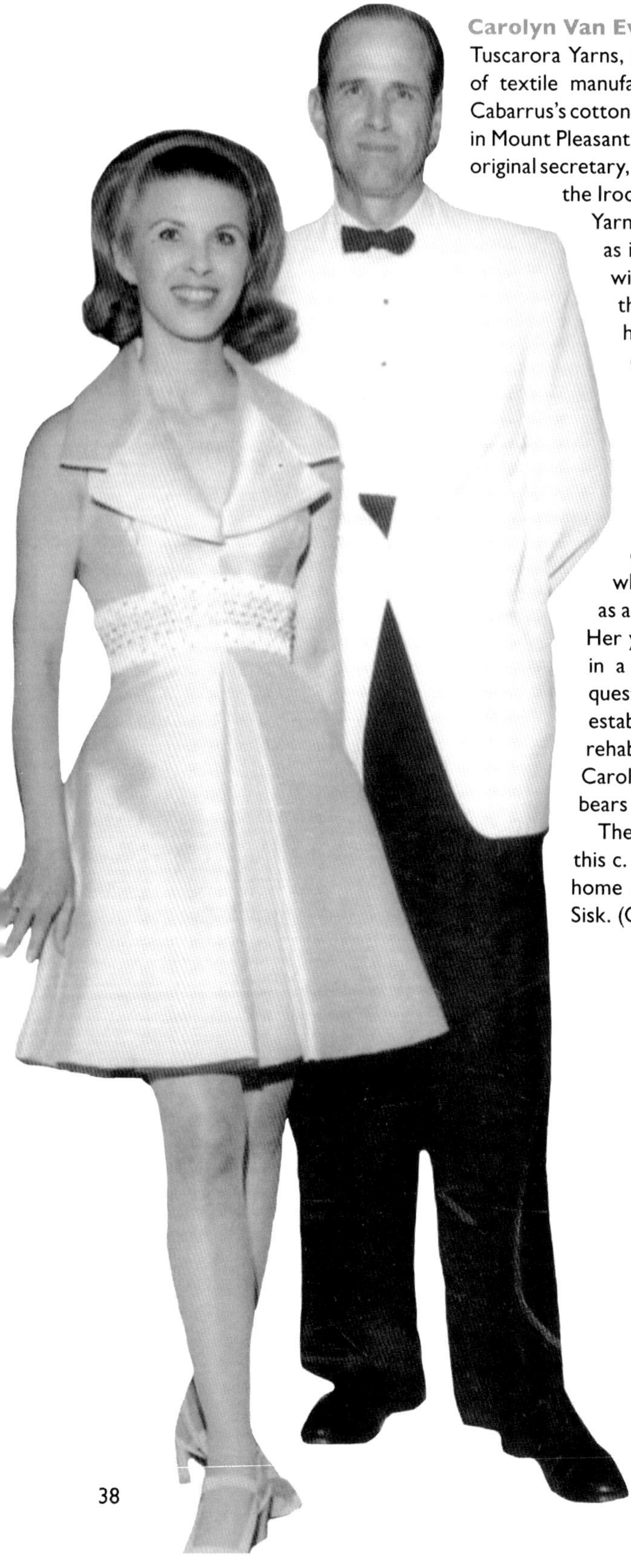

Carolyn Van Every and Martin B. Foil Jr.

Tuscarora Yarns, Inc., defies the trend of global exportation of textile manufacturing. It began in August 1899, during Cabarrus's cotton-mill heyday, when its factory was established in Mount Pleasant to provide jobs for locals. Paul Barringer, its original secretary, coined the company's name, borrowing from the Iroquois word for "hemp gatherers." Tuscarora Yarns still spins strong today, with Martin Foil as its chairman emeritus; he has been involved with the business since 1967. Foil's belief in the importance of American manufacturing has kept the firm's corporate headquarters entrenched at its original Mount Pleasant location. He is highly regarded for his industry knowledge and holds patents for textile-manufacturing devices.

His photogenic wife, Carolyn—known and loved by friends as "Puddin"—found tranquility in her magnificent garden, the envy of many of her friends. Yet Puddin Foil, who died in 2010, may best be remembered as a champion for individuals with brain injuries. Her youngest child, Phil, sustained brain trauma in a 1984 automobile crash, and her 16-year quest to find the best care for him led to the establishment of Hinds' Feet Farm, a 36-acre rehabilitative facility in Huntersville, North Carolina. A long-term care center on the farm bears her name: Puddin's Place.

The Foils make quite the handsome couple in this c. 1968 photograph, snapped at a party at the home of Puddin's sister, Mary Lance Van Every Sisk. (Courtesy of Quincy Foil.)

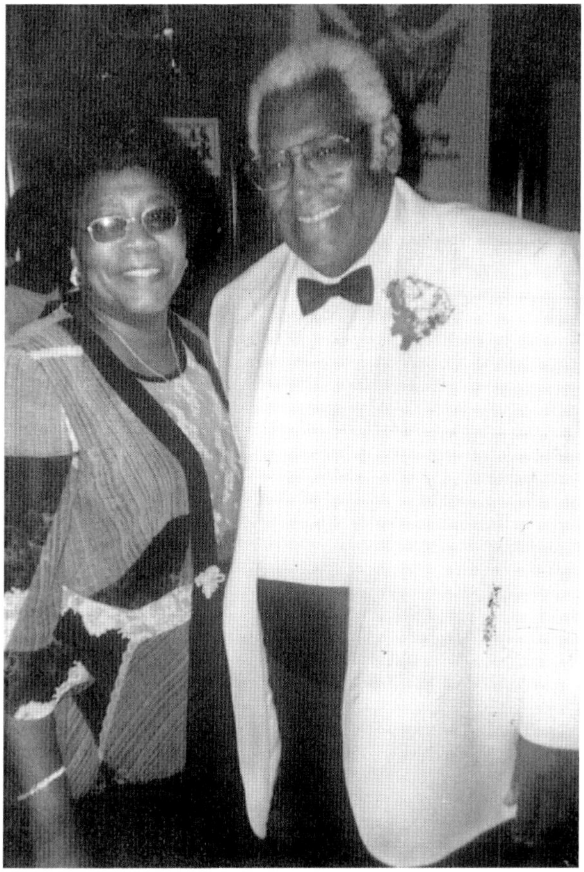

Allen T. and Ella Mae Small

"Don't talk it, but live it," Allen T. Small was known to say. And that he did. This cheerful Concordian transformed many students' lives as a dedicated educator and principal at Logan High School. Once desegregation shuttered that venerated African American institution, Small became principal of Coltrane-Webb Elementary during the earliest years of Concord's integrated school system, weathering the sometimes-difficult transition with unimpeachable grace and professionalism. He later served as principal of Wolf Meadow Elementary. But his community impact extended far beyond the hallowed halls of schoolhouses. The devoutly spiritual Small organized the Logan Optimist Club and was active with his church and with civic government on the local and state levels, being elected to the Concord City Council in 1997. He passionately represented District Three until his unexpected death in 2006. His legacy survives via Price Memorial AME Zion Church's Allen T. Small Family Life Center, whose name preserves his memory.

His legacy is also continued by his widow, the former Ella Mae Pompey, who filled his council seat upon his passing and was later elected to the post, becoming the first woman to serve on the Concord City Council. She was also its first female mayor pro tem. Prior to joining the council, she worked with some of its members on the committee that renamed US Highway 601 "Warren C. Coleman Boulevard" in honor of the trailblazing black business pioneer. Like her husband, Ella Mae Small's background is in education, having taught in the Concord and Cabarrus County School Systems, as well as in Charlotte and Atlanta and at Rowan-Cabarrus Technical School and North Carolina A&T University. Today, she is involved with numerous organizations in Concord's Logan community and throughout Concord and Cabarrus County, with several retired educators' associations, and as a city councilwoman. Small has been a proud member of Delta Sigma Theta sorority for nearly 60 years. (Courtesy of Ella Mae Small.)

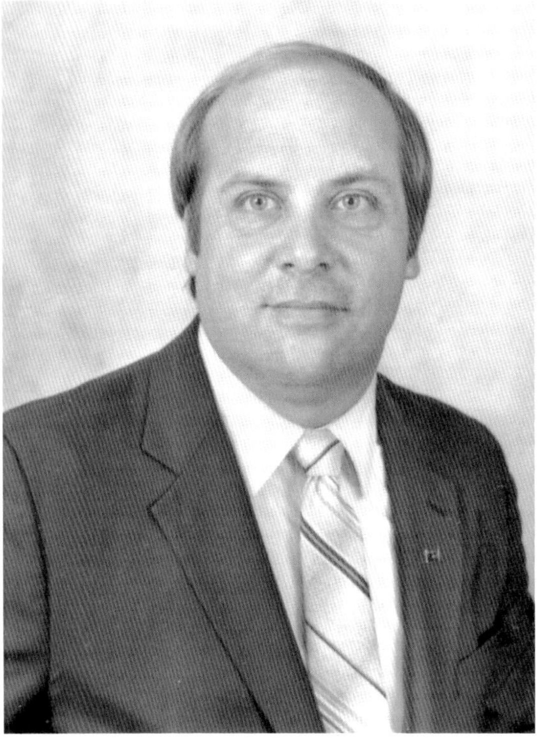

Lamar Barrier
Barrier, a Vietnam War veteran and semiretired mortician, has held a seat on the Concord City Council since 1985. His conviction to provide benevolent end-of-life treatment inspired his involvement with Hospice and Palliative Care of Cabarrus County, which he helped develop as a founding board member. Barrier also assisted with the development of two community health clinics. (Courtesy of Concord Public Library.)

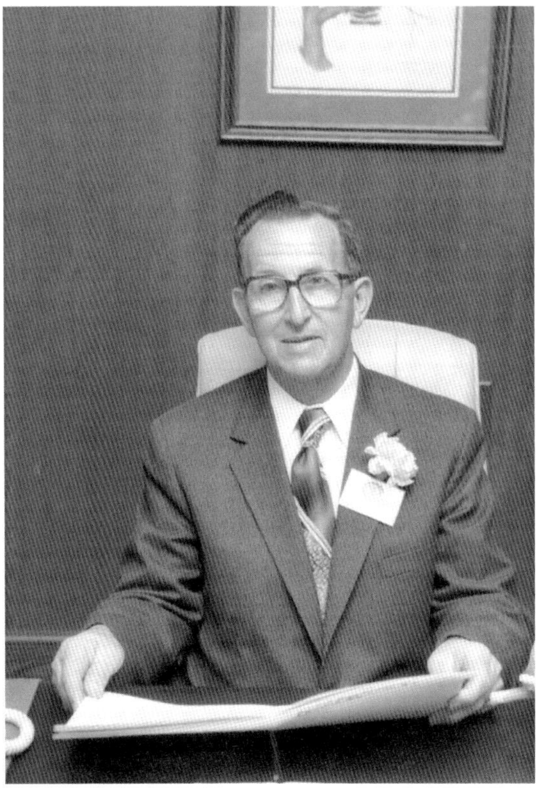

Everett Helms Sr.
Nicknamed "Mr. Banker," Helms shunned acclaim yet was fundamental in the economic growth of several charities, particularly the Boys and Girls Club, which he quietly encouraged donors to support through wills and trusts. A World War II veteran, he began his career in banking as a teller and ultimately climbed to the presidency of Citizens National Bank. Helms died in 1997 at age 79. (Courtesy of Neta Helms.)

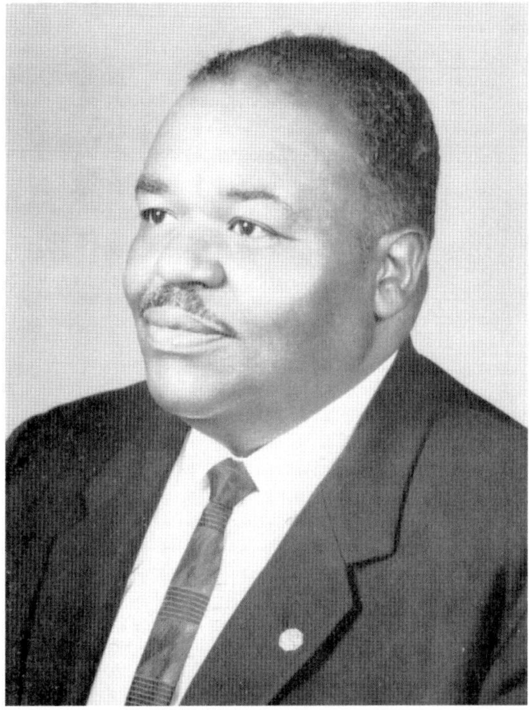

C.C. Griffin
Curl Caesar Griffin spent 15 of his 30 years in education as the principal of Logan High, Concord's pre-integration black high school. The first African American human resources director of Cannon Mills, he also founded a health clinic for Concord's Logan community. Blinded by diabetes during the last years of his life, Griffin died in 1986. A Concord middle school is named in his honor. (Courtesy of Concord Public Library.)

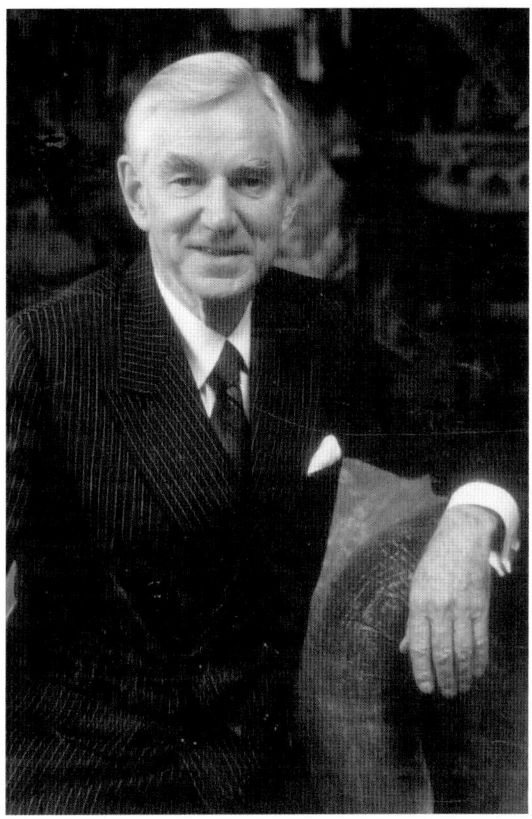

David H. Murdock
Kannapolis's metamorphosis began when billionaire Murdock purchased Cannon Mills and its surrounding 660 acres in 1982. Downtown was renovated into a retail village and the city was incorporated, but when the mill closed in 2003, another transformation occurred. In a move that was controversial for lifelong residents, Murdock razed Cannon Mills's historic grounds and on its site constructed the North Carolina Research Campus, which opened in 2008. (Courtesy of Concord Public Library.)

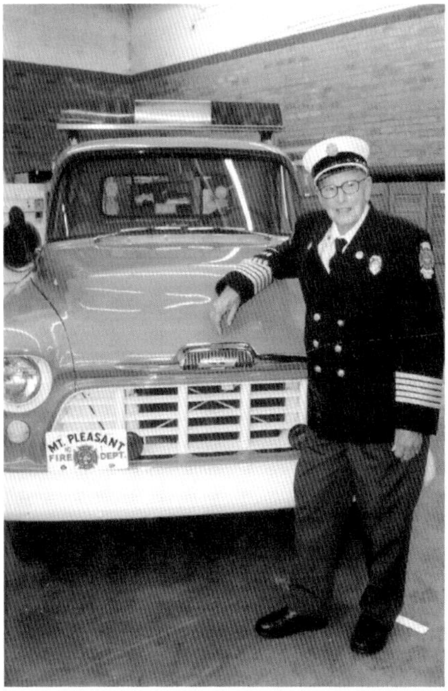

Arthur Lee Kluttz

This Miller Lumber Company owner's greatest "construction project" has been community development, including the improvement of Mount Pleasant's water supply and the building of its new fire station. A longtime town council member, in 2013, Kluttz was presented with this dress uniform, honoring his lifetime of service to the Mount Pleasant Fire Department, where he was fire chief for 29 years. (Courtesy of Arthur Lee Kluttz.)

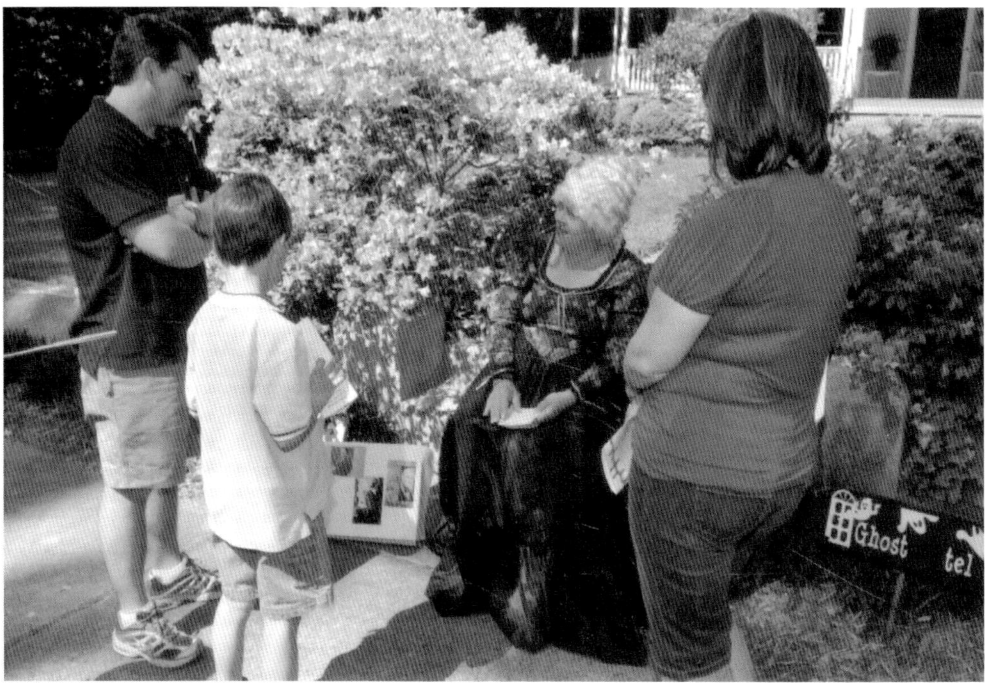

Carolyn Carpenter

This civil servant has been frequently elected to both the Cabarrus County School Board and the board of commissioners. Carpenter was the county's first woman chair of the commissioners and the youngest female commissioner to be elected. Her spirited passion for Concord's departed souls has become legend through her sharing of ghost stories and tales of characters of yesteryear, which she often does in period clothing. (Photograph by the author.)

George L. Govan

"At my age you have to keep moving or you may sit down and can't get back up," Govan said at age 83 in 2000. At that time, this Harrisburg hog and corn farmer, the son of sharecropper Henry Govan, was one of several area growers saluted in a celebration called Farm Games 2000. And Govan always kept moving, doing whatever was necessary to support his 11 children, including clocking in at Charlotte Pipe & Foundry Company for 36 years before "retiring" to farm life.

But it was at his house of worship that Govan became legendary in his community. He was one of the most cherished members of Harrisburg's historic Bellefonte Presbyterian Church. Bellefonte (meaning "beautiful fountain") was established by Rev. Luke Dorland in 1867, the same year that white Presbyterian minister founded Scotia Seminary (now known as Barber-Scotia College). Dorland founded Bellefonte as a church for African Americans who had previously attended Rocky River Presbyterian. Govan served Bellefonte in numerous ways, from fiduciary planning as a trustee to maintaining its grounds and cemetery. Immensely likable, Govan always sported a gentle smile, be he stylishly attired for church or in his comfy overalls on his farm. He passed away in 2011 at age 93, but his spirit remains through his large family (which extended to great-great-grandchildren at the time of his death) and in Bellefonte Presbyterian Church's life center, which is named in his honor. (Courtesy of Drucilla Govan.)

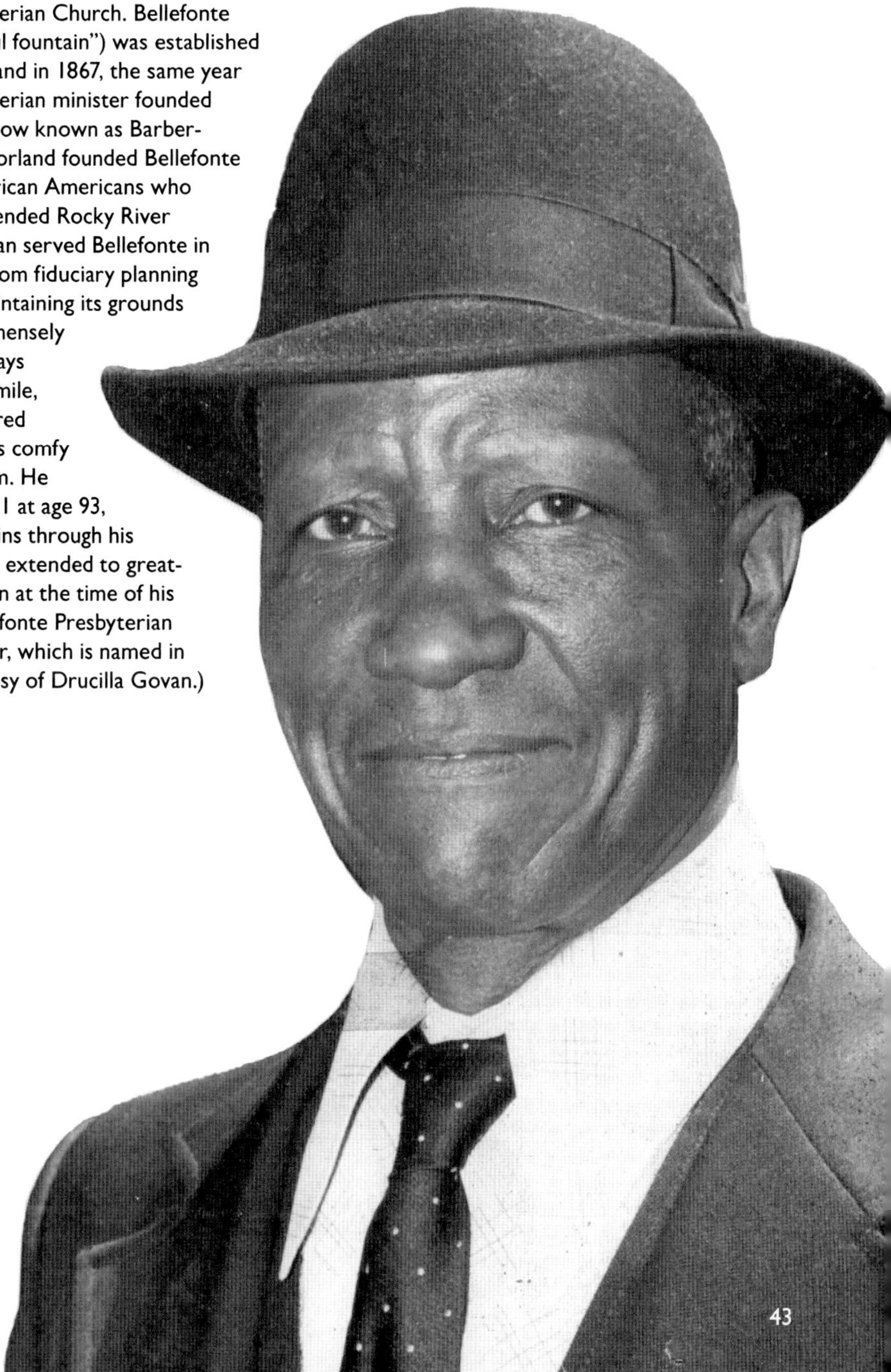

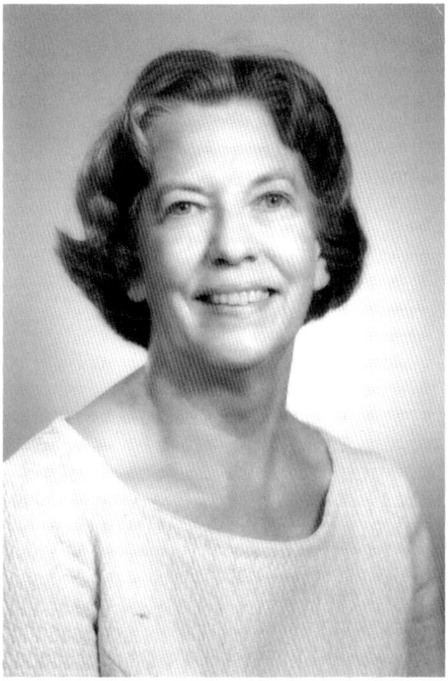

Margaret McConnell Holt

From the 1950s to her 1987 death, Holt, the wife of Cannon Mills executive Don S. Holt, was among the county's cultural cognoscenti, an accomplished musician, painter, sculptress, and author. Her arts and music education benefactions have enriched North Carolina universities and libraries. The Concord Public Library's *Story Time* statue (below), sculpted by Gary Price, is one of the community's most visible testaments to her generosity. The Concord Friends of the Library are custodians of an endowment made by Holt to support arts education within the library system. (Right, courtesy of Concord Public Library; below, photograph by the author.)

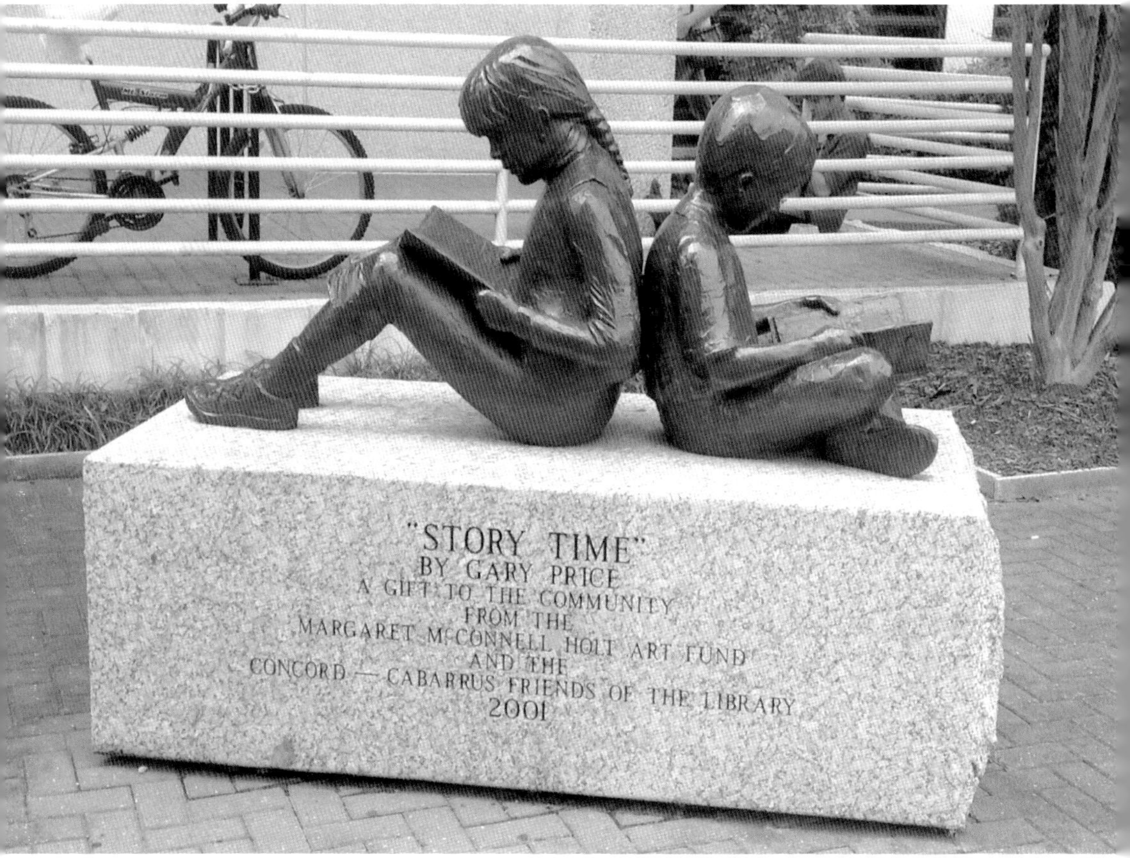

Anne Hege Wilson

As a young actress belting out "Hello, Mr. Charlie!" to the tune of "Hello, Dolly!" in honor of Cannon Mills's president at this May 1967 Charles A. Cannon Appreciation Day, Wilson could not have imagined her future as the matriarch of Cabarrus County's premier community theater family. Inspired by the indomitable will of arts patron Mary Snead Boger, whose mid-1970s crusade to spare the 1876 Historic Cabarrus County Courthouse from the wrecking ball ignited a campaign to preserve the building, Wilson became a familiar face on stage in numerous Old Courthouse Theatre (OCT) productions and as a member of its board of directors. Her backstage efforts, however, may not have garnered the applause of theatergoers, but they are nonetheless marquee-worthy. After the 1987 retirement of Boger as OCT's artistic director, Wilson stepped into a leadership role as the organization's volunteer business manager beginning in 1988 and continuing, with one brief interruption, for over 20 years. She devoted herself to the theater's success in matters small and large, from ticket sales to building sets to fundraising, rarely receiving compensation. Wilson helped guide OCT through a tumultuous period of site relocations. Her zeal has been shared by her family: her husband, Trent, has worked magic with inventive set and prop designs; son Chris, a trombonist, has performed in the pit orchestras of several musicals; and daughter Heather has acted in and directed myriad OCT productions, even serving as artistic director for 10 seasons. Each year, OCT presents the Wilson Family Volunteerism Award to a family that contributes their time and energies to the organization. Shown in this photograph are, from left to right, Linda Corbett, Wilson, Cannon, and Sue McMillan. At the time, the ladies were student nurses at the Cabarrus Memorial Hospital School of Nursing. (Courtesy of Anne Hege Wilson.)

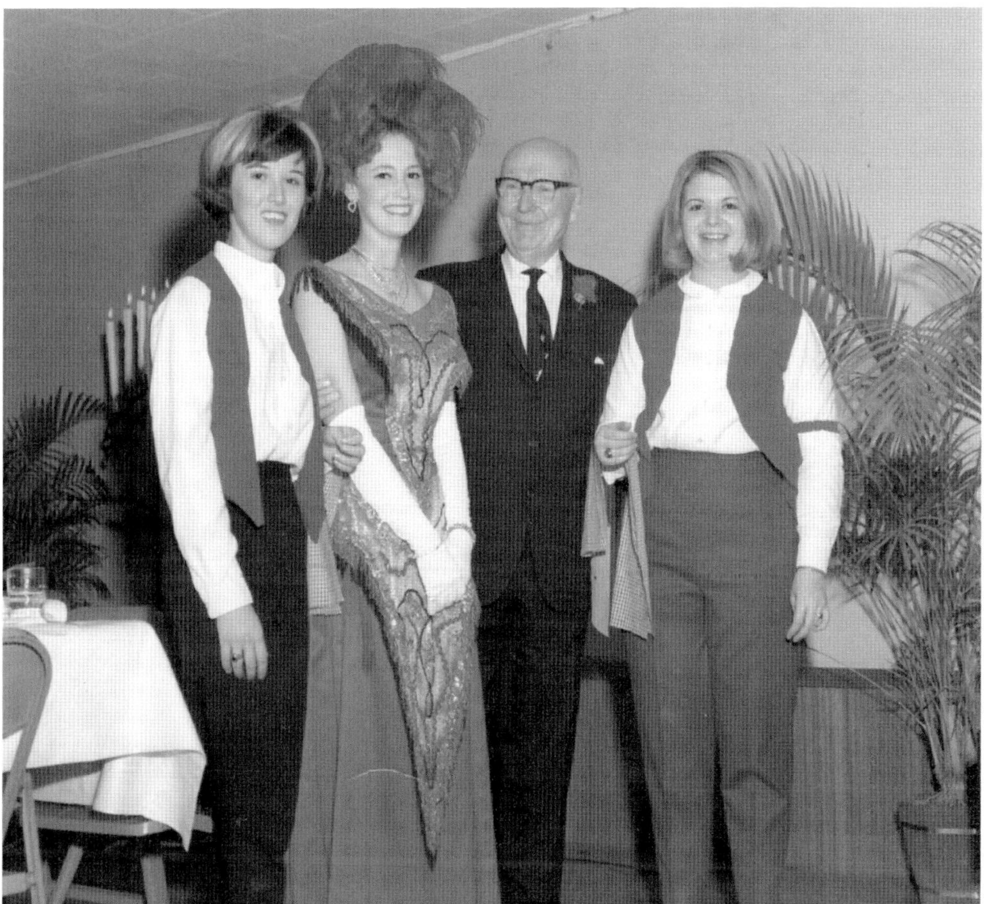

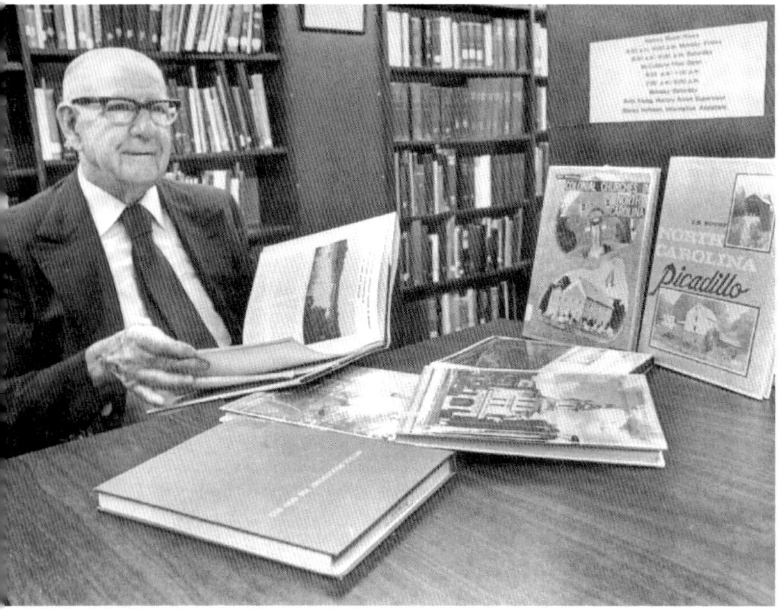

J.K. Rouse

Rouse, who died in 1992 at age 88, was visible in the community as a teacher, recorder's court judge, and associate secretary for the Cannon Memorial YMCA. His ineradicable contribution, however, is his impeccable historical research, shared with readers via numerous books, including *The Great Road through Cabarrus County* and *The Noble Experiment of Warren C. Coleman.* (Photograph by the *Salisbury Post*; courtesy of Concord Public Library.)

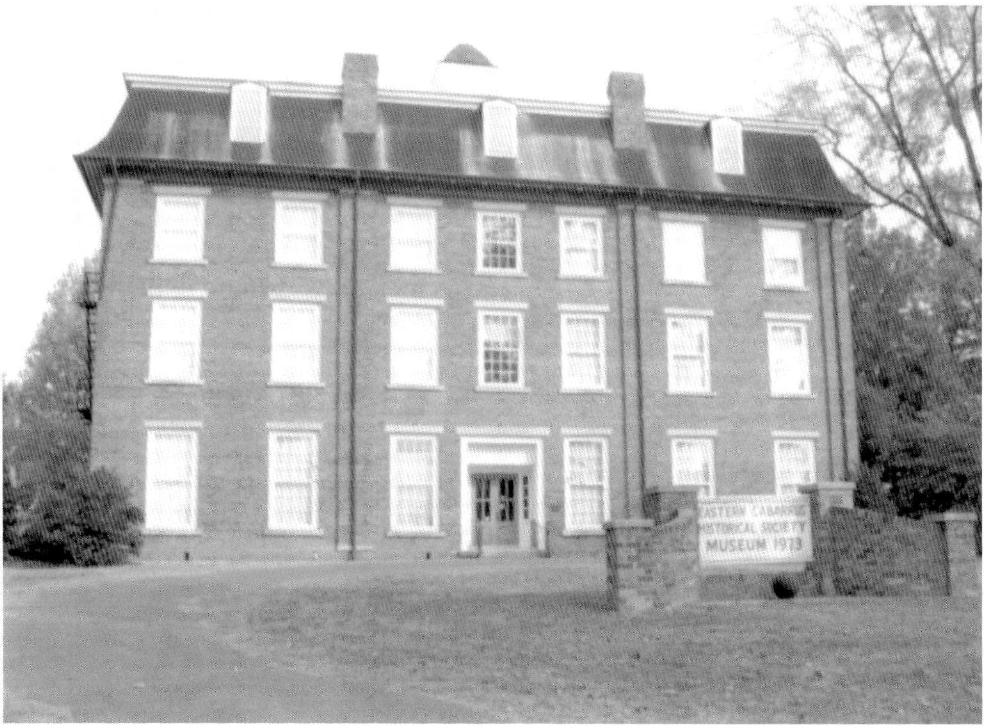

Eastern Cabarrus Historical Society

The august group of Mount Pleasant preservationists has filled this stately building, shown here in the mid-1970s, with artifacts, antiques, portraits and photographs, publications, and ephemera that recreate 19th- and early-20th-century life in Cabarrus County. The hilltop building itself was erected by the North Carolina Lutheran Synod in 1855 as the Western Carolina Male Academy. (Courtesy of Concord Public Library.)

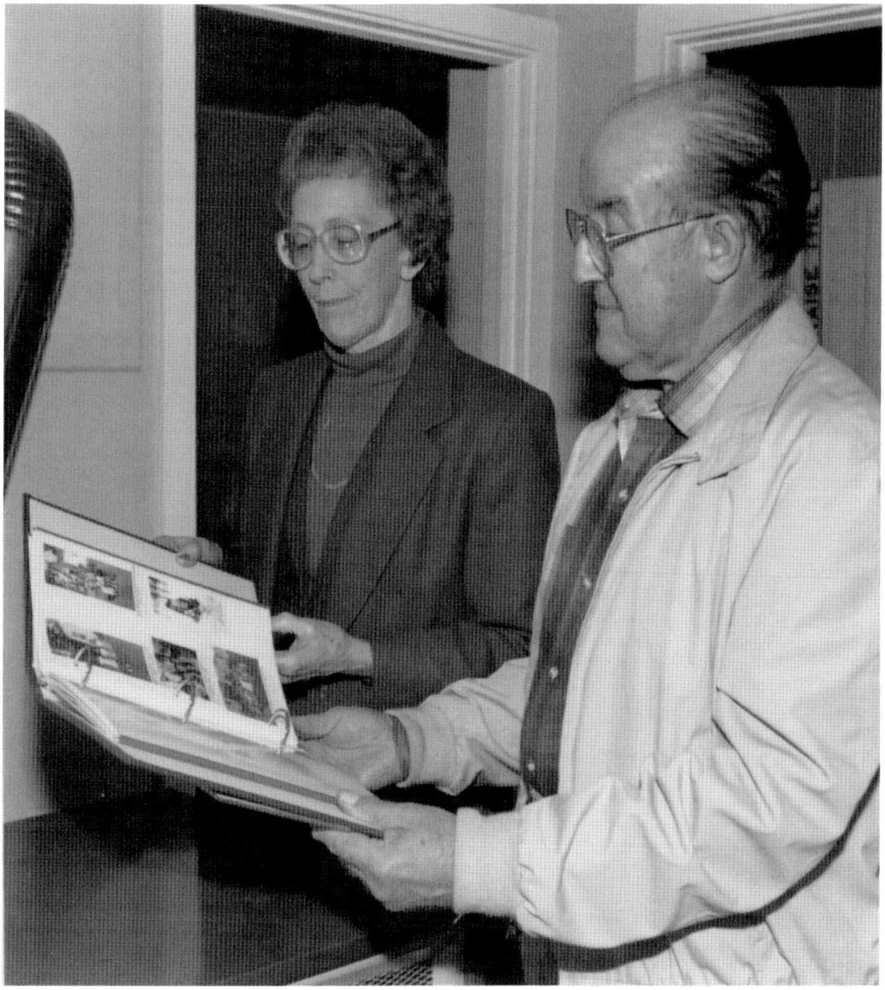

Kannapolis History Associates

In early 1987, Kannapolis first lady Mabel Brown (left), wife of Mayor Bachman S. Brown Jr., along with a few other citizens, quietly acquired items from an auction held at the city's old YMCA, tangible remnants of a bygone era. The Kannapolis History Associates (KHA), a group of preservation-minded volunteers, officially incorporated in April of that year, its mission being the creation of a permanent archival facility for the city's artifacts. While the group continued to collect pieces of the past—from executives' desks to sports memorabilia—the Cabarrus County Board of Commissioners decreed in 1992 the establishment of a history room at the Kannapolis Public Library. As overseers of the proposed history room, KHA began an extensive fundraising campaign to renovate and equip the facility, greatly abetted by a $50,000 donation from Gertrude Hinson, a gift that was originally made anonymously. By the time the facility was officially opened in 1998, the Hinson family's generosity was publicly acknowledged with the christening of the Foy and Gertrude Hinson History Room. Its chief caretakers were Cabarrus genealogist Larry Hayer and retired Cannon Mills employee and sagacious historian Norris Dearmon (right). A tumultuous turn of events in 2010 squeezed the history room out of the library, with KHA scrambling to find a new home. In 2011, the history room temporarily took residence in the Kannapolis Rotary Club's meeting hall until space became available in 2012 at A.L. Brown High School, the current home of the Hinson History Room and the headquarters of KHA. (Courtesy of Concord Public Library.)

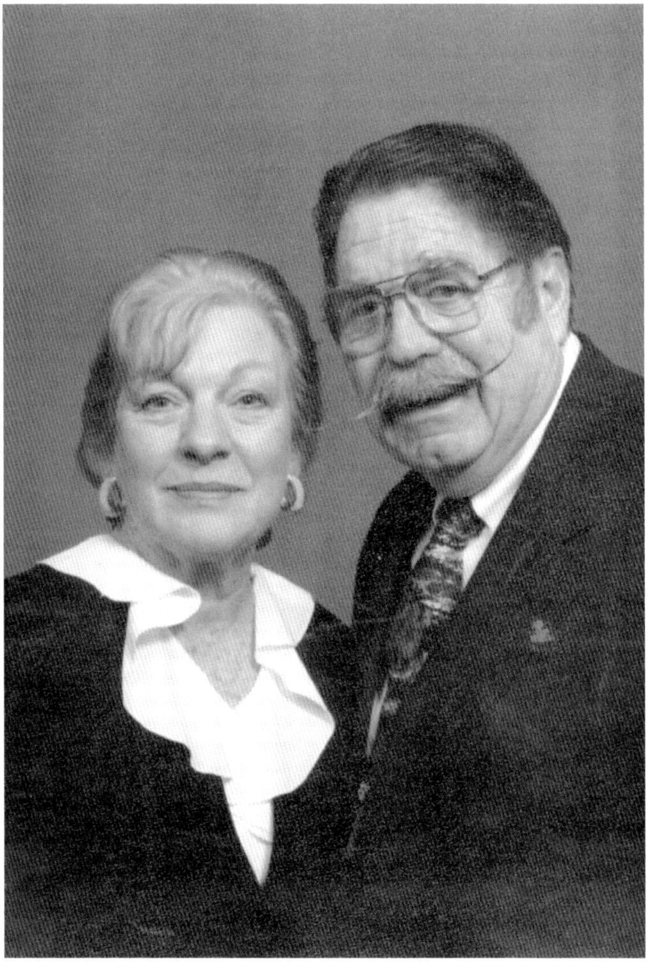

E.M. and Jennie Martin Tomlin

The Tomlins became a couple via a confluence of their respective fields. An acclaimed artist of local landmarks, Jennie, a widow, was hired by Dr. Tomlin to produce an illustration of a Cabarrus medical facility. One commissioned drawing led to another and another, until "Tommie" finally asked her out. They were married in 1980; it was also his second marriage.

The mustachioed physician was renowned in both the medical and political arenas of Cabarrus County. A decorated Korean War veteran, Tomlin served as a ship and battlefield surgeon before completing his military career at the Bethesda Naval Hospital, where his patients included Pres. Dwight D. Eisenhower and future presidents Lyndon B. Johnson and Richard M. Nixon. He settled in Cabarrus County after the war, founding the Cabarrus Urology Clinic, becoming chief of staff at Cabarrus Memorial Hospital, and serving on numerous prestigious statewide medical boards. He resuscitated Cabarrus County's ailing Republican Party as its chairman, helping to restore GOP representation in a region that had for generations been the domain of Democrats. A former mayor of Harrisburg, Dr. Tomlin died in 2010.

A recipient of the Kokenes Award for Proficiency in Visual and Creative Arts, the multitalented Jennie Martin Tomlin's acclaim extends beyond her native Cabarrus County. Her work has been frequently exhibited in the community—including a mural of historic county locations permanently displayed in the Harrisburg Town Hall—as well as in private and business collections across the globe. She is an in-demand art teacher who hosts classes in drawing, watercolor, and pastels, and she is active with the Cabarrus Art Guild and Cabarrus Arts Council. (Courtesy of Jennie Martin Tomlin.)

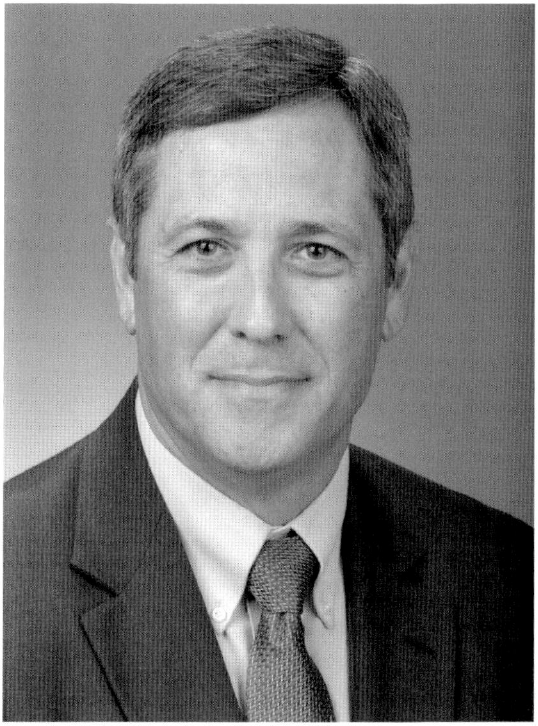

Ed Hosack
As a division manager at Pillowtex, Hosack had the arduous task of informing many employees of the mill's 2003 closing. Through prayerful consideration, he rejected job offers elsewhere and pursued a $1-million grant to help retrain displaced workers. Since 2005, Hosack has been the executive director of Cooperative Christian Ministry, Cabarrus County's foremost provider of crisis assistance. (Courtesy of Charlene Roof.)

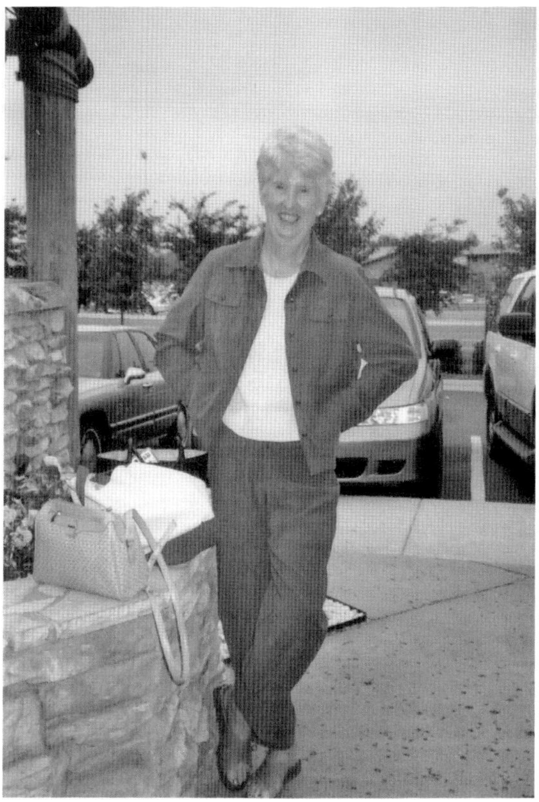

Pat Miller
The heart and soul of the Harrisburg Crisis Assistance Ministry, Miller magnanimously credits the people of her town, who provide vital resources whenever she asks. From families displaced from their homes to down-on-their-luck locals looking for food, she works closely with those in need and assesses how best to help. Miller is also the originator of Harrisburg's annual Fourth of July parade. (Courtesy of Pat Miller.)

David Goforth
Cabarrus County's greenest thumb belongs to this master gardener. During his three decades as the county's agriculture extension agent for the North Carolina Cooperative Extension, Goforth expanded Cabarrus's seasonal outdoor market, cultivated the Elma C. Lomax farm incubator, created the Master Gardener Volunteer Program, and provided horticultural education to both young and old via local access television and community presentations. Goforth retired in July 2015. (Courtesy of David Goforth.)

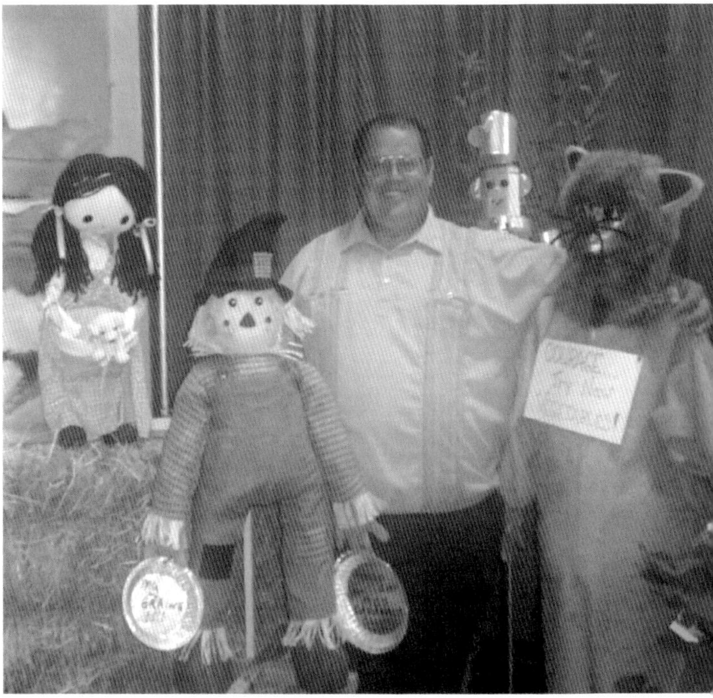

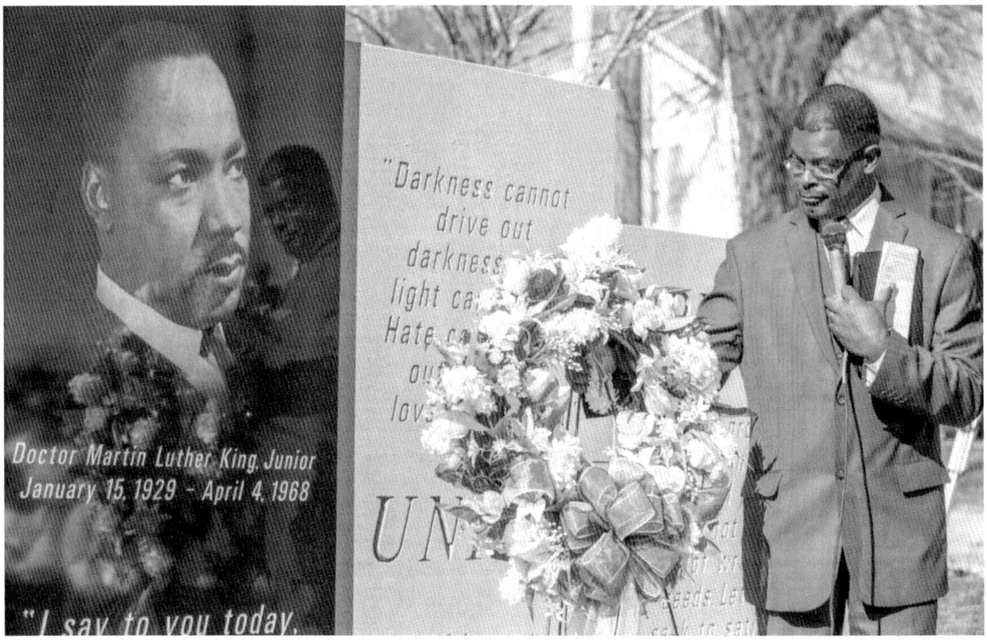

Rev. Donald E. Anthony
Since 1997, Anthony, an active community servant, has pastored Concord's Grace Lutheran Church, founded in 1883 by Rev. David James Koontz. A 2014 winner of Kannapolis City Schools' Champion for Children Award, Anthony chaperoned Cub Scout Pack No. 134 on a transformational March 2015 visit to Selma, Alabama, to commemorate the 50th anniversary of the landmark civil rights marches there. (Photograph by James Nix; courtesy of the *Independent Tribune*.)

CHAPTER THREE

Heroes

Each time the nation has taken up arms to uphold its values, the men and women of Cabarrus County have rallied without hesitation. Plucky patriot Elizabeth "Betsey" Phifer (Blackwelder) set out to liberate her family members from the clutches of the Redcoats, but she also compassionately nursed soldiers on both sides of the Revolutionary War during a smallpox epidemic. Kannapolis-born Glenn McDuffie became an American icon when his impromptu celebratory gesture etched his name into history as World War II's famous "Kissing Soldier." John A. Sweat Jr. retired from a career of military distinction to fight new battles as a Concord city councilman.

One must not overlook Cabarrus County's valiant law enforcement agents, firefighters, and medical personnel, who have unflinchingly safeguarded their neighbors' lives and property. Jack Moore and George Smith traded in their police uniforms for suits when they became Concord's first plainclothes detectives, while Richard Church was revered by a generation of children who regarded this approachable cop as a friend. Edie Moss is considered a trailblazer as the county's first African American female police officer, but it was her empathetic treatment of prisoners that made her legendary.

Bob Baucom was one of Cabarrus County's most treasured "uniformed" heroes, outfitted in the crimson costume of Santa Claus. With his lustrous white mane and beard and his cheery demeanor, he raised spirits during Christmastime and funds for the county's hospice center.

"The Intimidator," hometown hero Dale Earnhardt Sr., raced into residents' hearts and even earned the respect of those who never attended a NASCAR event. And the incomparable Bryson Foster, twice the national Muscular Dystrophy Association Goodwill Ambassador, reminds us that heroes come in all sizes.

The select heroes honored in this chapter represent thousands of others who have made Cabarrus County proud.

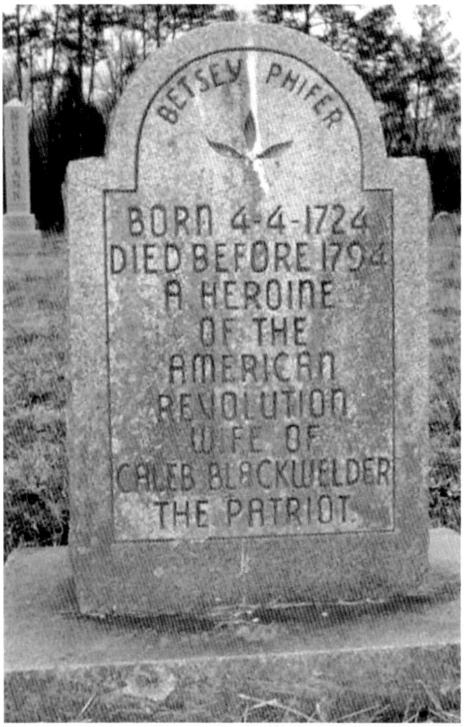

Elizabeth Phifer (Blackwelder)
When her husband, Caleb, son John, and son-in-law John Paul Barringer were captured by Tories (Loyalists) during the American Revolution, Betsey Phifer valiantly dashed from Mount Pleasant to their prison camp in Camden, South Carolina, to petition the British for their release. She encountered a smallpox outbreak there and humanely cared for the sick, both colonists and Redcoats. She is interred at St. John's Lutheran Church's cemetery. (Courtesy of Cabarrus Genealogical Society.)

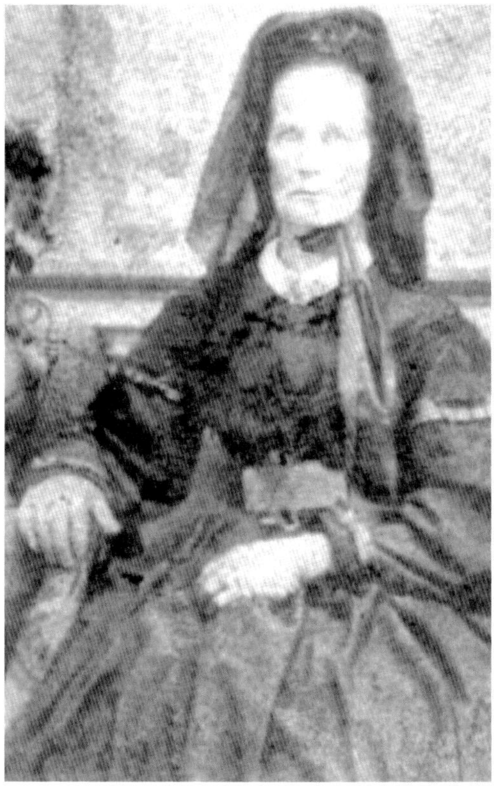

Margaret Mitchell Barrier
This photograph may have faded, but her Mount Pleasant legend still resonates. The mother of Confederate infantrymen Rufus and William Barrier, Margaret was at home with her two youngest children when a Union scout knocked on her door, demanding valuables. Purportedly, her single pistol shot felled the Yankee, whose body was hidden in her house's walls before being buried facedown so that he could "see Hell coming." (Courtesy of ECHS.)

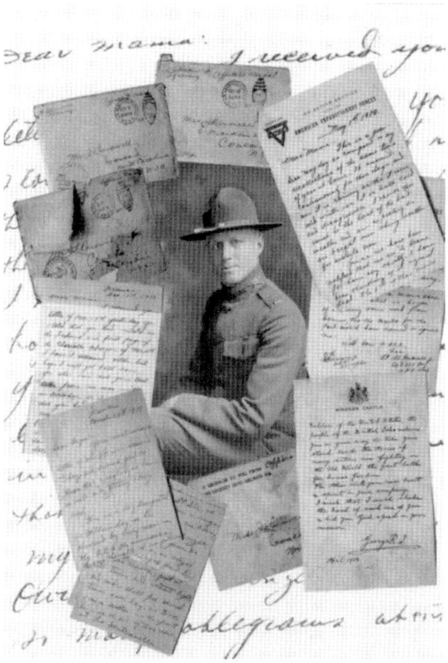

J. Lee Crowell Jr.
Second Lieutenant Crowell served his nation in combat during World War I but also by writing about his battlefield experiences in a series of letters mailed back home. After the war, he became a prominent Concord attorney. His father, lawyer J. Lee Crowell Sr., was a three-time Concord mayor whose major accomplishment was the implementation of the city's sewer system. (Courtesy of Robert D. Raiford and the *Independent Tribune*.)

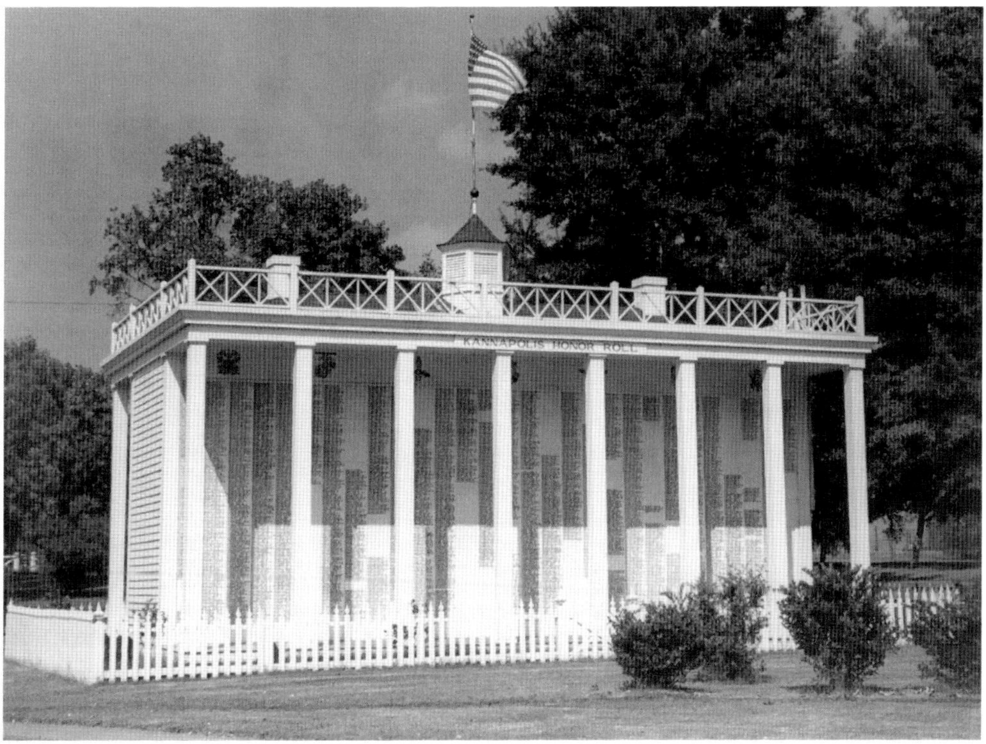

Little Mount Vernon
In 1943, the city of Kannapolis erected this facsimile of Pres. George Washington's residence, Mount Vernon, to salute those serving in World War II. Headquartered in Town Park and measuring 10 feet high by 36 feet wide, this American Legion–sponsored tribute listed the names of all of Kannapolis's servicemen and servicewomen. While it did not survive beyond the 1970s, the patriotism it engendered during its lifespan was immeasurable. (Courtesy of KHA.)

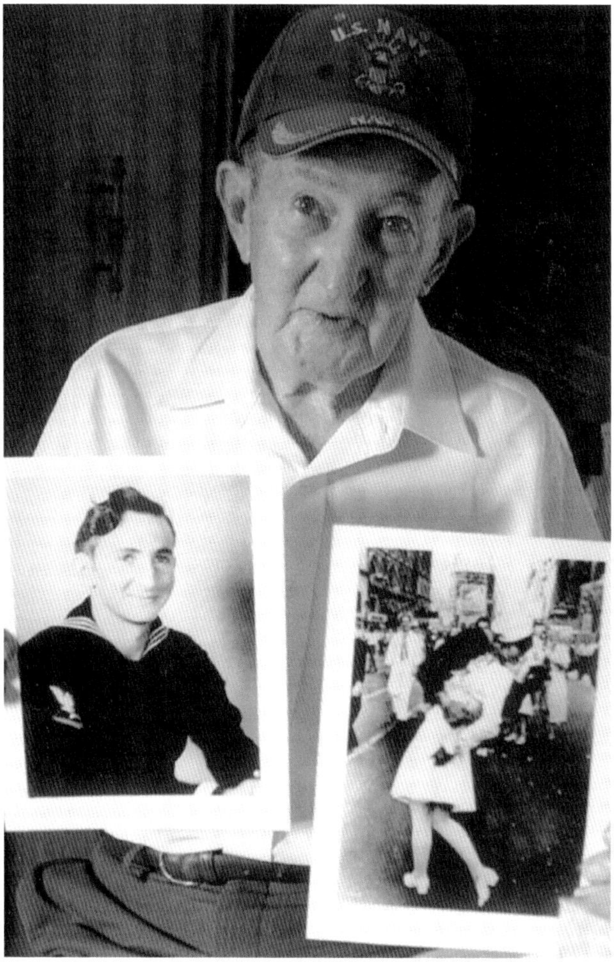

Glenn McDuffie

McDuffie was not the only bullheaded kid who lied about his age to enlist in the service during World War II (he was 15 at the time). Nor was he the only person who claimed to be the Times Square "Kissing Sailor" immortalized by *Life* magazine photographer Alfred Eisenstaedt during the jubilant V-J Day celebration on August 14, 1945. Yet many are convinced that this Kannapolis native was indeed the man in the famous photograph. Born in 1927 in a Packard Avenue mill house, McDuffie was a scrappy, athletic teen who convinced an adult grocer to sign his falsified enlistment papers. He was in New York City three years later, en route to Brooklyn to visit his girlfriend on the fabled day of the announcement of Japan's surrender. "I run out in the street, jumpin' and hollerin'," he said in a 2007 interview for the Library of Congress, thrilled not only of the conflict's end but particularly over the impending release of his older brother W.D., a prisoner of war. The contagious elation led him to grab a random nurse (believed to be Edith Shain) for the legendary lip-lock. After the war, McDuffie briefly played minor-league baseball before taking a post office job, eventually settling in Texas. It was there, in 2007, that a Houston Police Department forensic artist verified, through an extensive study, that McDuffie was indeed the man in the iconic image. The Kissing Sailor enjoyed a brief media blitz; he was interviewed by Diane Sawyer on television's *Good Morning America* and was zipped across the country for personal appearances, with starstruck ladies paying $10 to recreate the celebrated smooch with him. McDuffie died in 2014 at age 86 and was buried in the Dallas–Fort Worth National Cemetery. (Courtesy of the *Independent Tribune*.)

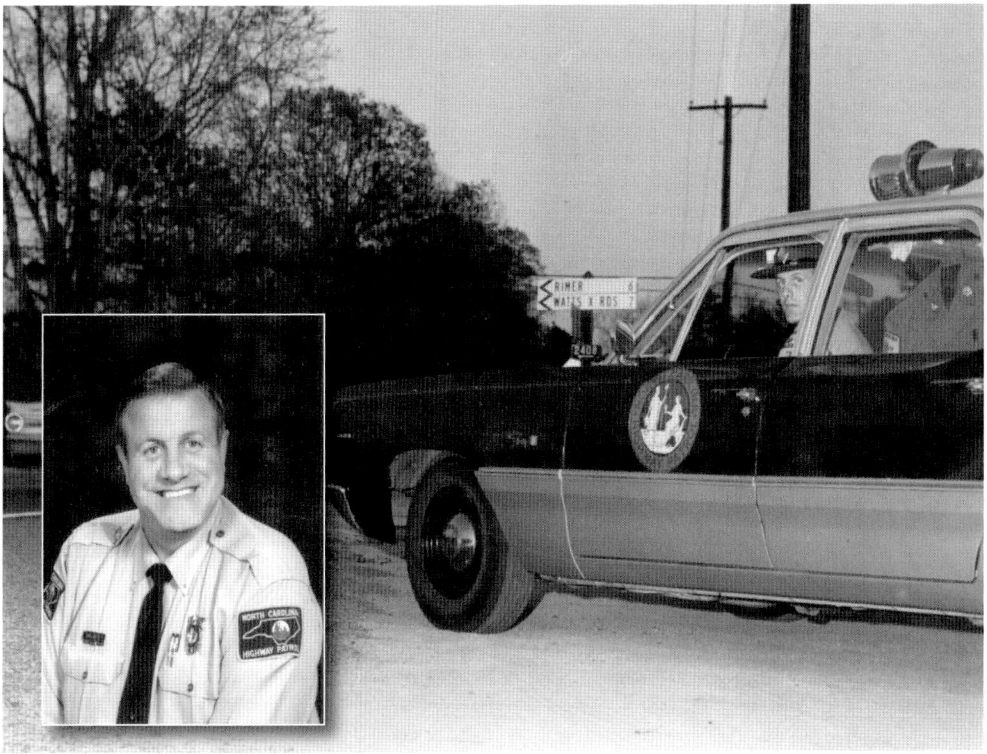

E.H. McAbee

Jack McAbee was a teenager working the family farm when a passing North Carolina Highway Patrol car struck his fancy. When he retired in 1995 after 30 years as Cabarrus County's resident state trooper, McAbee smiled and said, "If the good Lord ever allowed a man to enjoy his work more than me, I'd like to meet the man." (Both, courtesy of Kara McAbee Widener.)

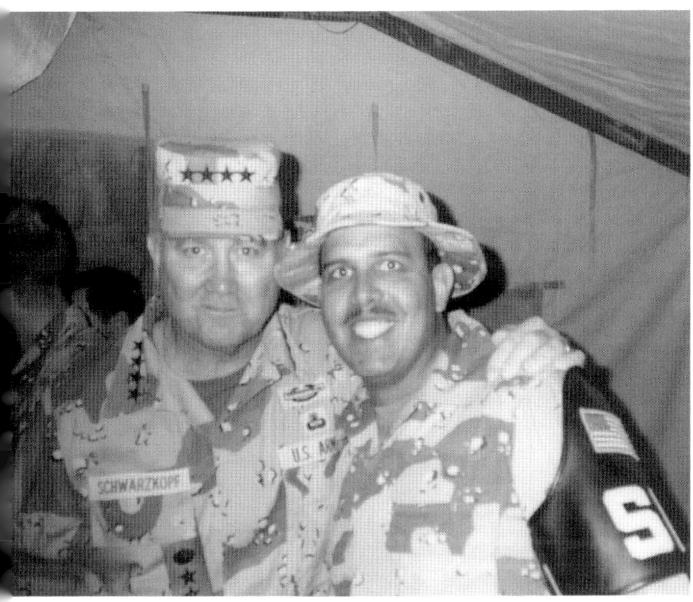

John A. Sweat Jr.

Concord city councilman, S&D Coffee executive, devoted husband and father—that is how most locals know this A.L. Brown High School alumnus. But Sweat's illustrious military career deserves public recognition. He was a highly decorated US Air Force and North Carolina Air National Guard officer, serving over 24 years. Sweat (right) met Gen. Norman Schwarzkopf during the 1990 USO Christmas show in Riyadh, Saudi Arabia. (Courtesy of John Sweat.)

Jack Moore and George Smith

In 1960, Moore (top, right) and Smith (top, left) became Concord's first plainclothes detectives, both having served with the Concord Police Department as uniformed officers in the 1950s. They protected the city through myriad changes, from periods of racial unrest in the 1970s to rapid geographic expansion and economic development in the 1980s. Moore, shown in uniform at bottom left, led the department as police chief from 1975 through 1987. Smith, in his dress blues at bottom right, was chief of police from 1987 through 1990. For many years, Smith's family owned a popular gas and oil company on North Church Street. (Top, courtesy of Lisa Linker; below left, courtesy of Concord Public Library; below right, courtesy of George Smith.)

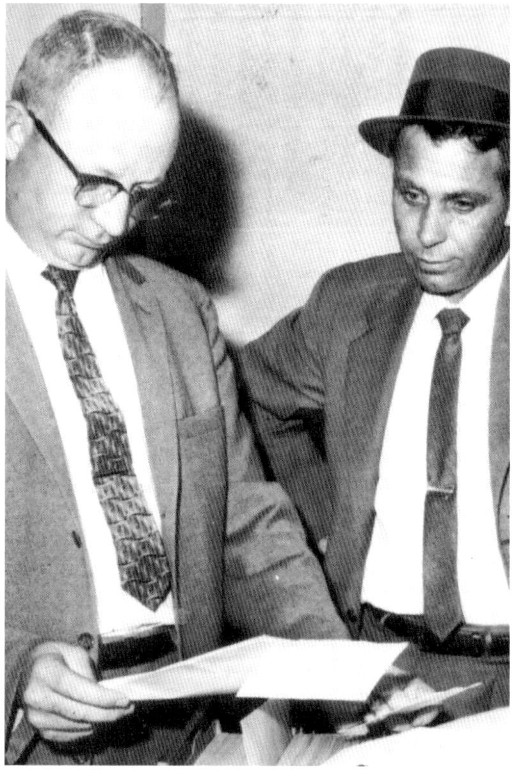

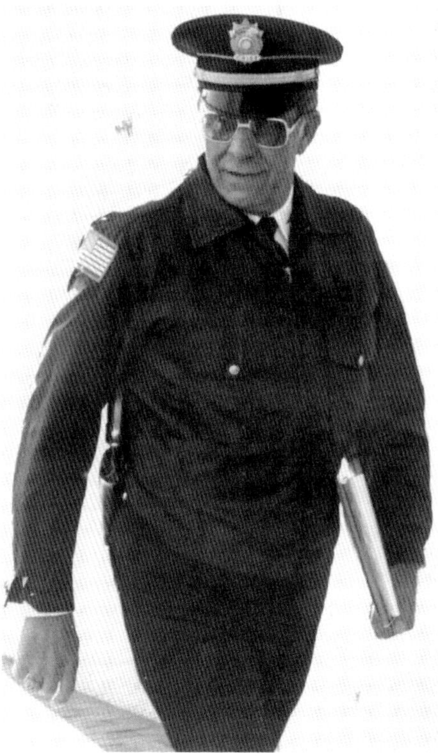

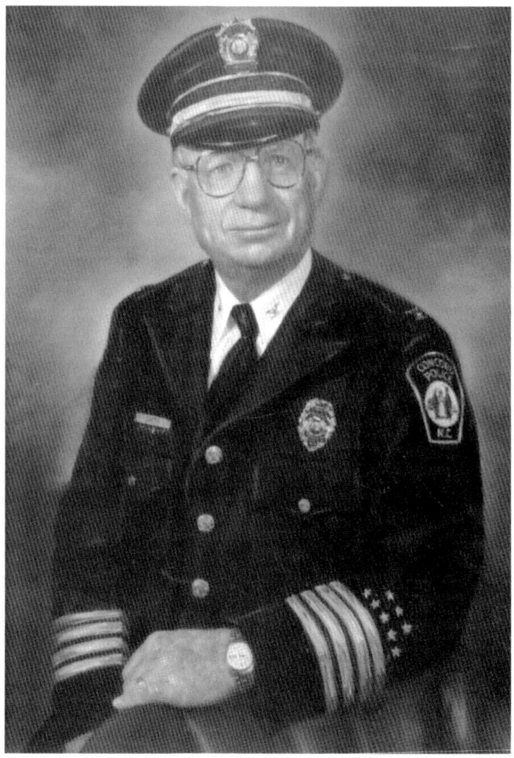

 56

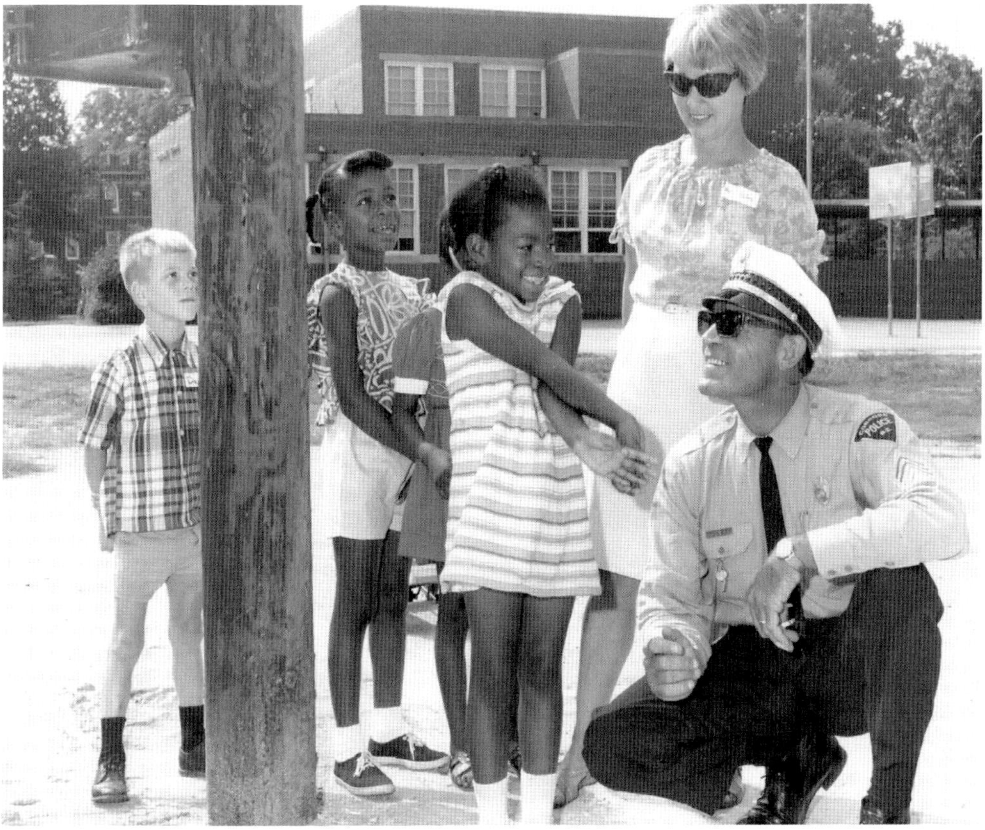

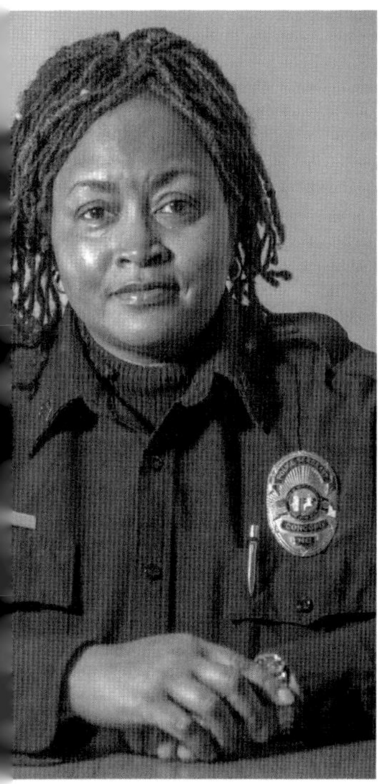

Richard Church
Concord schoolchildren of the 1950s through the 1970s had no friend more devoted than Church, the city's public school officer who shared safety tips with kids on campus and conducted tours of the police department. Of the many tributes he received during his 30-year career, none meant more than the Concord High School Class of 1964's dedication of its yearbook to him. Church died in 2005. (Courtesy of Sharon Luquire.)

Edie Moss
While her 1985 hiring made Moss the first African American woman to become a law enforcement agent in both the city of Concord and Cabarrus County, she may be best remembered for the compassion she showed to those she arrested. "I treated them how I wanted to be treated," she told the *Independent Tribune* in an article about her 2015 retirement. (Photograph by James Nix; courtesy of the *Independent Tribune*.)

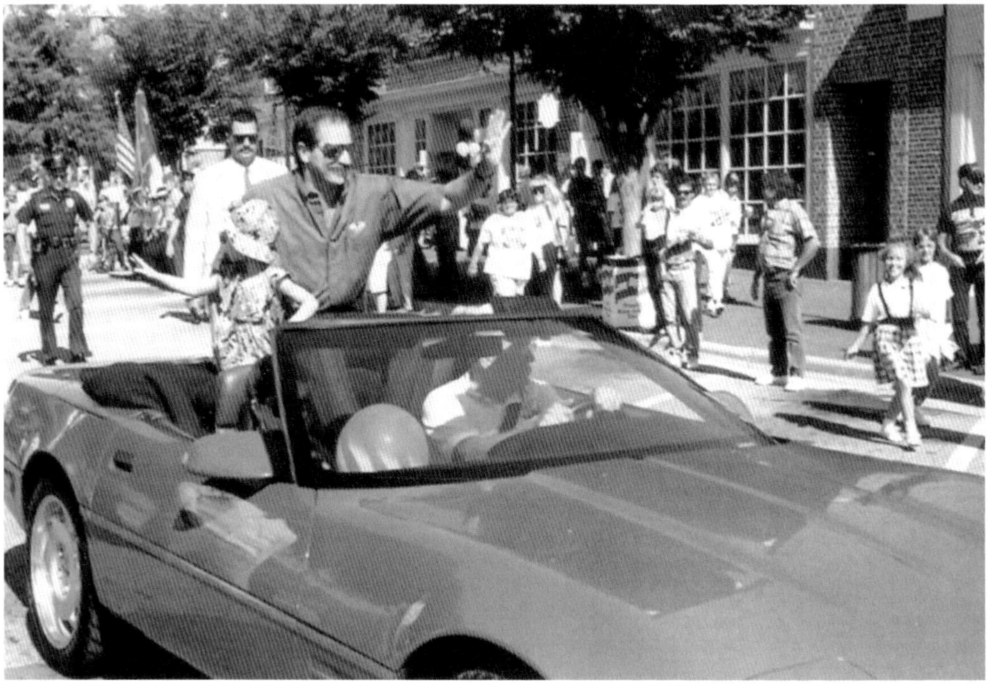

Dale Earnhardt Sr.
Many people in Cabarrus County remember where they were "the day Dale died." Kannapolis's most famous son, "the Intimidator," was more than a winning NASCAR racer. He epitomized the American dream, a small-town boy who made it big. His genuineness is on display in this photograph of the 1993 Dale Earnhardt Appreciation Day in Kannapolis. Earnhardt died in a crash during the 2001 Daytona 500. (Courtesy of the *Independent Tribune*.)

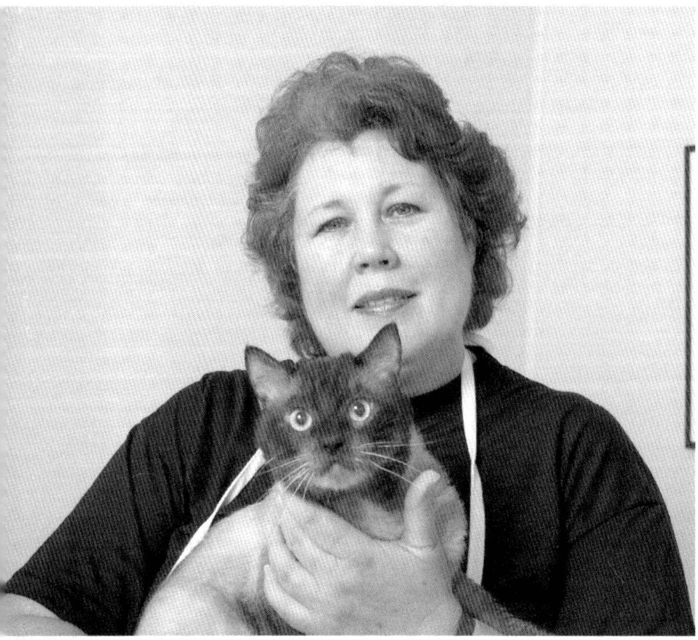

Patsy Beeker
With a soldier's fortitude, she trudged through the mire to liberate abandoned dogs. And with a nurse's empathy, she tended to the physical and psychological needs of unwanted felines. Beeker ran downtown Concord's liveliest location, the no-kill shelter Kitty City, a project of Cabarrus CARES (Coalition of Animal Rescue Efforts and Services). Established in 2005, Kitty City helped arrange vaccinations, adoptions, and pet-owner education programs until its 2015 closing. (Courtesy of Patsy Beeker.)

Bob Baucom

This jolly southeast Concord resident was known and loved by neighbors as "the mayor of Miller Avenue." He also made countless friends when he worked at the City of Concord's Light and Water Department and when he attended area cruise-ins in his restored 1961 Ford Falcon Ranchero pickup. But to the community at large, Bob Baucom was Cabarrus County's own Santa Claus. For years, Baucom traded on his resemblance to Saint Nick by appearing at Christmas parties and nonprofit benefits, soliciting donations for Hospice and Palliative Care of Cabarrus County in lieu of payment for his services. As he aged, he retired his fake beard and grew his own snowy whiskers. He charmed children, including his granddaughter Hailee Evans, shown with Baucom in the below photograph. Hailee was told that Grandpa was "Santa's helper," to avoid confusion with the "real" Kris Kringle.

Among Baucom's other fundraisers for the hospice center were his guided tours of his colossal collection of Santa Claus figures, which could be viewed for a hospice donation, and his seven-year stint of hand-crafting more than 1,000 crystal angels, which were sold from the spectacular "Angel Tree" at Carolina Mall. He died in 2015. (Courtesy of Phyllis Baucom.)

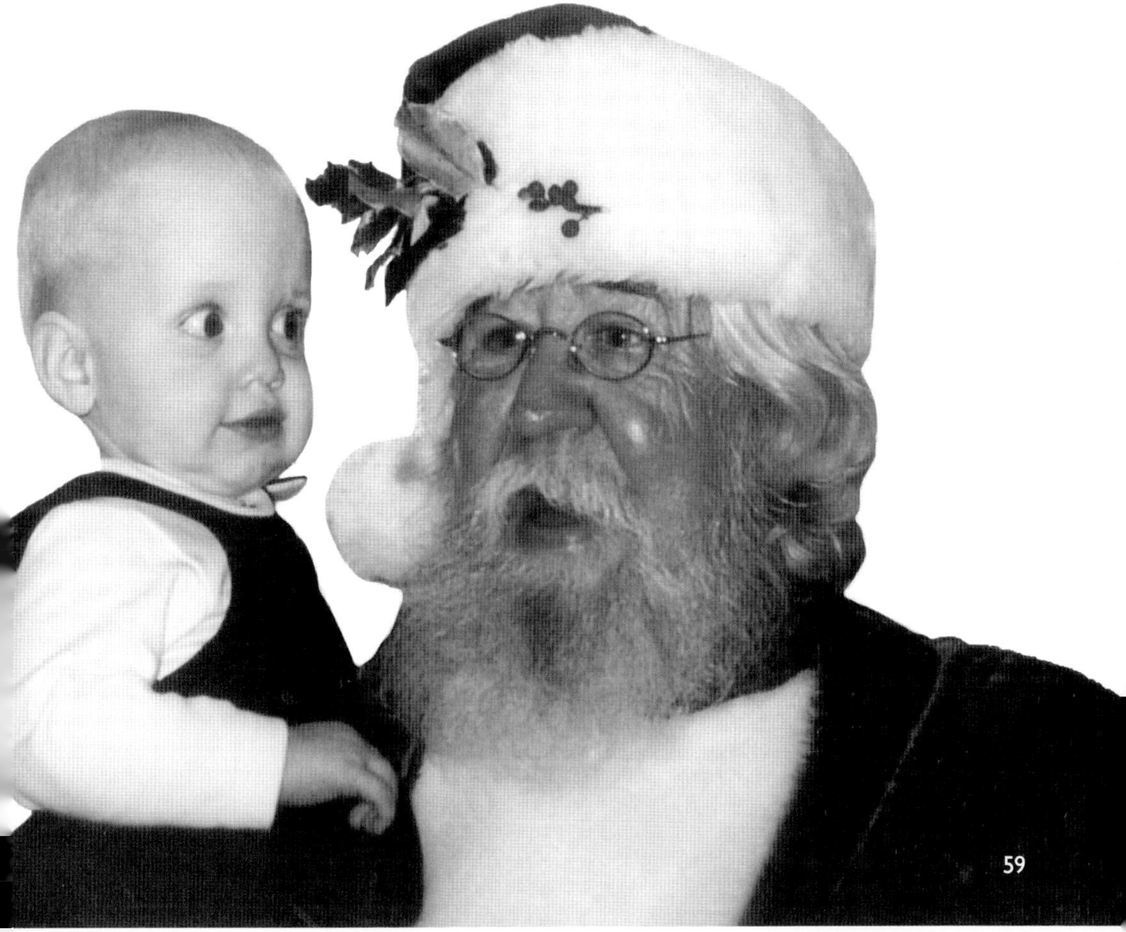

Kathy Kitts

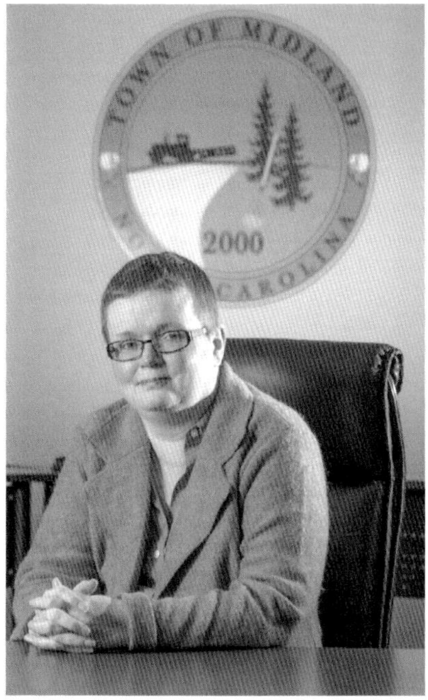

The Honorable Kathy Kitts is no stranger to challenges. Midland's mayor since 2009, she has been fighting to manage her town's development without sacrificing its pastoral charm. She has also been fighting cancer, handling municipal matters while undergoing treatments, to the awe of family and friends. Kitts reveals her motivation: "I want to make sure I'm there for my kids." (Photograph by James Nix; courtesy of the *Independent Tribune*.)

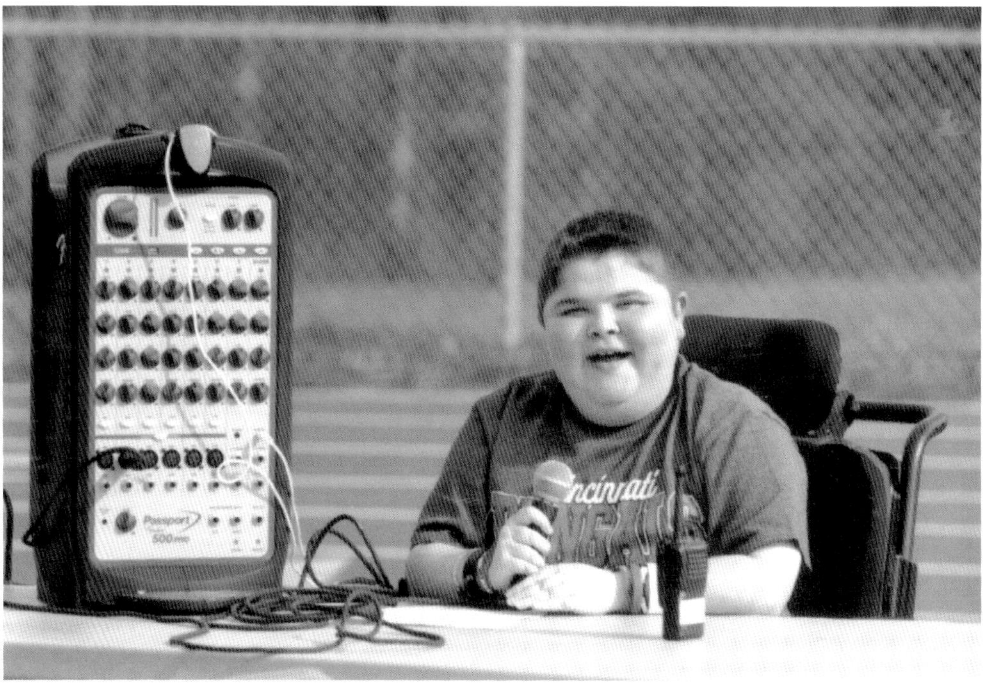

Bryson Foster

Concord's cheerful child activist was diagnosed with Duchenne muscular dystrophy at age five. A few years later, Bryson's parents discovered that their son was a natural communicator. Since then, Bryson has used his gift for gab and his infectious enthusiasm as an award-winning advocate for the Muscular Dystrophy Association, becoming the national MDA Goodwill Ambassador in 2012 and 2013. (Courtesy of Claire Foster.)

CHAPTER FOUR

Business Leaders and Professionals

For most of the 20th century, Cabarrus County was economically buttressed by the powerhouse Cannon Mills and numerous smaller but profitable plants. While textiles provided jobs and spending power, entrepreneurial locals saw great promise for new ventures.

It did not take long for these startups to discover that, in this intimate region, their name recognition was tantamount to their product. Drop the family names Baucom, Dover, Moose, Whitley, and Wilkinson, and identifiable businesses spring to mind—whereas the name Safrit has meant community service for three generations. E.L. "Eb" Bost got a taste of success when his What-A-Burger franchise became a county mainstay, and Don Frye introduced big-city amusements to Cabarrus kids by creating a roller rink and fun center that has spanned the decades.

Cabarrus County's citizens have been served by highly competent municipal governors, medical practitioners, and legal representatives. Some of them have enjoyed multifaceted careers, including Bill Hefner, the gospel singer who became a congressman. Attorney Clyde L. Propst Jr. proudly represented his constituents in both the North Carolina House of Representatives and Senate. In the minds of the people of Cabarrus County, however, he is forever remembered as the director of the county fair.

As the county's saga unfolded, homegrown shutterbugs captured each day's events for an inquisitive public. Edgar Readling's and Frankie Furr's photographic flair transformed routine experiences into memorable images.

Some legendary locals have reached beyond the confines of Cabarrus County to stake their claims to fame. Janet Ward Black, the county's first female prosecutor, now fronts a successful legal firm in Greensboro, North Carolina. Concord's own Judge Johnnie B. Rawlinson and Dr. R. Rodney Howell have attained national achievements.

From the perennial merchant to the convivial go-getter, these business leaders and professionals netted premiums that raised the bar for those who have followed.

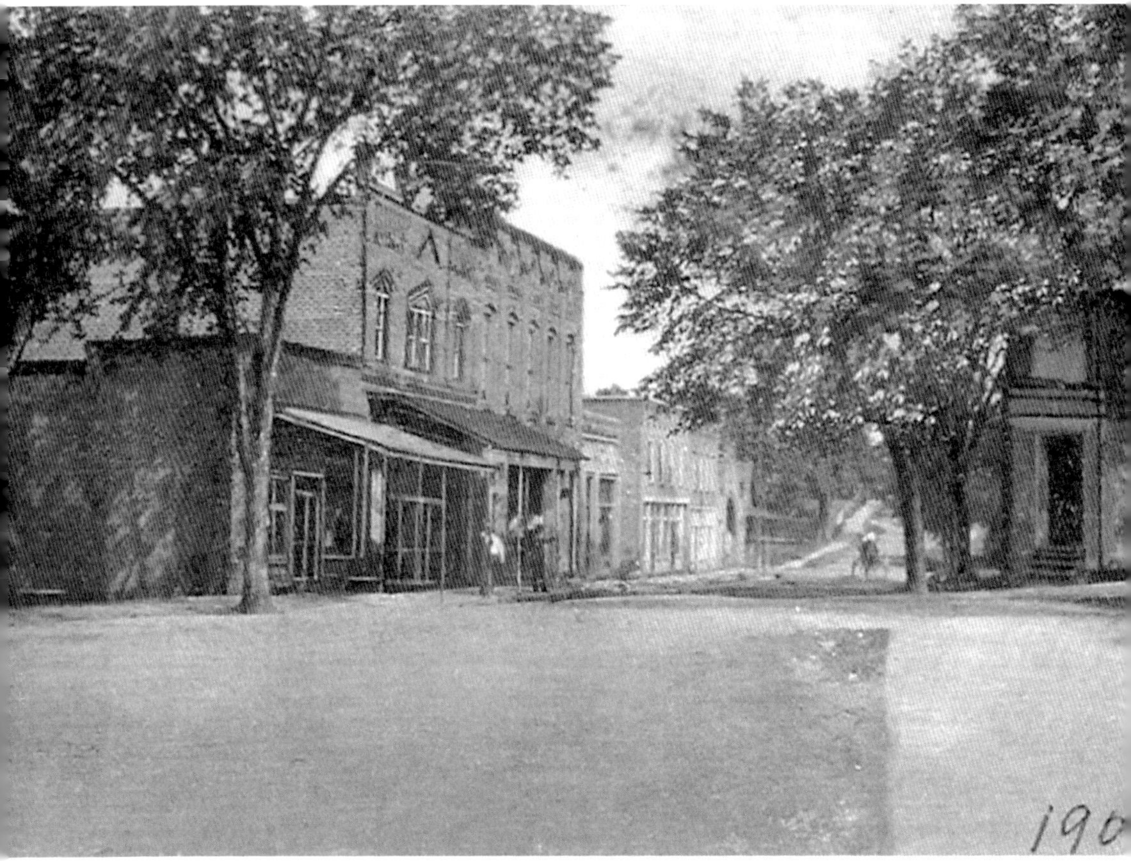

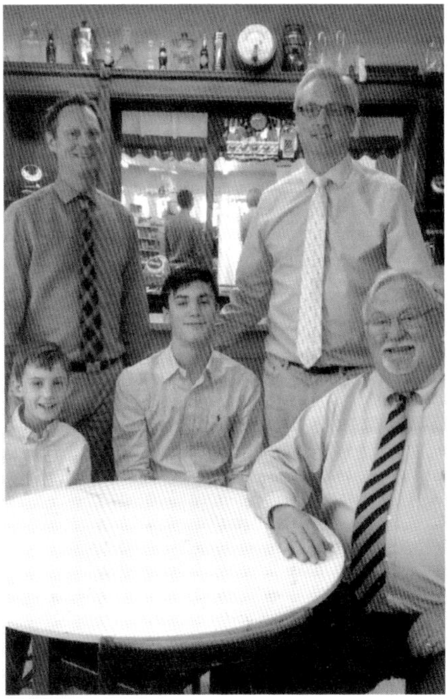

Moose Family

Cabarrus County's first name in pharmacies started in 1882 in downtown Mount Pleasant when A.W. Moose Drug Company opened. Druggist A.W. provided medicines prescribed by his physician brother, John. In 1927, A.W.'s youngest son, Hoy, became a second-generation pharmacist. Hoy rebuilt the pharmacy after it was leveled by a 1928 wildfire and added its popular soda fountain. Whit Sr., Hoy's son, joined the business in 1960, ultimately expanding it into other Cabarrus communities. Today, his sons Whit Jr. and Joe operate the multigenerational pharmacy.

The 1908 postcard above shows the original store (left). The current pharmacy stands on this exact site. Today's Moose family is gathered in the photograph on the left. Shown are, from left to right, (seated) Jacob, Walter, and Whit Sr.; (standing) Whit Jr. and Joe. (Above, courtesy of ECHS; left, courtesy of the Moose family.)

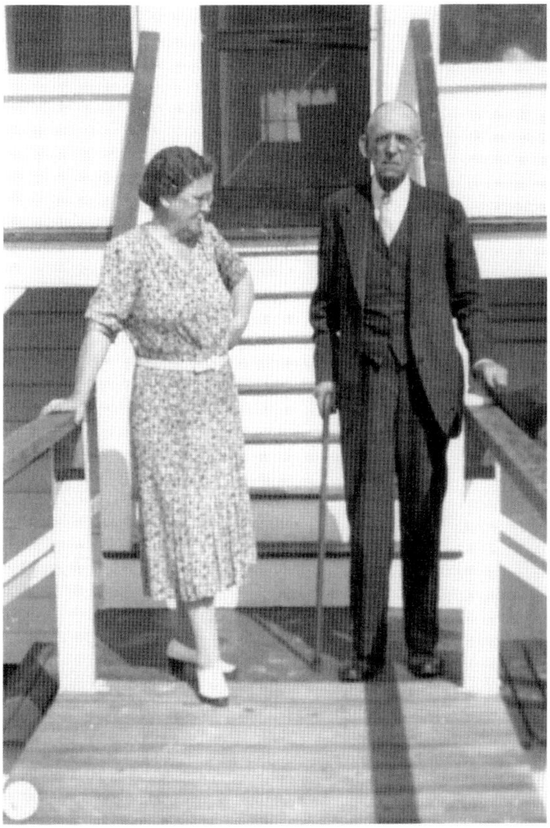

Heilig B. Wilkinson
In the early 1900s, this Concordian opened Wilkinson Furniture Store in a two-story brick structure at Church and Buffalo Streets. When he expanded into Kannapolis in 1913, his addition of wooden caskets to the product line birthed Wilkinson Furniture & Undertaking Company. Four generations later, Wilkinson Funeral Home, now in Concord, remains one of the county's leading providers of interment services. In this photograph, Heilig poses with his wife, Cornelia. (Courtesy of Wilkinson Funeral Home.)

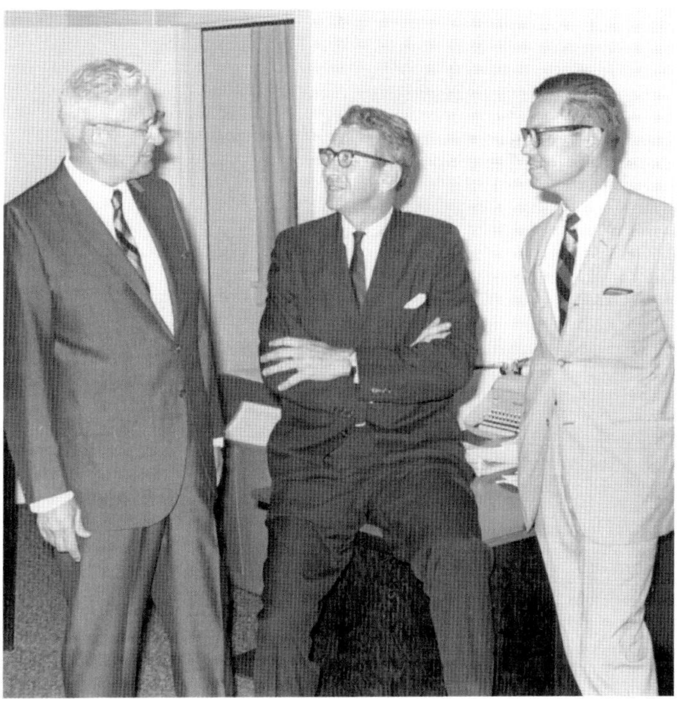

John K.P. Odell
This Concordian was the midcentury president of Kerr Bleachery and sat on the executive committee of the North Carolina Textiles Manufacturing Association. Odell's civic service included terms as Concord Rotary Club president and Cabarrus Memorial Hospital Board chairman. He died in 1991 at age 68. Odell is seen here in 1968 with Concord mayor S. Les Myers (left) and J. Melville Broughton (center). (Courtesy of Concord Public Library.)

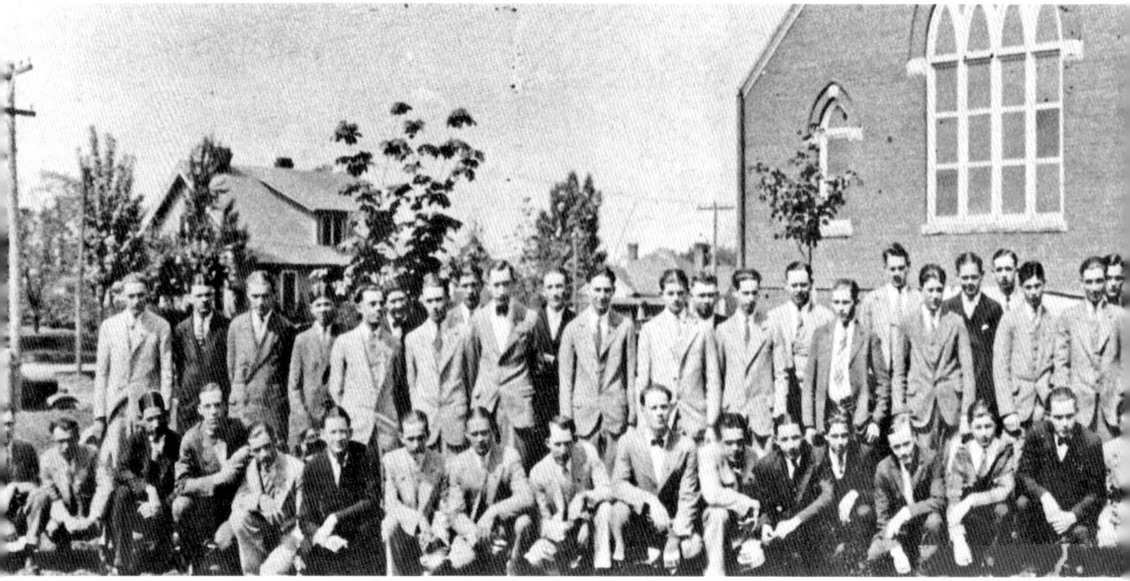

Whitley Family (ABOVE AND OPPOSITE PAGE)
In 1918, William H. "W.H." Whitley Sr. began working at Heilig B. Wilkerson's Furniture & Undertaking Company in Kannapolis, planting the seeds of a business dynasty that would stretch a century. Whitley's role in the company grew to manager, then partner, and in 1938, he purchased the enterprise, renaming it W.H. Whitley & Sons, operating it with his eldest sons, Ralph and Fred. In 1940, after several relocations, the business settled into the South Main Street site where it would remain for close to five decades. Another of W.H.'s sons, William L. "Bill" Whitley Sr., joined the family business after military service in World War II, where he heroically flew over 30 bombing missions. His brothers Ralph and Fred segued out of the company to pursue other professions. Bill eventually ascended to the roles of president and treasurer, helping Whitley's Funeral Home—as the company was renamed in the 1960s, its furniture roots a relic of the past—adapt to meet the needs of the ever-changing Kannapolis. William L. "Whit" Whitley Jr. started the third generation of Whitleys to enter the business in 1971. Debunking the stereotype of stoic morticians, Whit moonlights as a stand-up comic. His siblings David and Jane eventually joined the family's funeral business.

The amazing photograph above, taken around 1920, shows patriarch W.H. Whitley standing at the far right, with the Sunday school class he taught at Kannapolis's Trinity Methodist Church. The photograph on the opposite page was taken around 1986, shortly after Whitley's opened its newly constructed (and current) location in Kannapolis. Family members populating this staff assemblage are as follows: (seated) Whit Whitley (far left), Johnette (Mrs. Bill) Whitley (center), Jane Whitley (second from right), and David Whitley (far right); (standing) Bill Whitley (center). (Both, courtesy of Whitley's Funeral Home.)

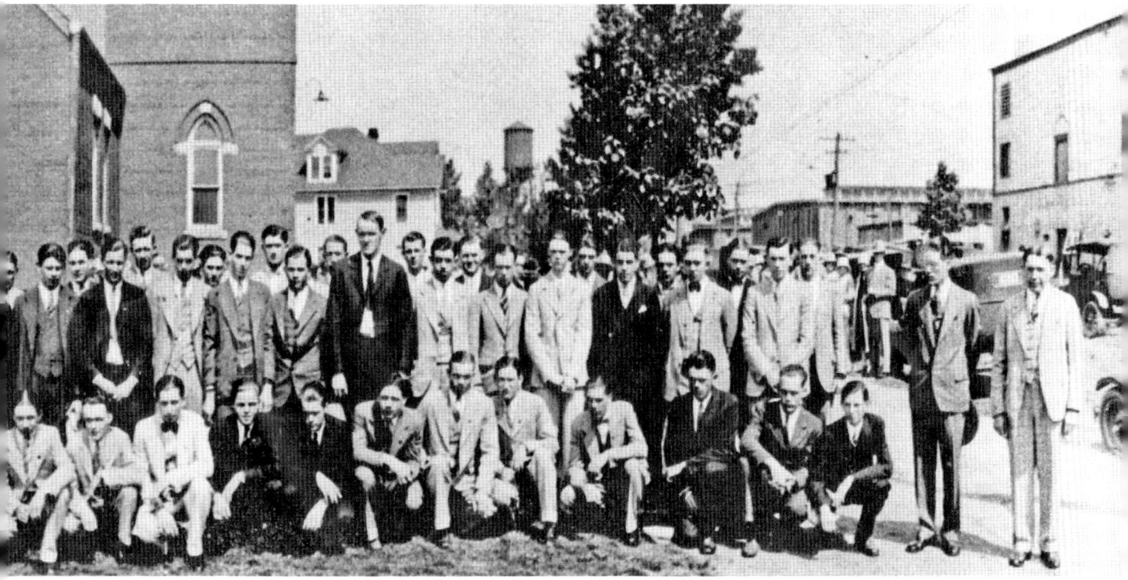

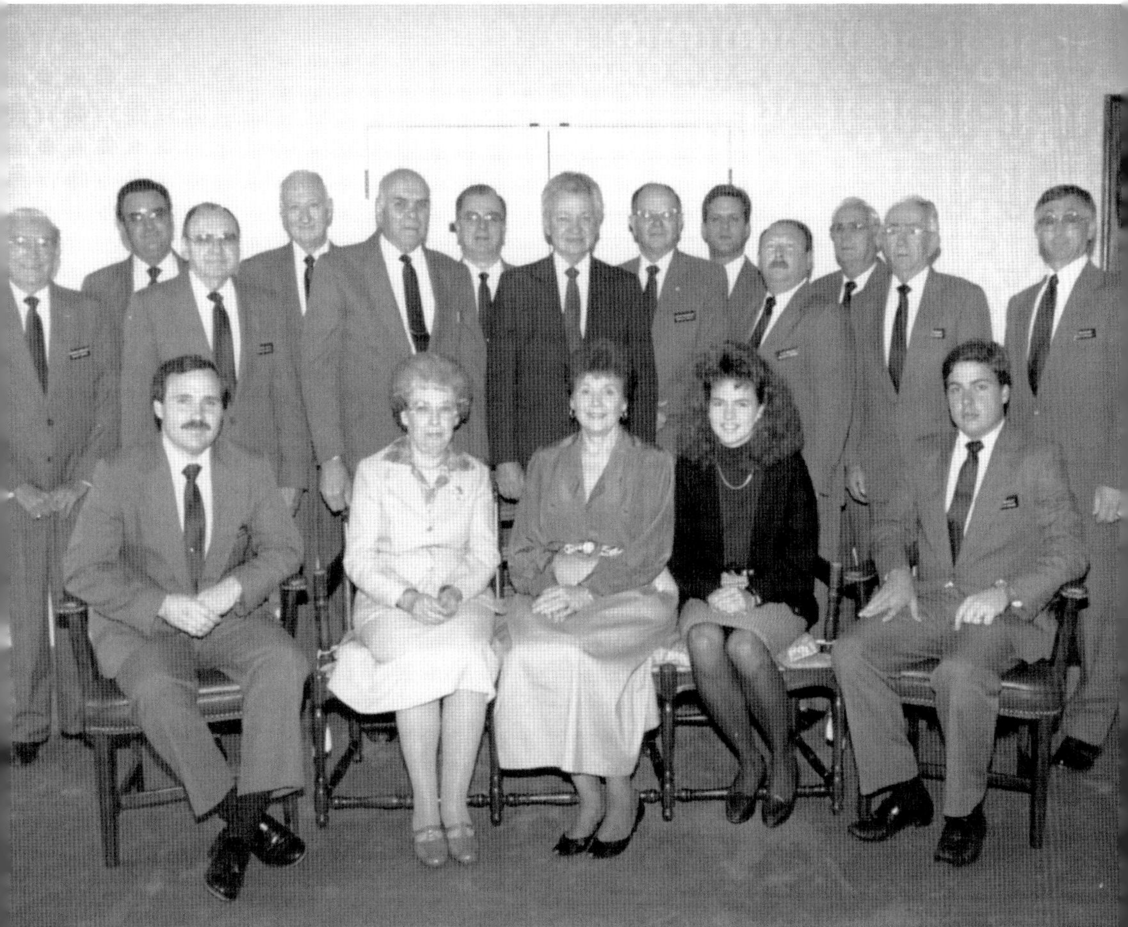

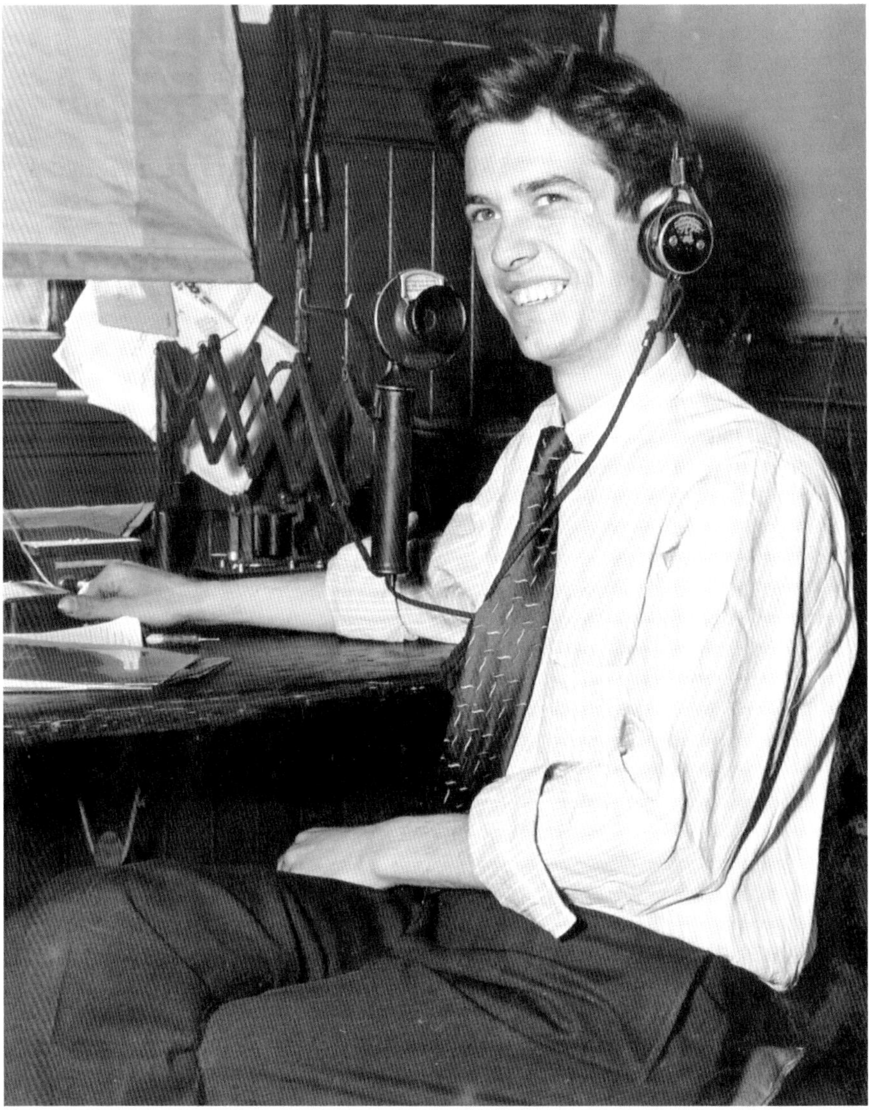

Harry R. Higgins (ABOVE AND OPPOSITE PAGE)

Harry R. Higgins (above) remembers how his grueling first day on the job at Southern Railway nearly derailed the 17-year-old's desire to follow in his father's footsteps: "When I got done, I was about ready to quit!" But he persevered, spending his professional life working at different depots in Cabarrus and Rowan Counties, chugging ahead from his early days as a ticket clerk to his position of depot agent at the Kannapolis train station, where he retired in 1982. His father, Jesse Carl Higgins (opposite), moved his family to Harrisburg for a job at the Harrisburg Depot during the Great Depression, when Harry was a child. The station was in its final days of operation at that time, but the senior Higgins went on to become a depot agent in China Grove and elsewhere in the area. Today, locals desiring a history lesson on the railroad's importance to the community need look no further than Harry for information: he gleefully describes how trains were the source of mail pickups and deliveries, the transport of goods for establishments from country stores to Cannon Mills, and the means of business and recreational travel. These photographs, taken in 1949 or 1950 by Sam L. Braswell of Concord, show son and father at work at the Concord Depot. (Both, courtesy of Harry R. Higgins.)

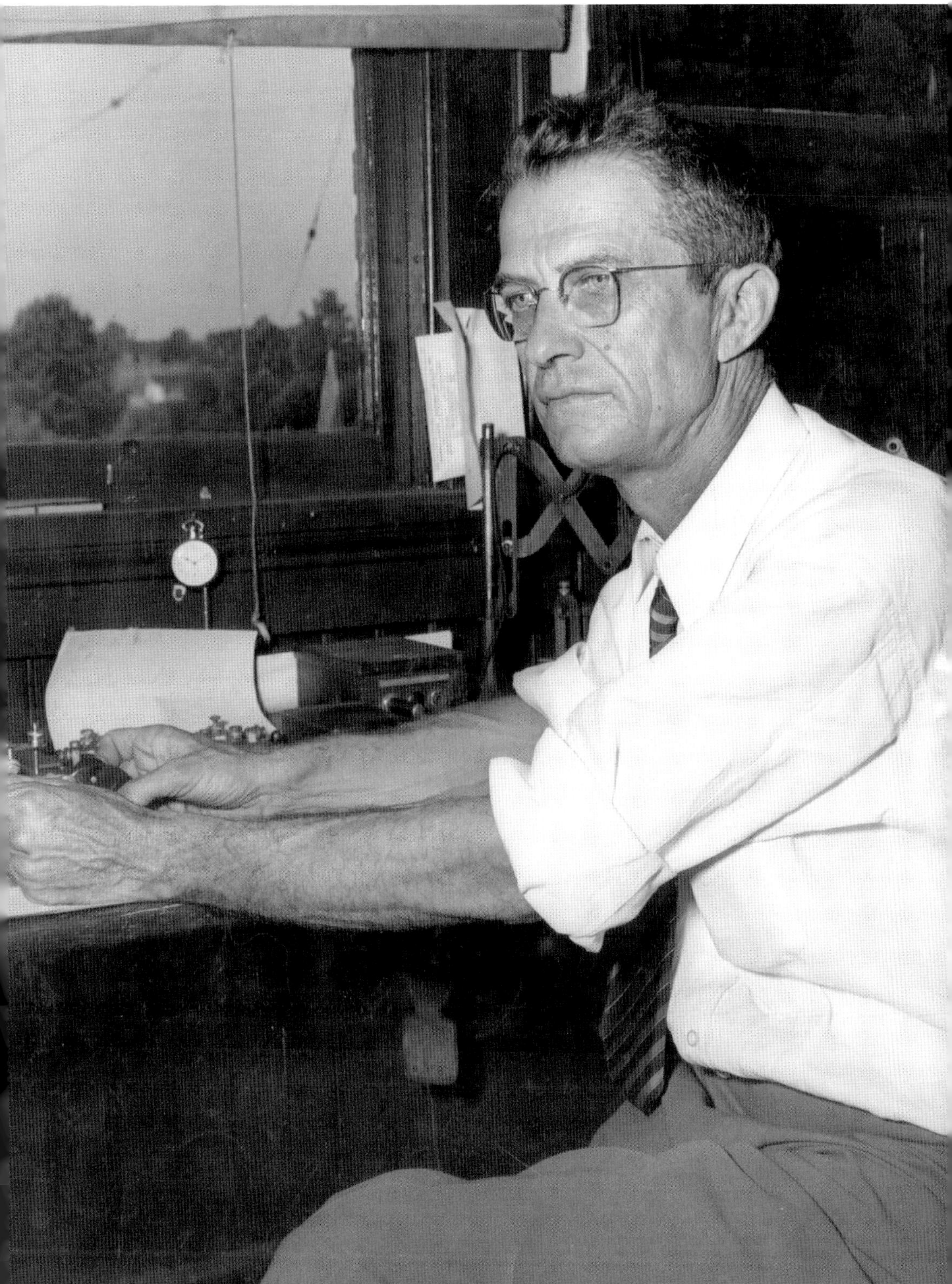

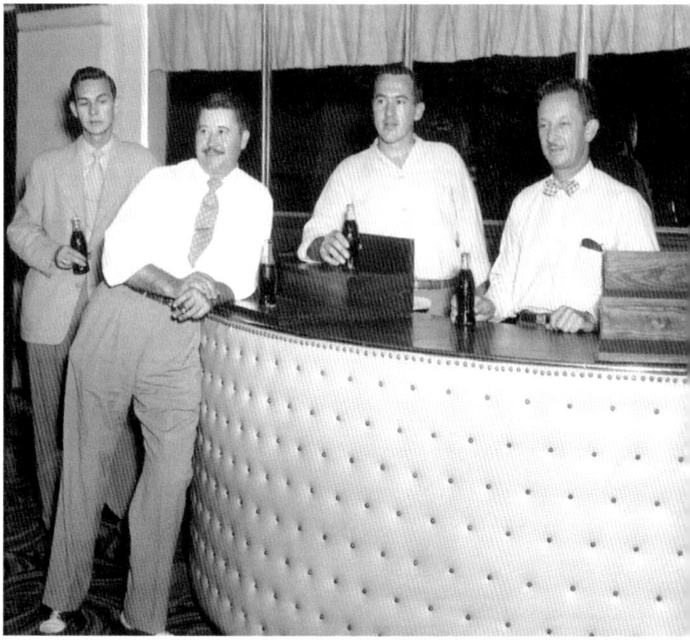

Julian K. Whitley

The Gem Theatre, which opened in 1936, was the first of four Kannapolis cinemas under the auspices of Towel City Theaters, and it is the only one in business today. Whitley became the Gem's manager in 1941, beginning a five-decade career. Joining Whitley (far right) in this 1948 photograph at the Gem's concession stand are, from left to right, Wayne Reece, Gene Corbin, and Glenn Phillips. (Courtesy of the Gem Theatre.)

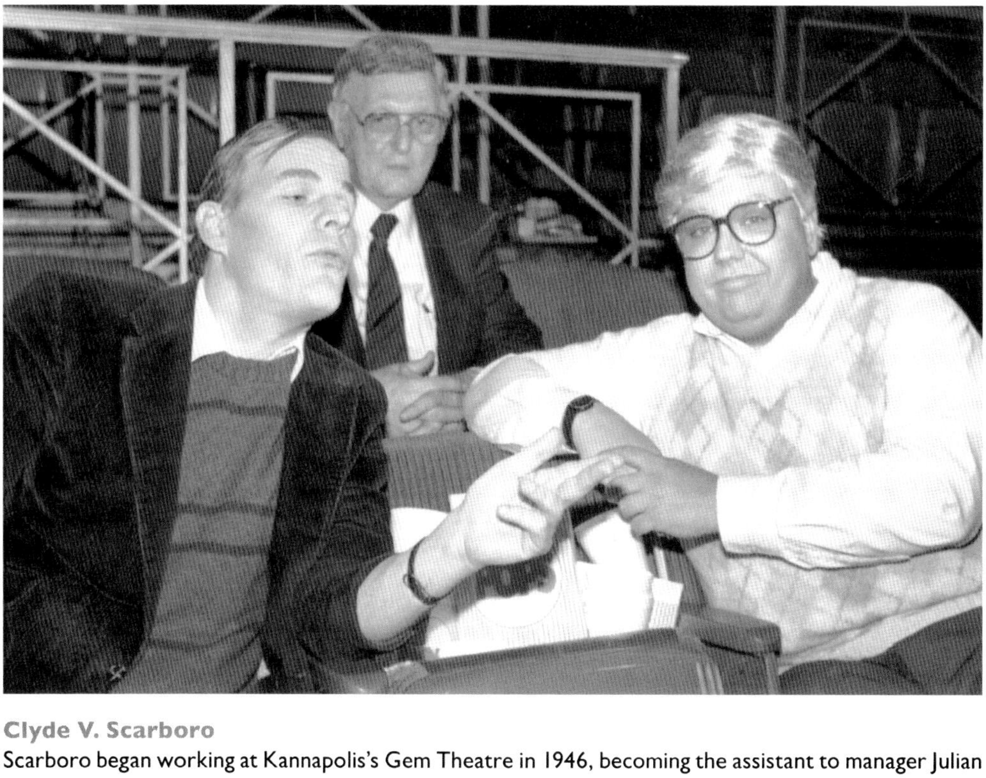

Clyde V. Scarboro

Scarboro began working at Kannapolis's Gem Theatre in 1946, becoming the assistant to manager Julian K. Whitley. He was elected a vice president of its board of directors in 1972 and succeeded Whitley as general manager, ultimately spending 49 years in the Gem's employ. In this 1992 photograph, Scarboro (center) observes two unidentified actors rehearsing for a Belk's department store commercial filmed inside the theater. (Courtesy of the Gem Theatre.)

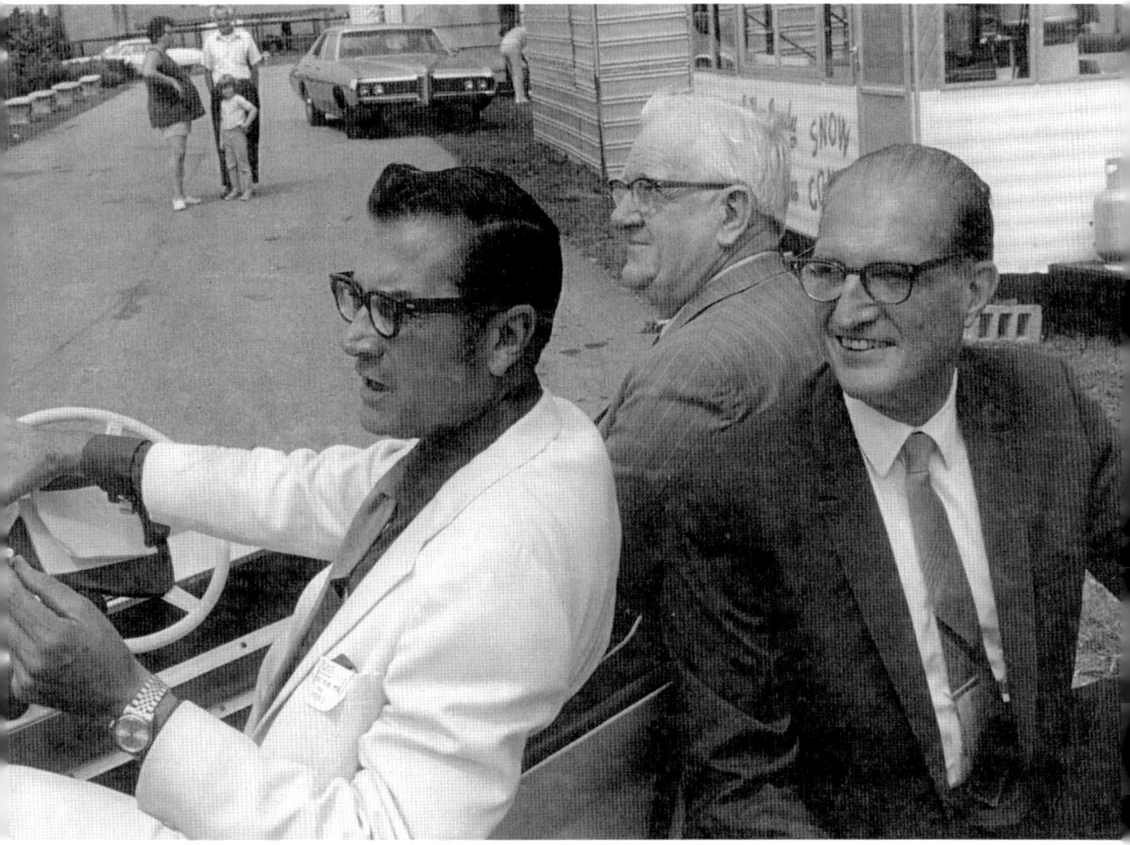

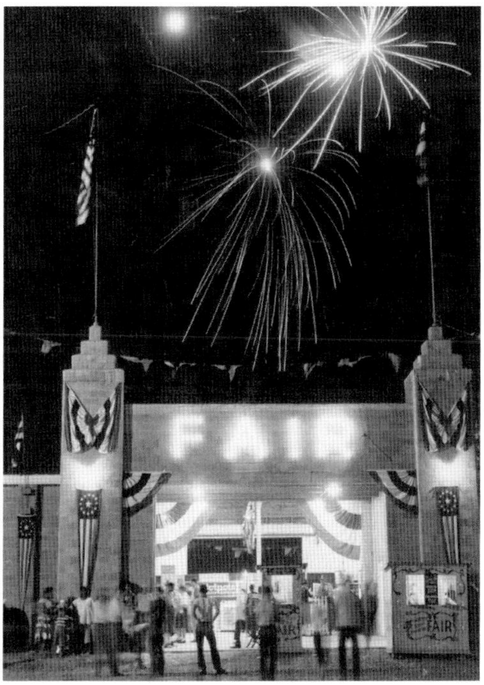

Clyde L. Propst Jr.

This World War II veteran and Duke University Law School graduate enjoyed an illustrious career as Concord's city attorney and as a Cabarrus County recorder's court judge. He also made his mark in Raleigh, the state capital, being elected to both the North Carolina House of Representatives and Senate. But generations best remember Propst as the general manager of the Cabarrus County Fair, which he oversaw from 1954 until his 1991 death. Under his watch, the fair witnessed unparalleled growth, adding numerous music acts and attractions, such as the double Ferris wheel. In the above photograph, Propst (left) is seen with Cabarrus County Fair board members Gene Bost (center) and Tom Ross. Below is an exterior shot of the fair during the Propst era. (Above, courtesy of Susan Propst Hannah; left, photograph by Edgar Readling, courtesy of Irene Readling Russell.)

Don and Larry Frye (BELOW AND OPPOSITE PAGE)

Don Frye was the Walt Disney of Cabarrus County. He imagined an amusement park for area children and started saving to realize his dream while in the military during World War II. His mother sent him cigarettes, and Don sold them to his fellow soldiers, squirreling away his profits. In 1946, Frye purchased 60 acres on Poplar Tent Road in Concord, and the next year, he opened the 3.5-acre Frye's Lake for swimming. A roller-skating rink was added in 1949, and in the decade that followed, more attractions debuted: an archery range, chairlift, carousel, go-karts, driving range, picnic facility, and, in 1959, Frye's Lake Lanes, a bowling alley. In 1964, the Cabarrus & Western Gold Mine Railroad joined the franchise, a quarter-mile track winding through a family-constructed Old West village and ending at a zoo. Along the route was the site where the legendary Cabarrus Black Boys patriots detonated their pilfered British munitions shipment. A ride pass (opposite, top) would guarantee one lucky person a gleeful getaway. Despite his nonstop dedication to his enterprise, Frye, shown below operating his steam engine, would make time to shuttle kids who needed a ride to and from his park in his long-bed truck. He died in 1985.

Working alongside Don and his wife, Nell, was their only child, Larry. At age nine, he started in the family business by shoveling sand around the lake. Like his father, Larry was hands-on, applying his various skills—from lifeguarding to carpentry—to the myriad attractions, assisting his dad with their construction and maintenance. A certified Brunswick bowling machine mechanic, Larry assisted his father in opening skating facilities in other cities. For numerous Cabarrus kids who spun away the hours at Frye's Roller Rink, Larry was its friendly "cop," patrolling the rink with a whistle. He died in 2015.

Today, the bowling alley and roller rink remain in operation (with renovations from their original incarnations), as well as the driving range. Another venue, Cabarrus Dance Academy (formerly Peggè Lee School of Dance), is also on the Fryes' property, with the next generation of the Frye family in charge. The fuzzy but fabulous photograph (opposite, bottom) shows, from left to right, Larry, Don, and Nell at the original Frye's Roller Rink. (All, courtesy of the Frye family.)

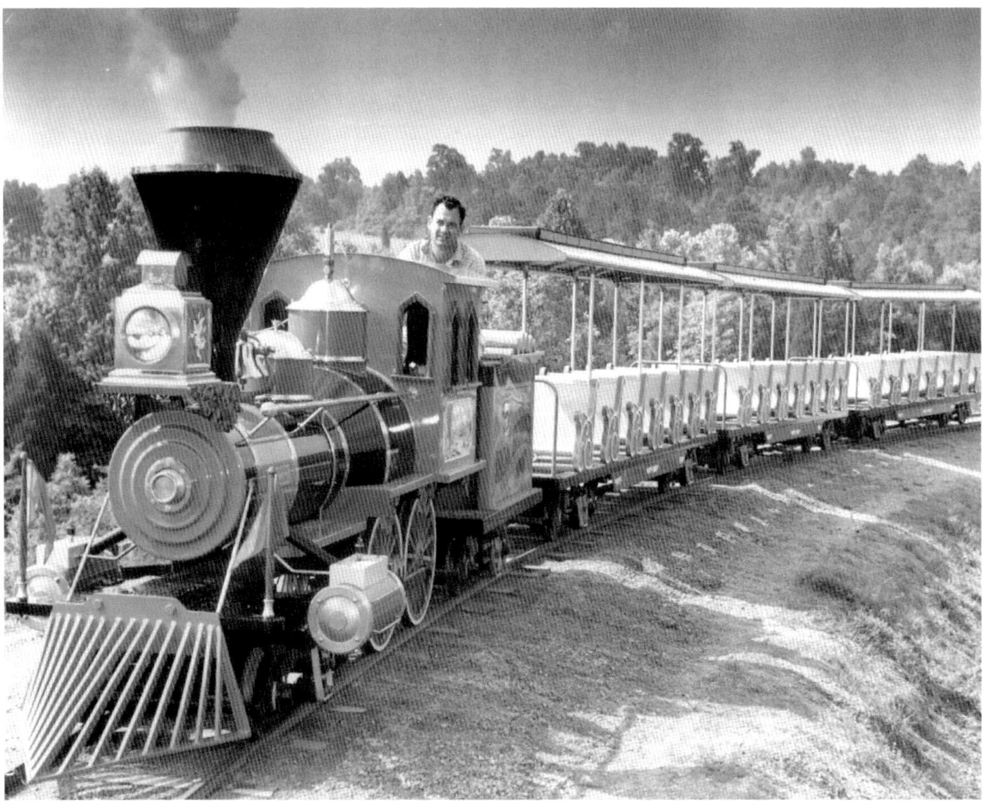

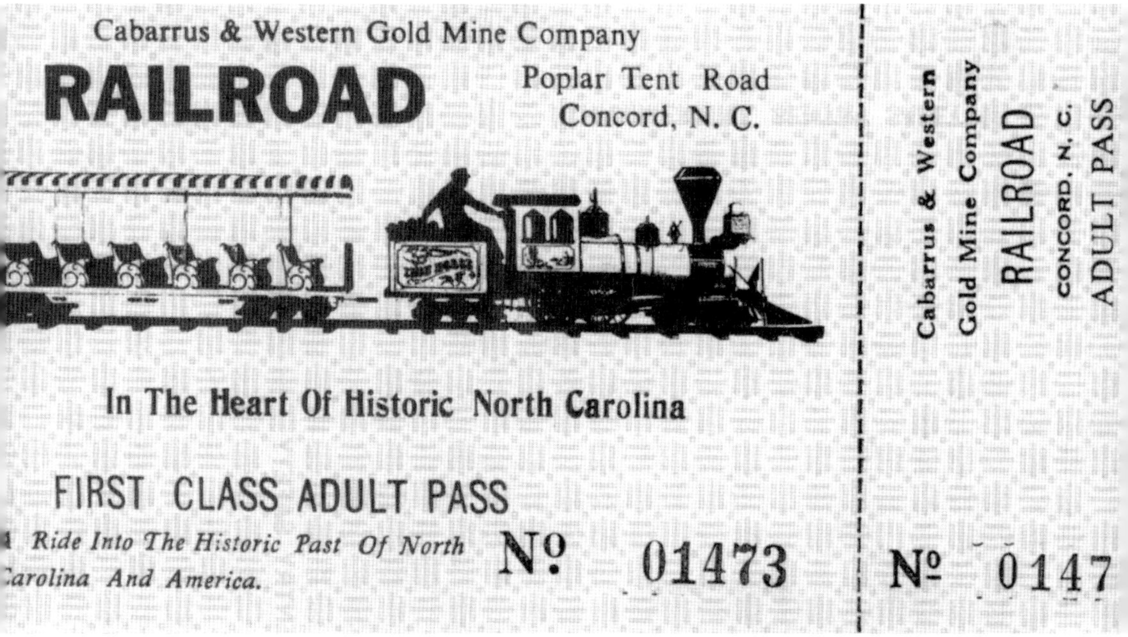
Cabarrus & Western Gold Mine Company
RAILROAD
Poplar Tent Road
Concord, N. C.
In The Heart Of Historic North Carolina
FIRST CLASS ADULT PASS
Ride Into The Historic Past Of North
arolina And America.
№ 01473
Cabarrus & Western
Gold Mine Company
RAILROAD
CONCORD, N. C.
ADULT PASS
№ 0147

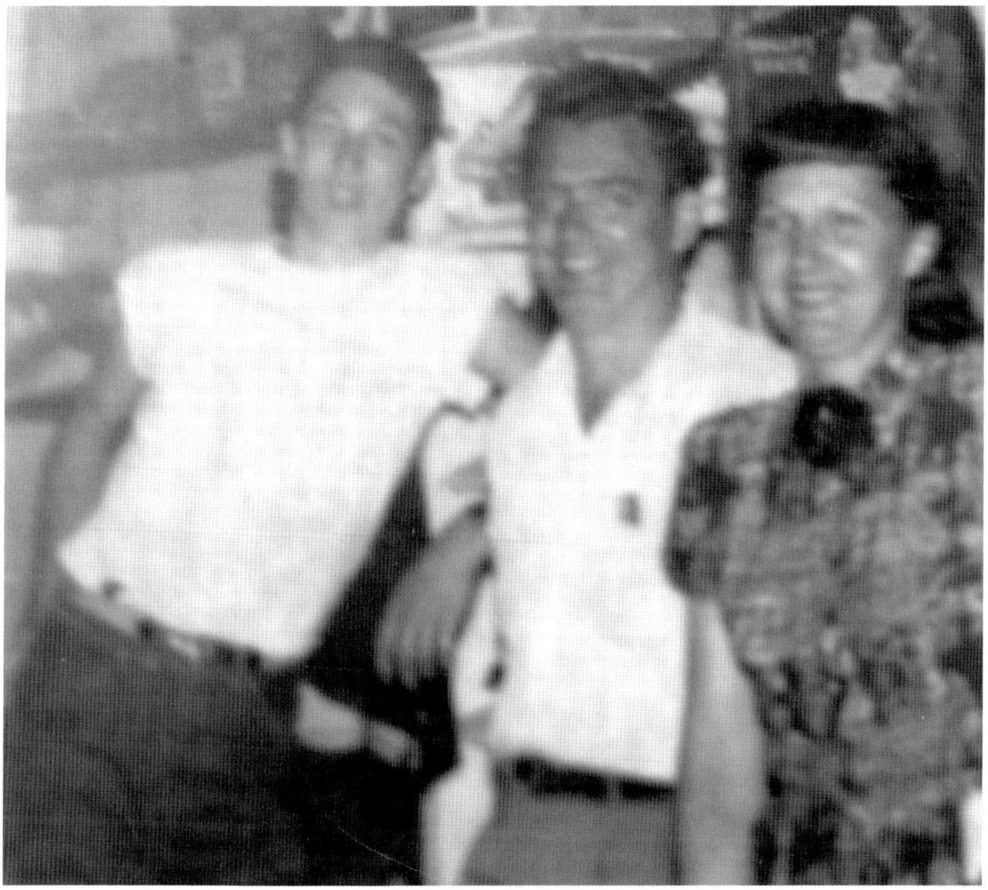

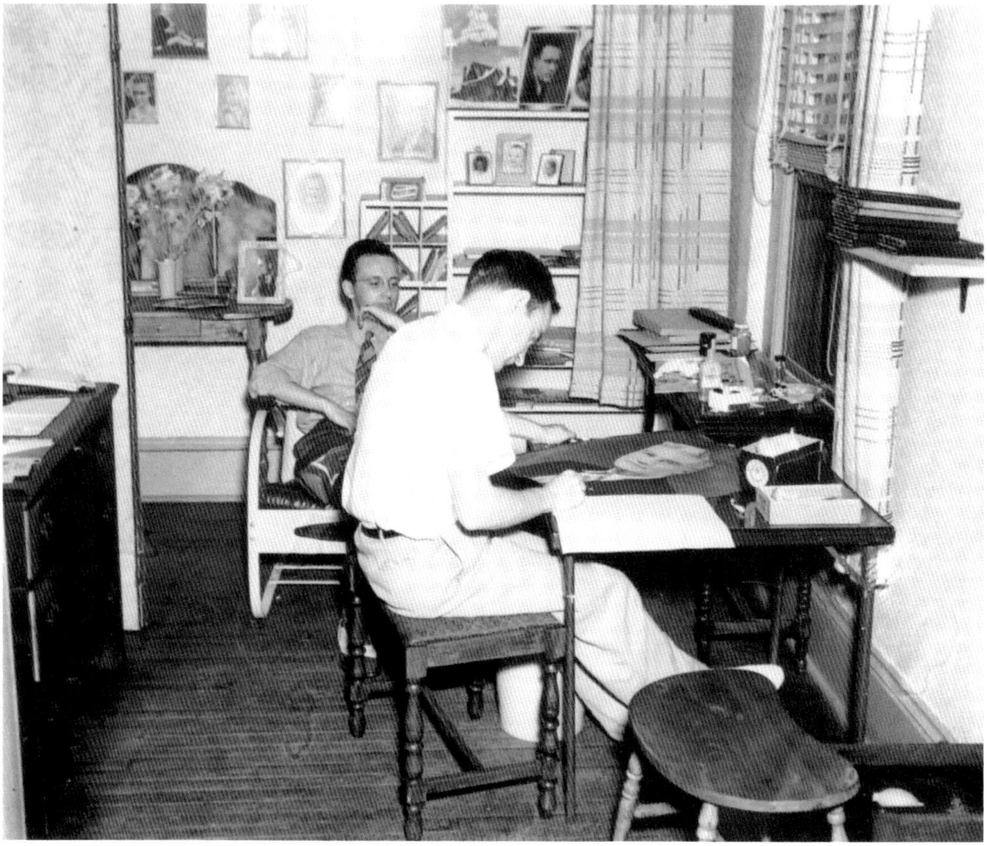

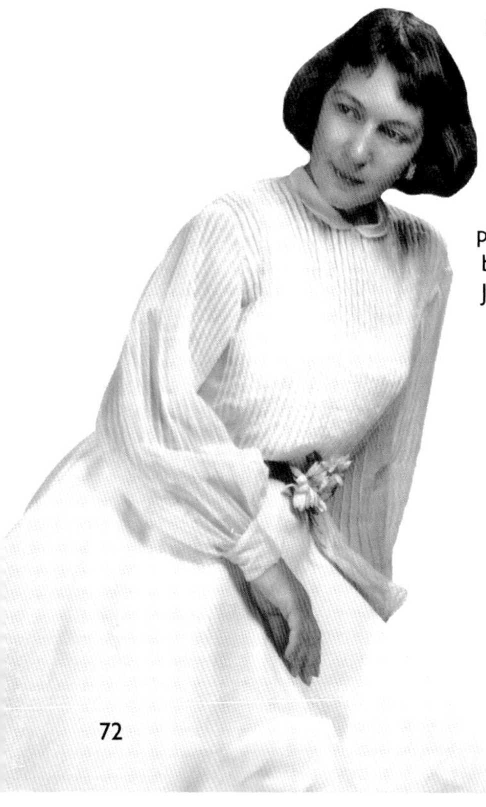

Healy and Foye Jones

Glamour shots were a specialty of this versatile husband-wife photography team, who snapped everything from yearbook headshots to society party pictures from 1939 until Healy's untimely death in 1952. Foye (left) relocated the studio from downtown Concord into her home after her husband's passing and continued the business until 1962. In the above photograph, Healy is hand-coloring a portrait in oils while his brother Marshall Jones observes. (Both, courtesy of Martha Jones Sisk.)

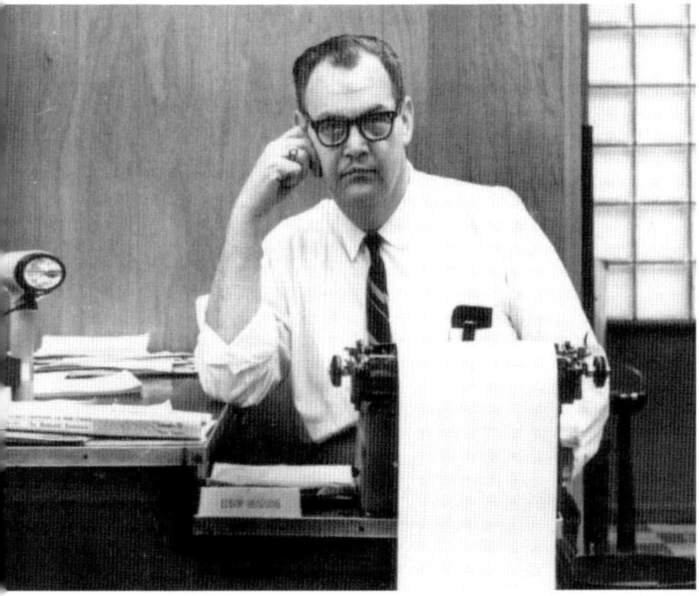

Edgar Readling
Readling captured many of Cabarrus's most significant midcentury stories as a reporter and religion editor for the *Concord Tribune*. Yet his greatest gift was his photographic eye: his skill for image composition created photographs that told rich stories in a single, memorable frame. A World War II veteran who also worked at the Hugh-Grey Hosiery Mill, Readling died in 1994. (Courtesy of Irene Readling Russell.)

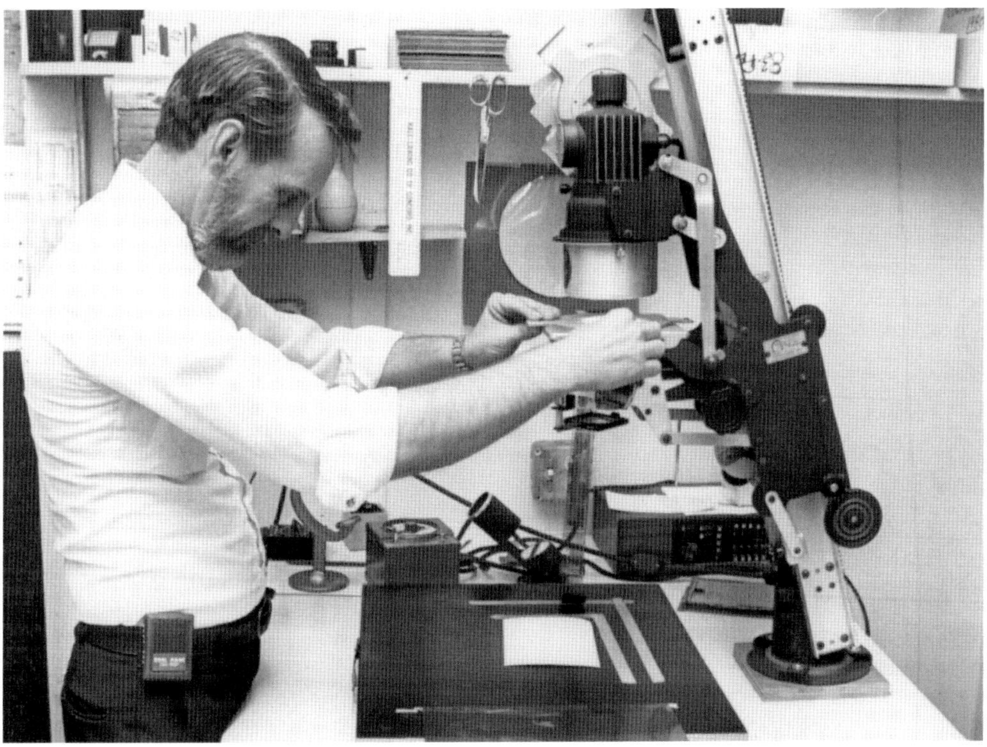

Frankie Furr
This newspaperman had already logged nearly two decades working at the *Concord Tribune* in the 1970s when he slid into the role for which he is best known: photographer. Many recall his "View Finder" spotlights of young ladies. Furr's favorite photograph was his shot of a Jesus statue, its arms extended, behind which he superimposed a background of clouds, creating the illusion of Christ ascending into heaven. (Courtesy of Frankie Furr.)

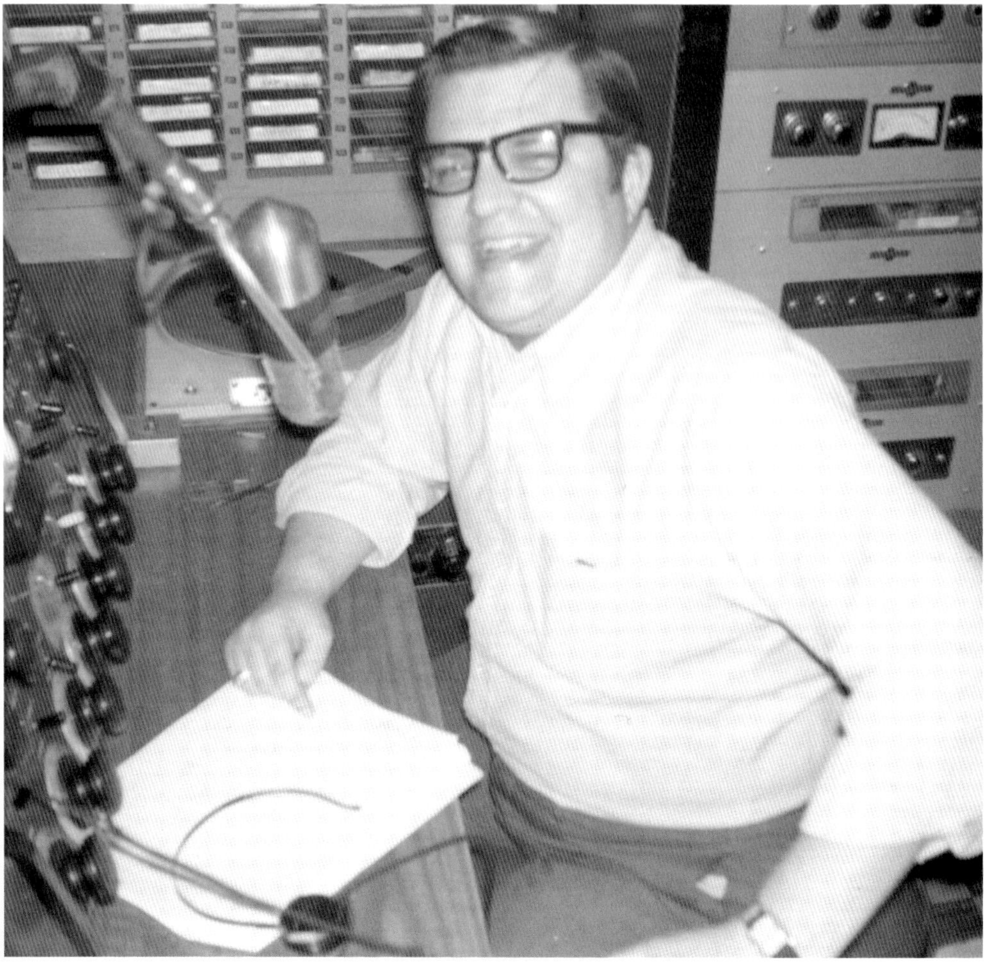

Bill Biggerstaff

In the era before 24/7 social media and copious television affiliates, local radio stations were essential to the small communities comprising Cabarrus County, offering not only music but also news, farm reports, and religious programming. Biggerstaff got his start at Concord's WEGO-AM in February 1966, when he was hired as a sportscaster by manager Jim Keel, broadcasting from the control room in WEGO's Highway 29 (now Concord Parkway) studio, as shown here. His voice was well known to fans of the Concord Spiders, as he announced everything from football to basketball games for years. Biggerstaff was tapped to become a local newscaster once Keel expanded his station's programming in 1968. One of Biggerstaff's first on-air news interviews was with civil rights activist Golden Frinks, who was leading a march down Union Street in Concord after the April 1968 assassination of Rev. Dr. Martin Luther King Jr. Tensions were high in the small Southern town. The defiant Ku Klux Klan was present, yet the WEGO interviewer soldiered on in the front lines for his dialogue with Frinks.

As Biggerstaff's community profile grew, he segued into radio sales at WEGO and its FM sister station WPEG—never relinquishing the microphone for his beloved sports broadcasts—and was eventually promoted to sales manager. When gospel crooner Bill Hefner and his business partner, Bob Warren, purchased Kannapolis radio station WKRB from Gertrude Hinson, wife of Foy Hinson, the station's original owner, Biggerstaff was hired as its vice president/general manager. Among his on-air duties at WKRB was a midmorning show he cohosted with Hefner. Biggerstaff retired from WKRB in 1980. (Courtesy of Bill Biggerstaff.)

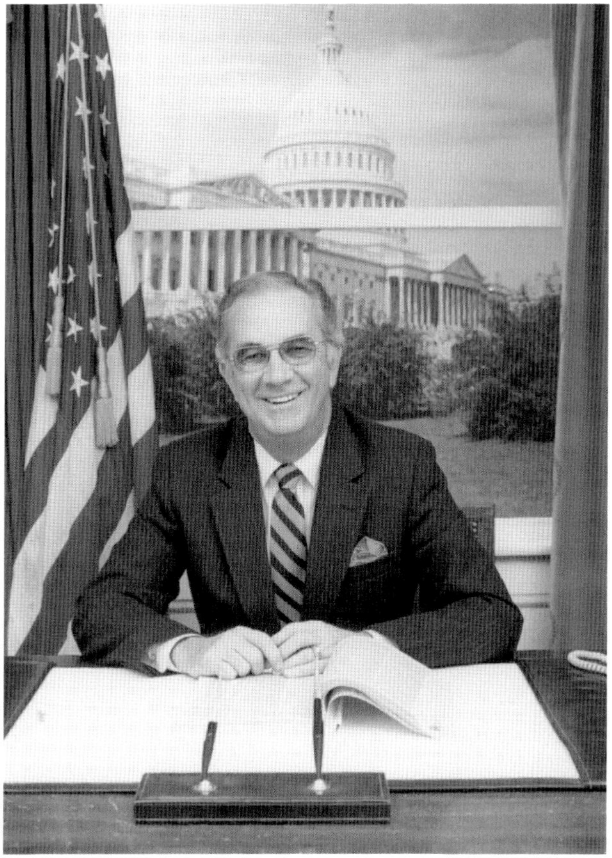

Bill Hefner

Bill Biggerstaff, a broadcaster at WKRB, the Kannapolis radio station co-owned by Hefner, was surprised when Hefner announced his intentions to run for US Congress in 1974. Hefner had no political experience; he was a radio and television singer with the Harvesters Quartet gospel group. "How do you get to be a congressman?" Biggerstaff asked. "You get elected," Hefner replied. After performing gospel tunes while stumping for votes, Hefner, a Democrat, won the 1974 election, part of a Watergate-inspired nationwide referendum on Republicans. He became a Washington institution from 1975 to 1999, serving a remarkable 12 terms in the US Congress representing the Eighth District. An advocate for veterans' rights, he was honored in 1999 when Salisbury's veterans hospital adopted his name. (Right, courtesy of Nancy Hefner; below, courtesy of the author.)

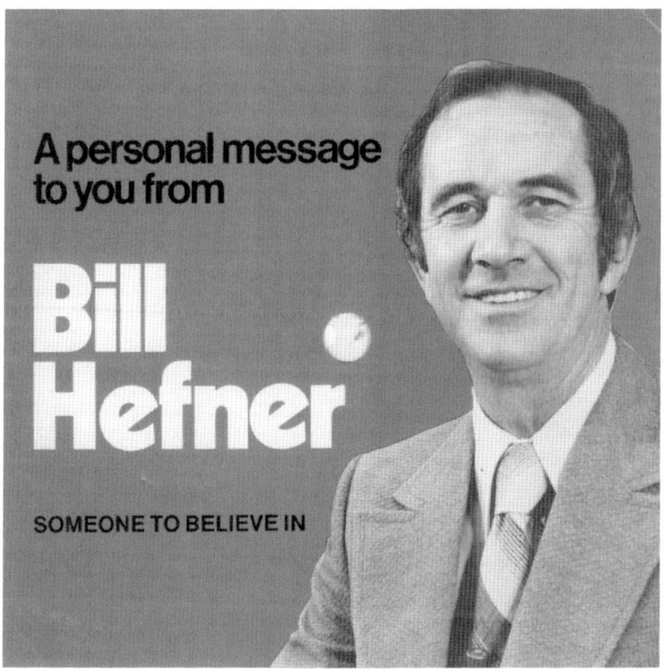

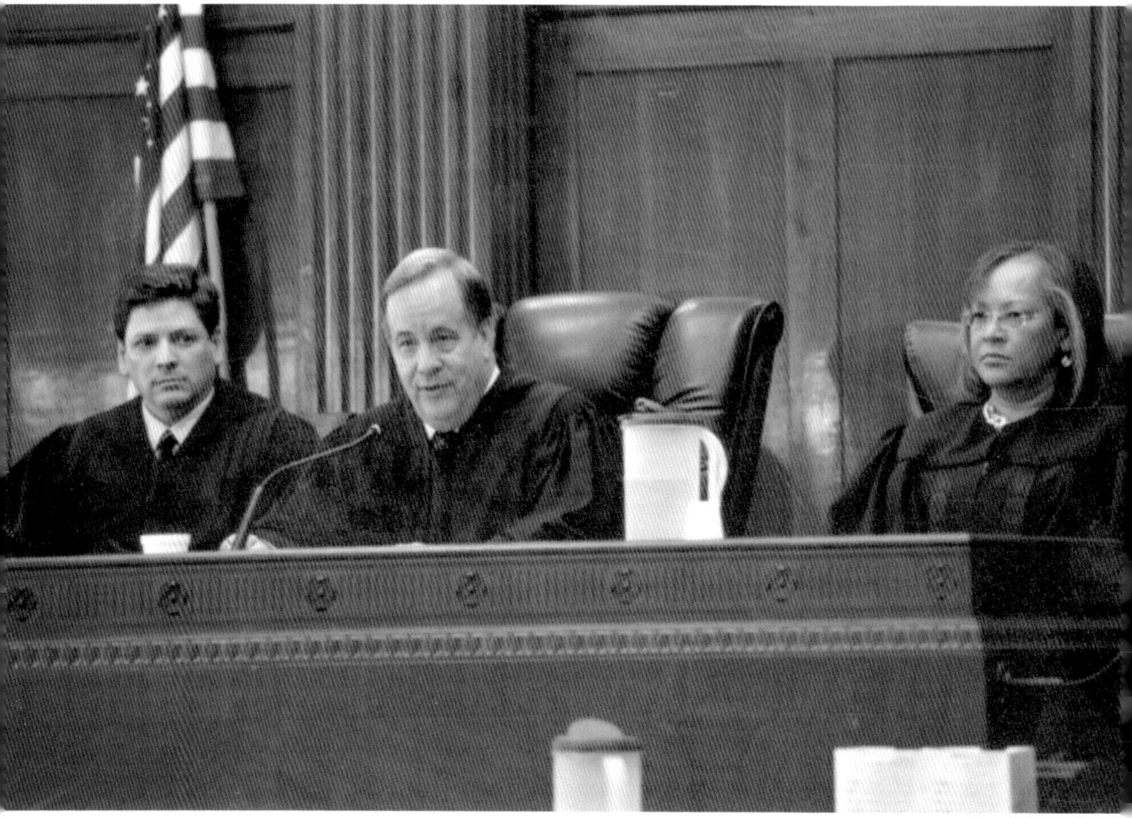

Erwin Spainhour

The Honorable Erwin Spainhour remembers a nail-biting, three-week ordeal during his earlier days as a trial lawyer, when he and colleague Fletcher L. Hartsell Jr. (now a state senator) defended a mistakenly accused client in a first-degree murder case. With little regard for his own health during the trial, Spainhour sacrificed nights of sleep and dropped close to 20 pounds while fighting to save the defendant's life; he succeeded, the trial concluding with a verdict of not guilty. Decades later, during his nearly 17 years as Cabarrus County's superior court judge, Spainhour experienced déjà vu while presiding over an Innocence Commission case in North Carolina's Buncombe County, where his three-judge panel released a wrongly jailed person from prison.

Spainhour's steadfast devotion to justice has guided him through a long and storied career. He proved himself a man of veracity shortly after college while serving in the Army, where, as a courier officer, he was entrusted with global deliveries of classified documents. As a Cabarrus County attorney, he earned the respect of his colleagues. "Instead of trying to persuade someone to a particular point of view as a lawyer, my only concern was to follow the law and the correct procedure to ensure that a fair trial occurred and that the result was fair for everybody," he told the *Independent Tribune*. That conviction led to his 1996 election as president of the North Carolina State Bar, followed two years later by his appointment by Gov. Jim Hunt to become Cabarrus County's superior court judge. When retiring from the bench in late 2014, he humbly remarked, "It takes a whole courthouse to make a judge." At the time of his retirement, Spainhour also became a recipient of the state's highest civilian honor, the Order of the Long Leaf Pine.

Shown in this September 2011 photograph from the Innocence Commission case in Buncombe County are, from left to right, Judge Bradley Letts (Jackson County), Senior Judge Spainhour, and Judge Patrice Hinnant (Guilford County). (Photograph from the *Asheville Citizen-Times*; courtesy of Erwin Spainhour.)

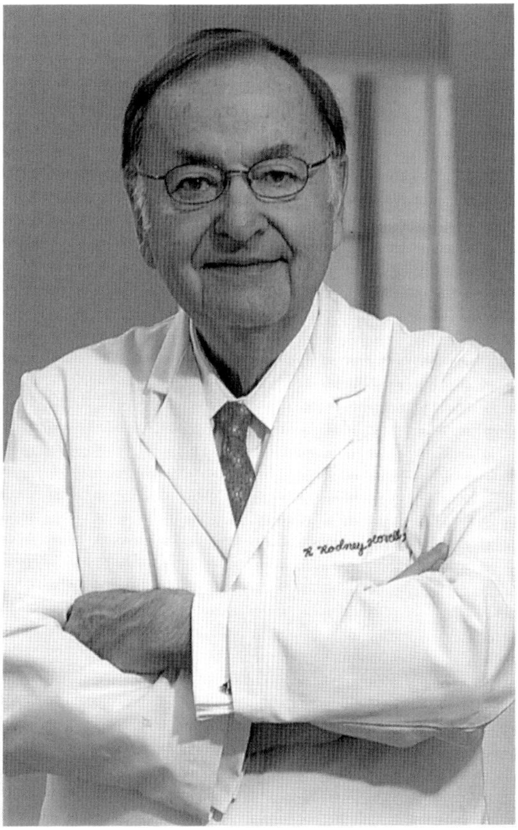

R. Rodney Howell
Dr. Howell is the University of Miami Health System's professor of pediatrics and chair emeritus of the Department of Pediatrics, previously serving as an advisor to the National Institutes of Health. Those with long memories recall him growing up in Concord's Forest Hill area; his father, Fred L. Howell Sr., opened his own machine shop after being laid off from a mill job. (Courtesy of Rodney Howell, MD.)

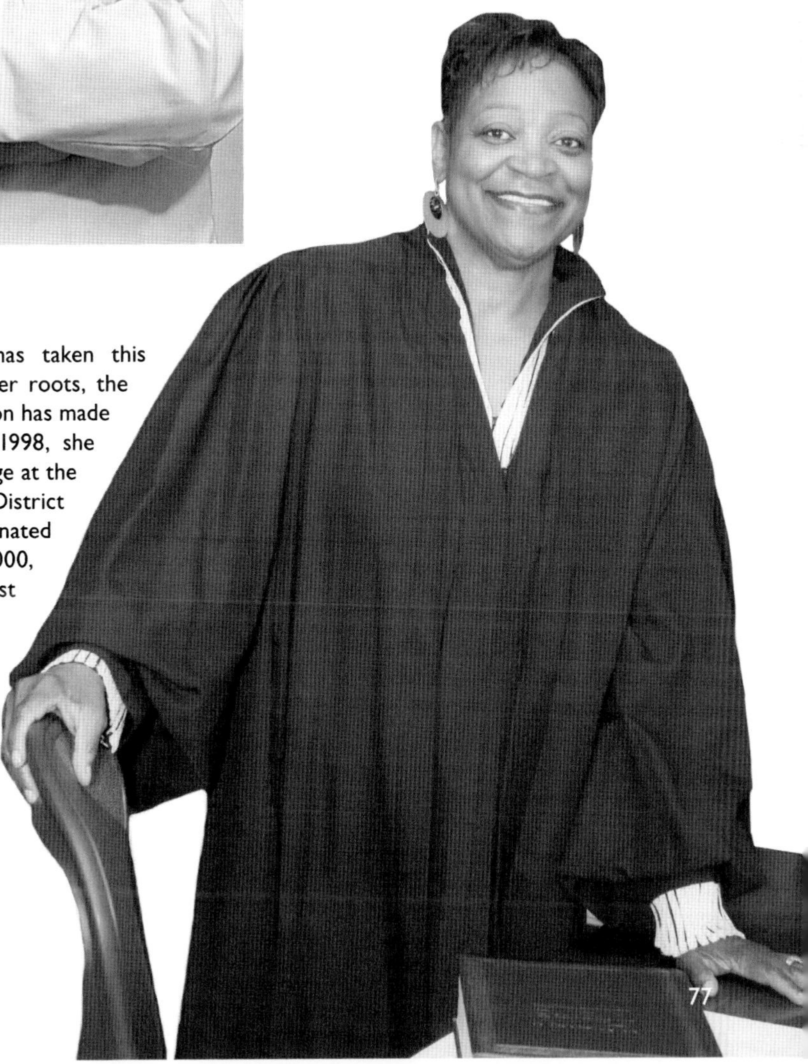

Johnnie B. Rawlinson
While her legal career has taken this Concord native far from her roots, the Honorable Johnnie Rawlinson has made her hometown proud. In 1998, she became the first female judge at the US District Court for the District of Nevada. After being nominated by Pres. Bill Clinton in 2000, Rawlinson became the first woman of color to serve on the US Court of Appeals for the Ninth Circuit. (Courtesy of Johnnie B. Rawlinson.)

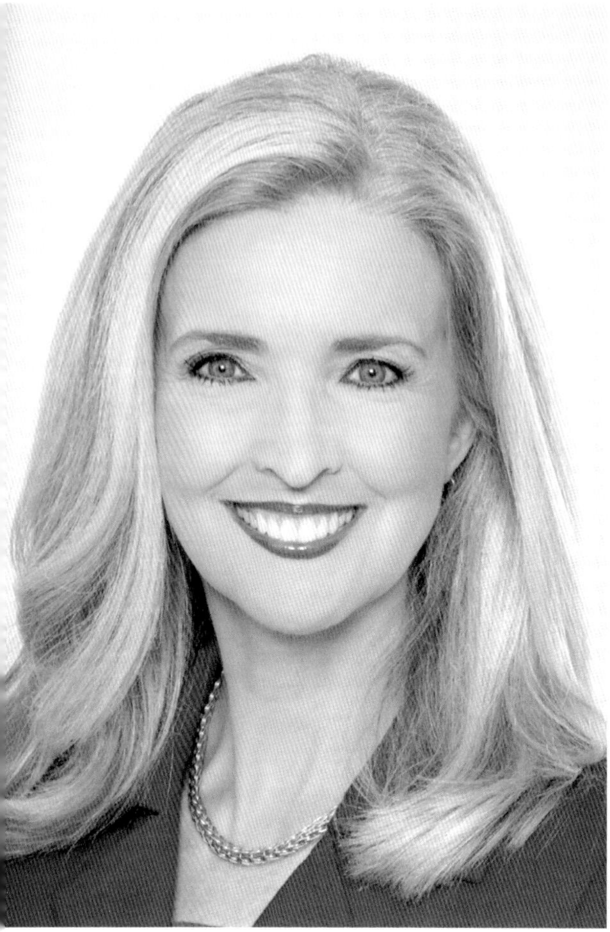

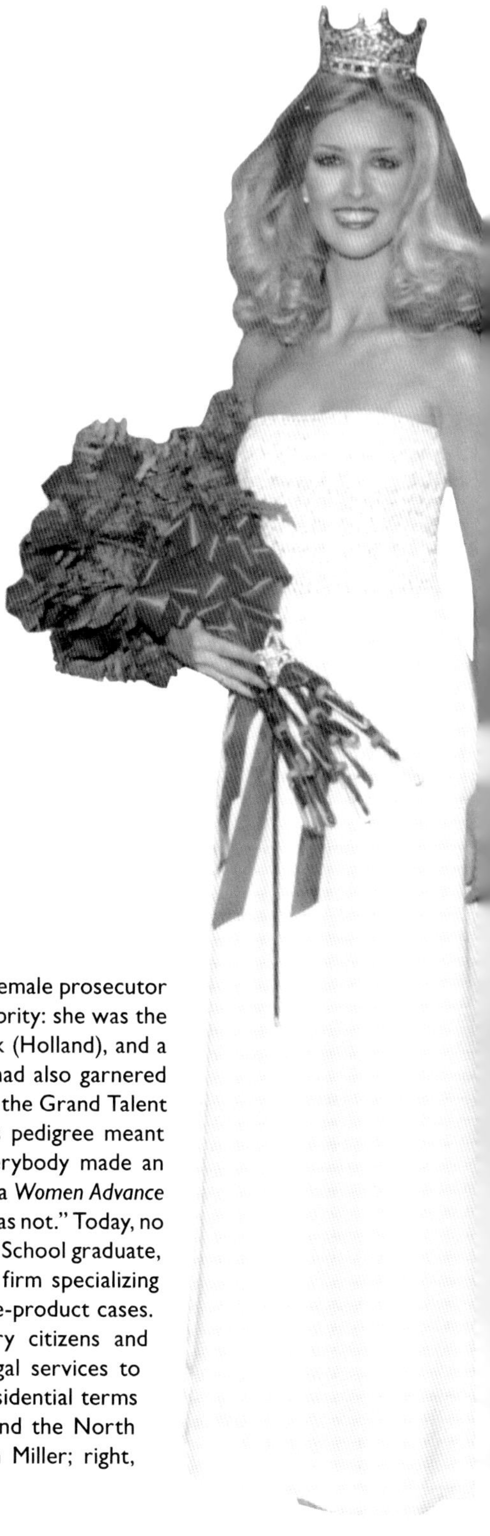

Janet Ward Black

When she became Cabarrus and Rowan Counties' first female prosecutor in 1985, Janet Ward Black was already a hometown celebrity: she was the honor-student daughter of a popular teacher, Fran Black (Holland), and a successful Kannapolis druggist, Baxter F. Black Jr. She had also garnered headlines as the 1980 Miss North Carolina (right) and as the Grand Talent Award winner in the 1981 Miss America pageant. This pedigree meant little to courtroom judges and opposing counsel. "Everybody made an assumption that I was an airhead," she once remarked in a *Women Advance* interview. "I had to convince them by competence that I was not." Today, no one underestimates this Davidson College and Duke Law School graduate, the primary owner of Ward Black Law, a Greensboro firm specializing in personal injury, workers' compensation, and defective-product cases. Black regards herself privileged to represent ordinary citizens and is the creator of "4 ALL," a program offering free legal services to disadvantaged clients. Among her many honors are presidential terms for the North Carolina Association of Trial Lawyers and the North Carolina Bar Association. (Above, courtesy of Hannah Miller; right, courtesy of Fran Black Holland.)

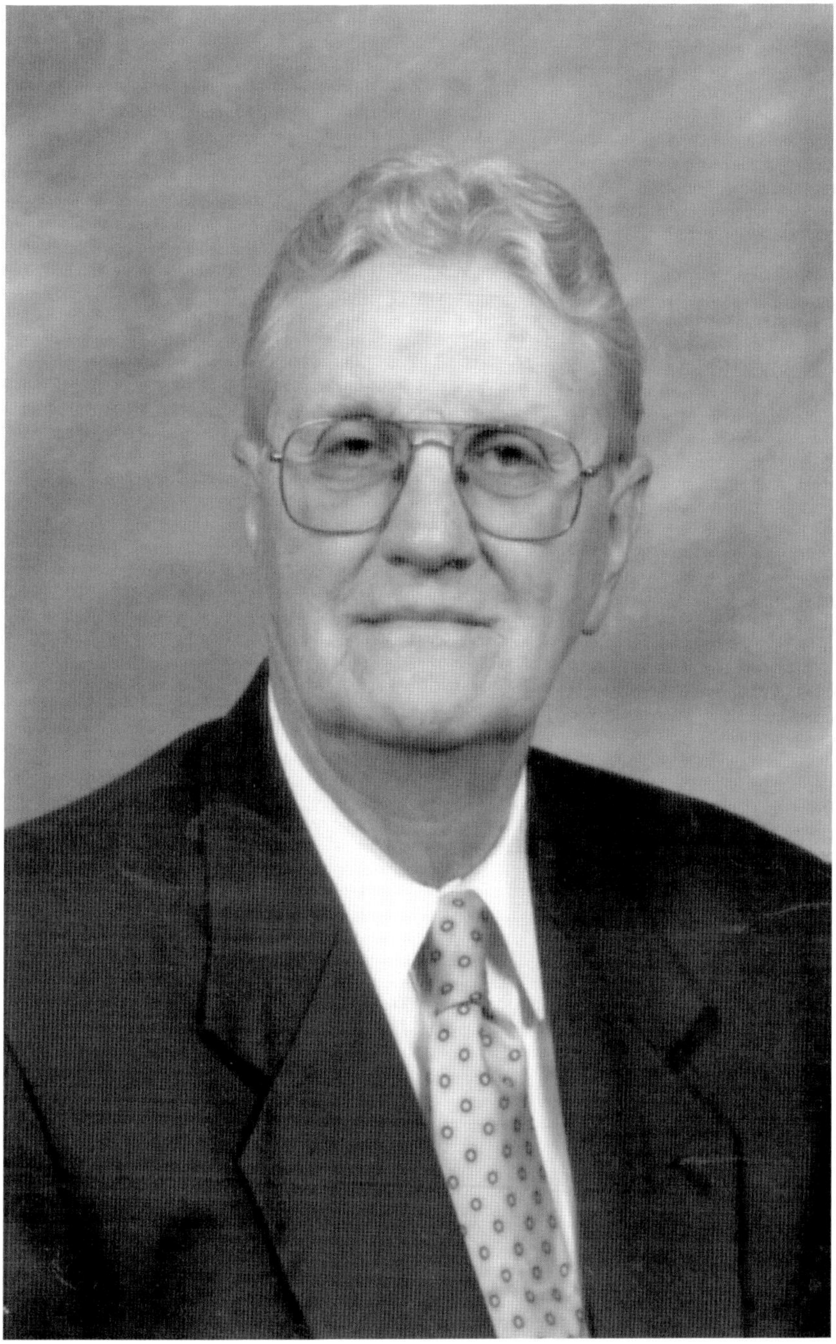

J.W. McGee Jr.
"Mickey" McGee epitomized the term "community leader" with his astonishing record of public involvement that lasted from the 1950s through the early 1990s. In this time, he was school commissioner, a Concord city councilman for 12 years, a Light and Water Department commissioner, and a member of the Historic Preservation Commission. A Concord city park is named after McGee, who died in 2015. (Courtesy of City of Concord.)

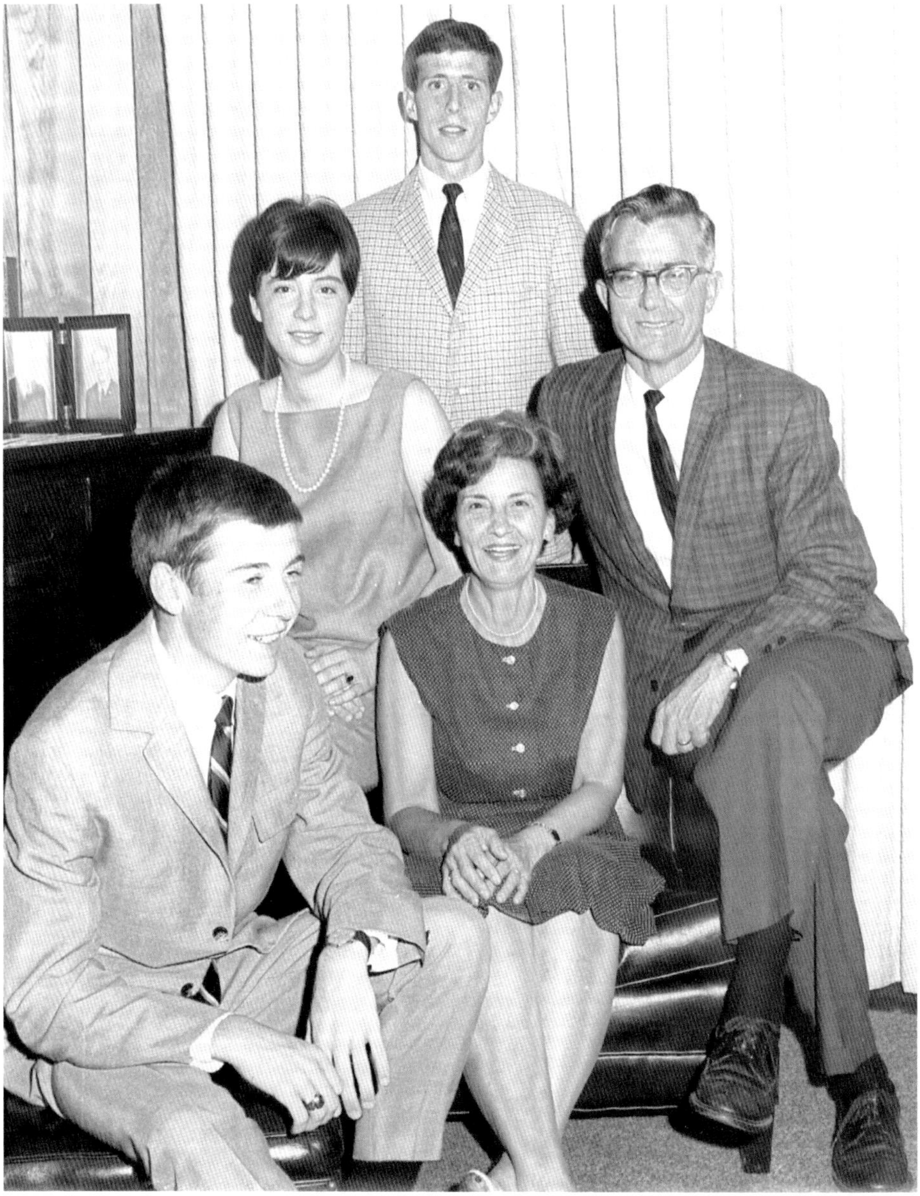

Walter M. Safrit (ABOVE AND OPPOSITE PAGE)
Safrit spent 41 years working for the YMCA, 29 of them as executive director of Kannapolis's Cannon Memorial YMCA. The association's events were often family affairs for the Safrits, especially Camp Elliott summer programs, which featured tasty Southern delicacies like cheese biscuits and cherry cobbler, a menu selected by Safrit's wife, Hope. In 2001, the 17-acre Walter M. Safrit Park on Bethpage Road in Kannapolis was dedicated in his honor. Safrit died in 2003.

Pictured above in the 1960s are, from left to right, (seated) Peter Decker, a German foreign exchange student, and Hope Safrit; (on chair arms) Susan Safrit and Walter Safrit; (standing) Walter M. "Wally" Safrit II, who, at this writing, is the Kannapolis city attorney. The photograph on the opposite page, taken in the 1950s, shows the city's third and best-remembered YMCA, located in Cannon Village. (Both, courtesy of KHA.)

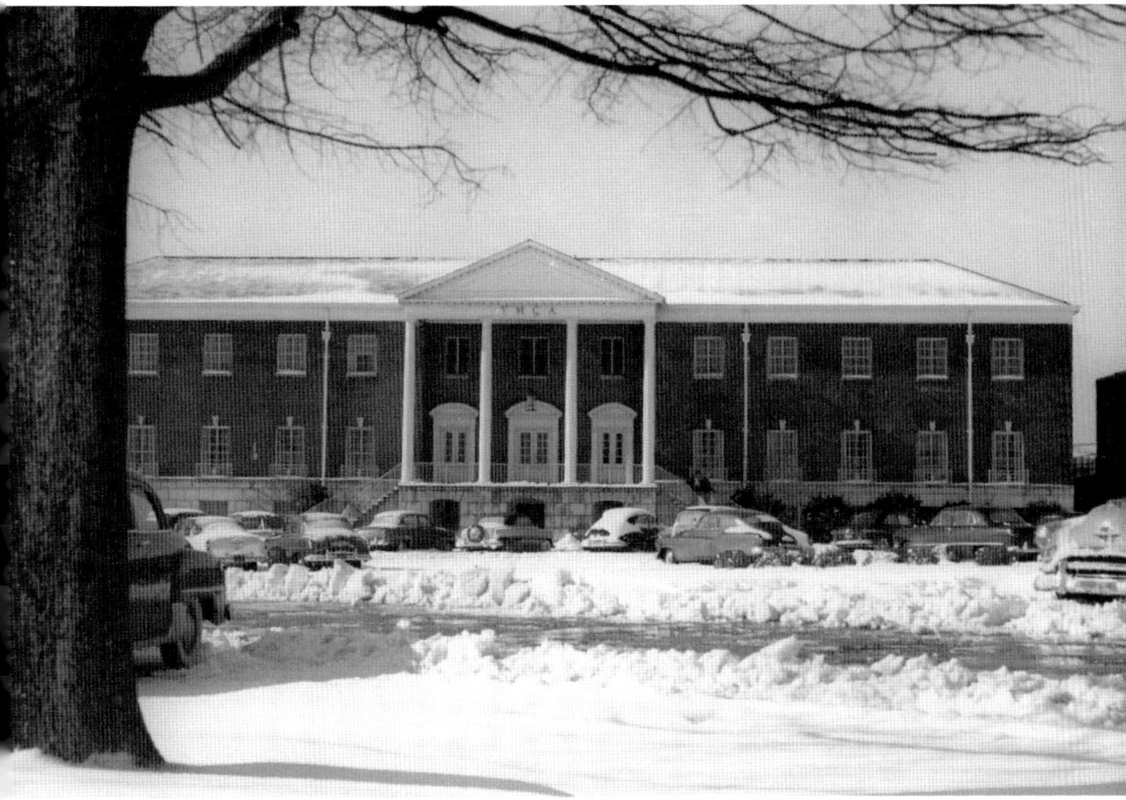

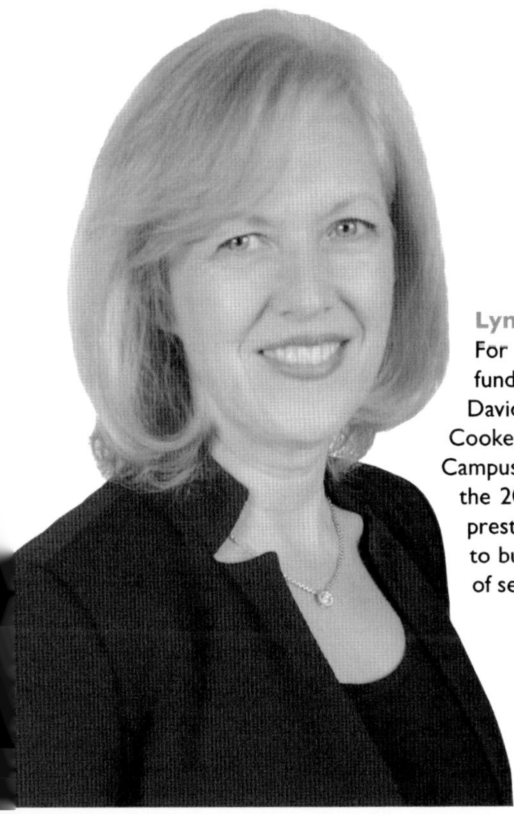

Lynne Scott Safrit
For 33 years, Dr. Safrit, a Kannapolis native, was fundamental in her hometown's reinvention, overseeing David L. Murdock's real estate company, Castle and Cooke, LLC, and later leading the North Carolina Research Campus (NCRC). She and her daughter Elizabeth Safrit, the 2014 Miss United States, received Pfeiffer University's prestigious 2015 Heart of Grace Award, presented annually to businesswomen "whose lives and work embody a spirit of servant leadership." (Courtesy of NCRC.)

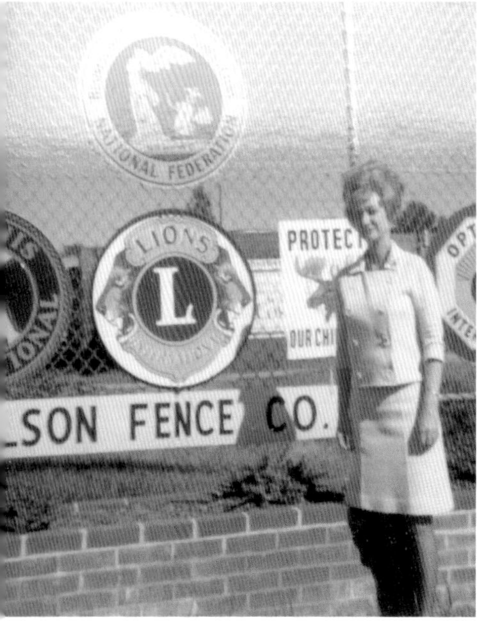

Concord-Cabarrus Business and Professional Women

This multigenerational club of working women was chartered in Concord in 1947 with 40 members and Annie M. Pemberton as its president. Over the decades, its membership has mirrored societal changes, with the teachers once populating its ranks being joined by professionals from diverse fields. Today known as the Concord-Cabarrus BPW, the club administers the Frances B. Long Scholarship, named after one of its influential former members, awarding subsidies to high school graduates and businesswomen seeking to further their educations. In the 1970 photograph at left, president Carolyn B. Williams proudly poses with the BPW emblem after victoriously petitioning the hesitant Concord City Council to allow its display alongside those of male-dominated civic groups. In the 1977 photograph below, BPW members Mary Lentz (far left) and Anna Lois Bulla (far right) congratulate scholarship winners Emily Hogan (second from left) and Judith McAnulty. (Both, courtesy of Debbie Morse.)

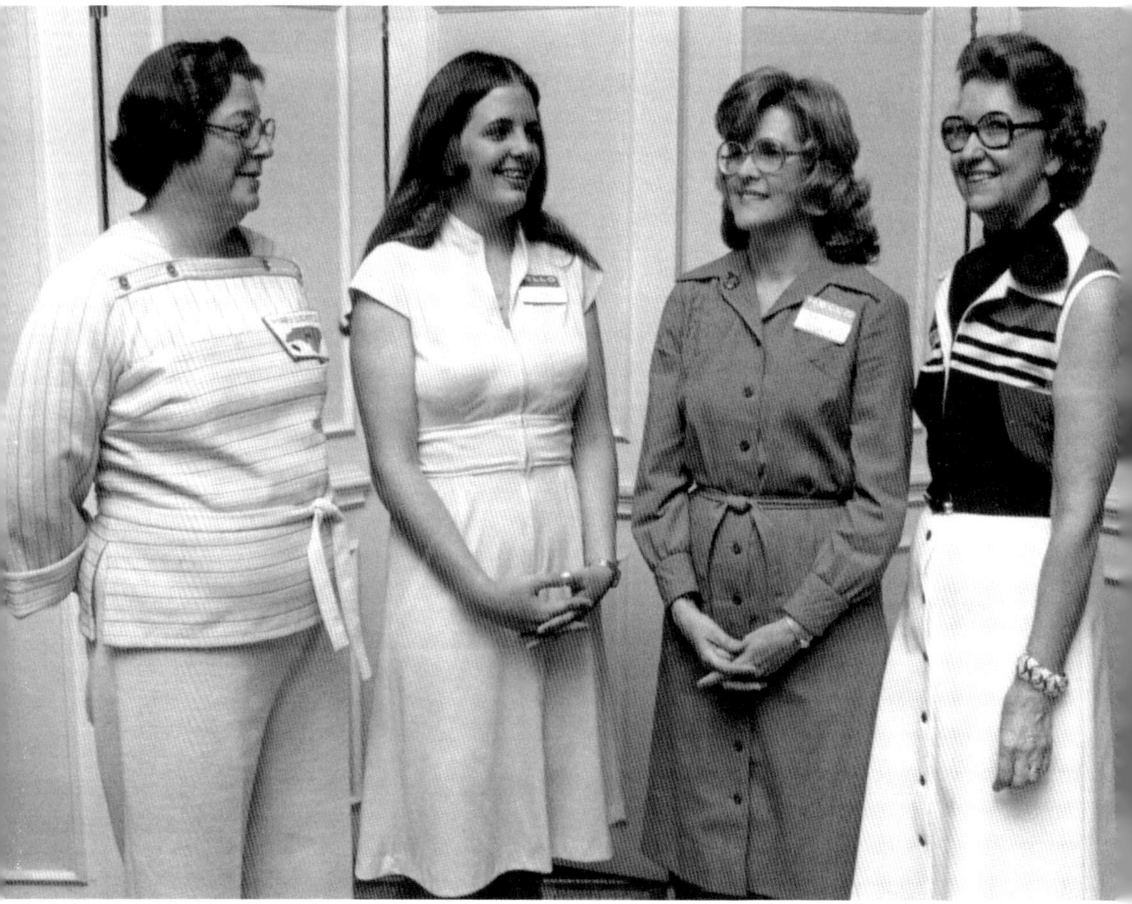

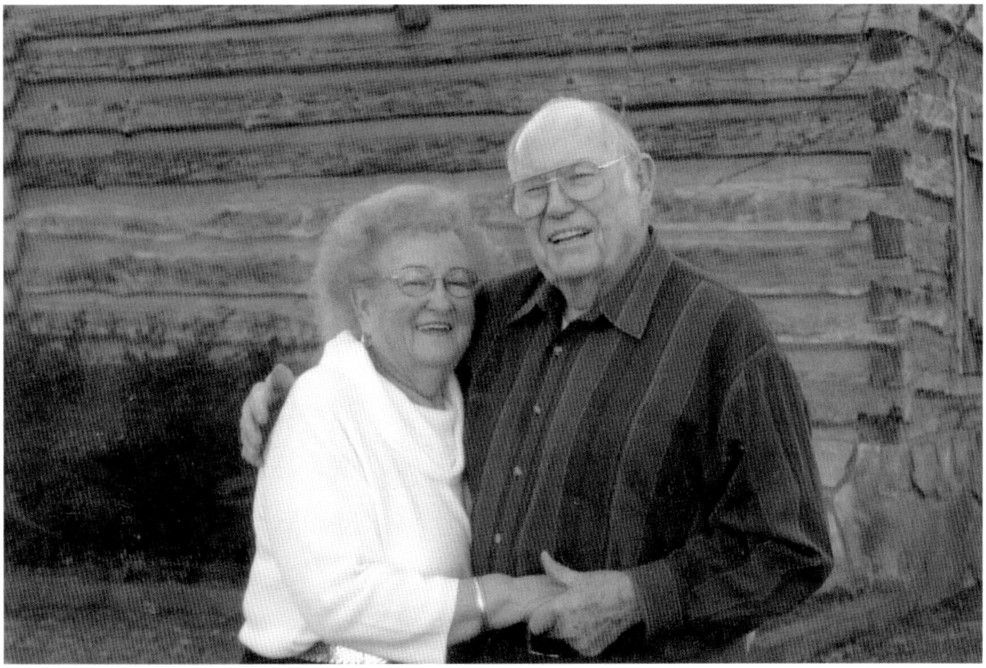

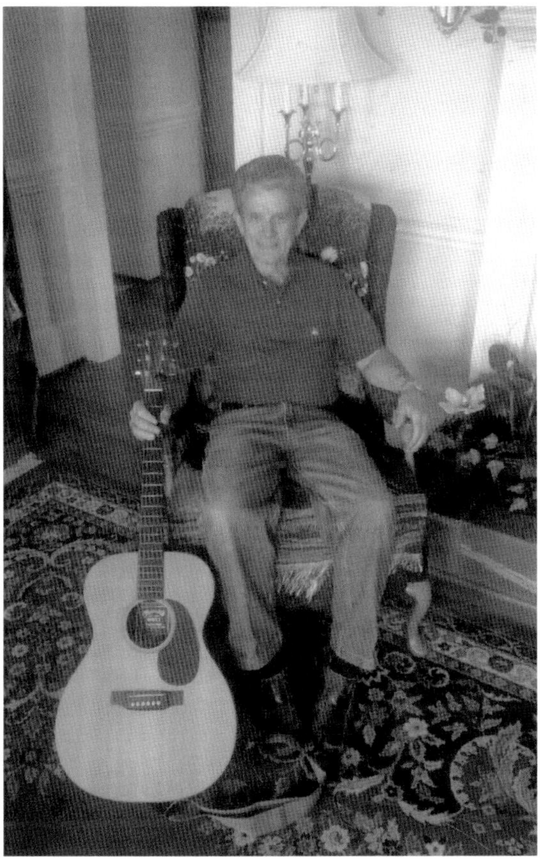

Janie Queen Lyles
In the 1960s, when proprietorship in Harrisburg was exclusively a male domain, this trailblazer bought Harrisburg Florist and operated the flower shop for decades. Prior to that, Janie was known from working at Queen's Grocery, a store owned by her then-husband, Marshall Queen. Janie's impressive collection of antiques, accumulated from decades of auctions, fills the log cabin she owns with her husband, Louis Lyles, shown here with her. (Courtesy of Linda Gibbs.)

Roy Kee
While Harrisburg was experiencing a whirlwind of change, Kee held a lock on the barbering market, running the Harrisburg Barber Shop for over four decades. Even when new barbers came to town, Kee's expertise and the down-home, chatty atmosphere of his shop kept his customers coming back year after year. When he is not holding his clippers, Kee can be found strumming his guitar. (Photograph by Rose Rummel-Eury.)

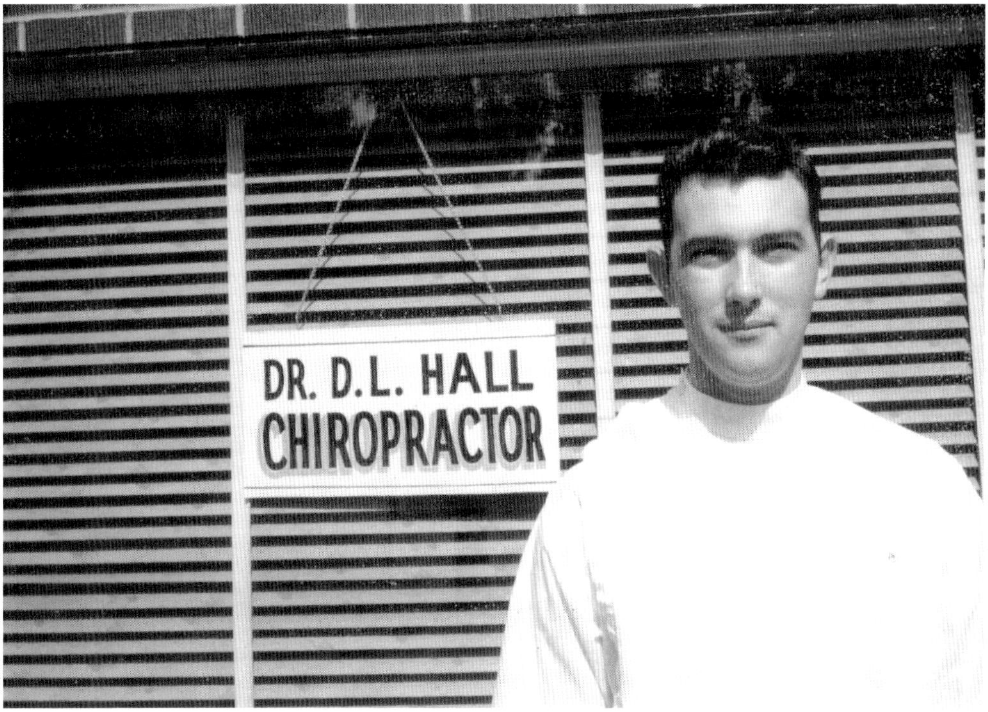

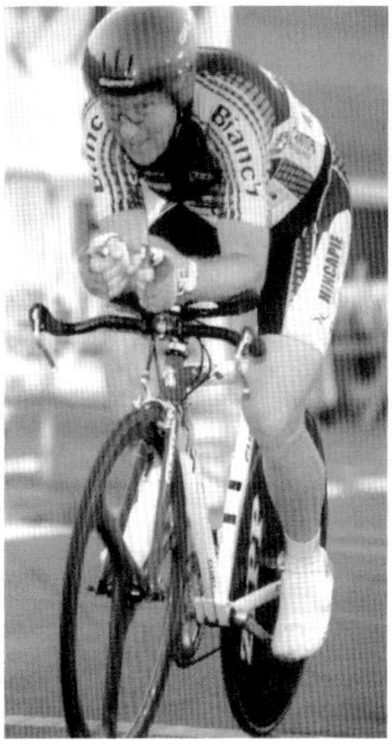

Dennis L. Hall Sr.
Chiropractic treatment was a new and unfamiliar concept in Concord when Dr. Hall opened his practice in 1965. His clinic continues to thrive 50 years later, as does the doctor himself, an award-winning bicycle racer. On three occasions, Hall has received gubernatorial appointments to the North Carolina Board of Chiropractic Examiners, and he has twice served as president of the North Carolina Chiropractic Association. (Both, courtesy of Hall Clinic of Chiropractic.)

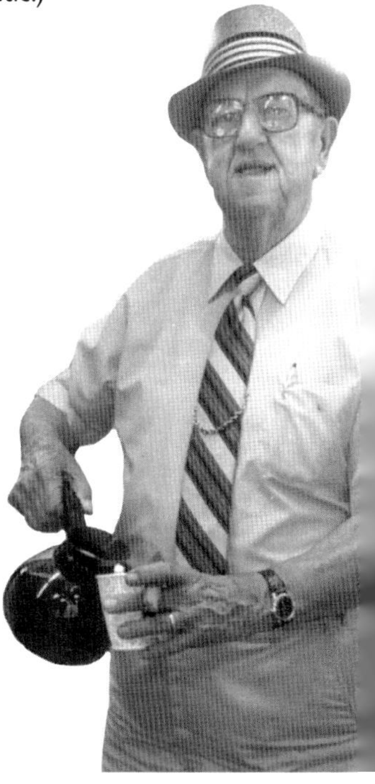

E.L. Bost
"Eb" Bost, who previously ran a taxi service, partnered with C.W. Bost (no direct relation) in 1956 to open the first of a regional chain of drive-ins, What-A-Burger. The name was inspired by the eatery's signature huge hamburger bun. One of its specialties is the Witch Doctor, a soft-drink blend with dill pickle slices added. Several What-A-Burgers remain hotspots today, with Bost's son Mike running the business. (Courtesy of What-A-Burger.)

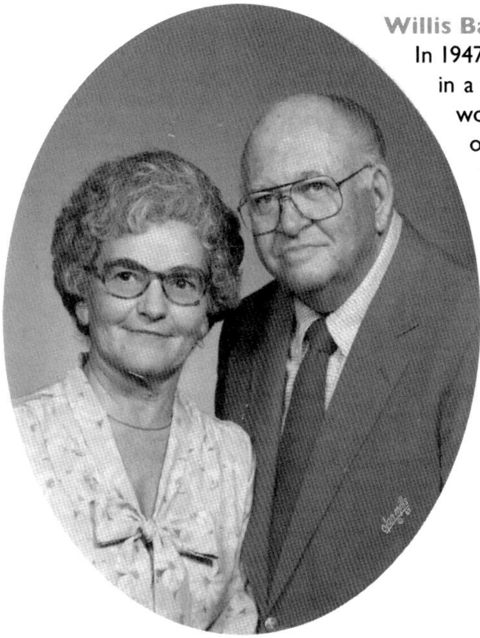

Willis Baucom Jr.

In 1947, Baucom (shown with his wife, Joyce) invested $300 in a selection of shoes, which he hoofed door-to-door, working from his 1939 Dodge. Then, two years later, he opened Baucom's Shoe Store in downtown Concord, where it prospers today. In 1991, Baucom sold the business to his son Randy, who said, "He always wanted me to earn what I got . . . and I learned from that." (Courtesy of Randy Baucom Sr.)

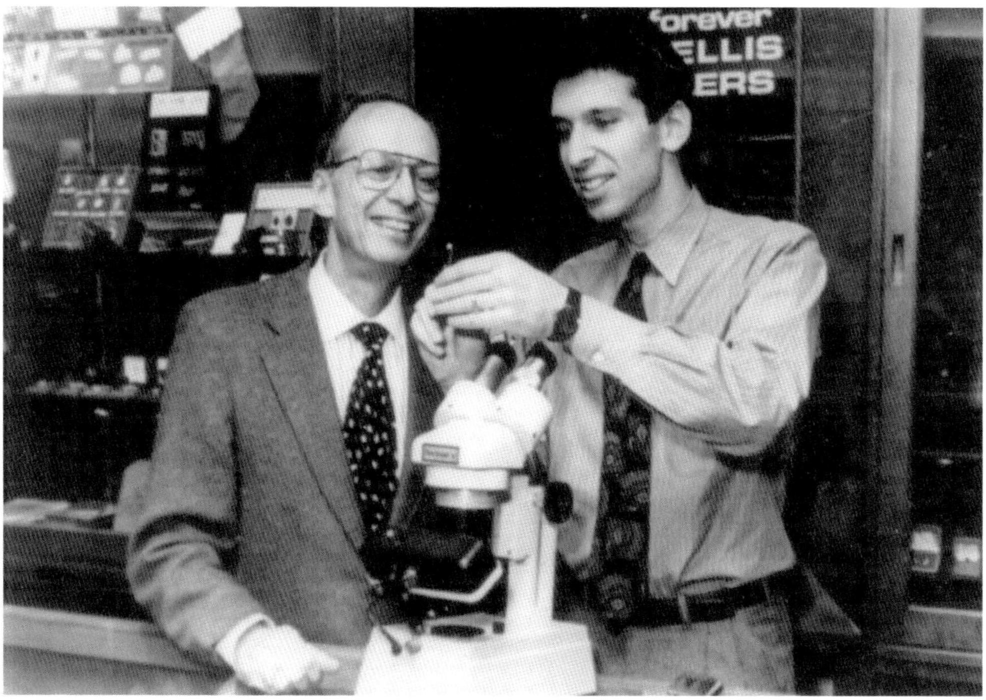

Ellis Levinson

The promise of free prizes packed Ellis Jewelers with customers when Levinson opened his enterprise in downtown Concord on Thursday, July 23, 1953. What continues to bring them in over 60 years later is this independent firm's commitment to artistry and customer service. This 1990 photograph shows Levinson (left), who has since retired, welcoming his son Dan on his first day on the job. (Courtesy of Justyna Bernacki.)

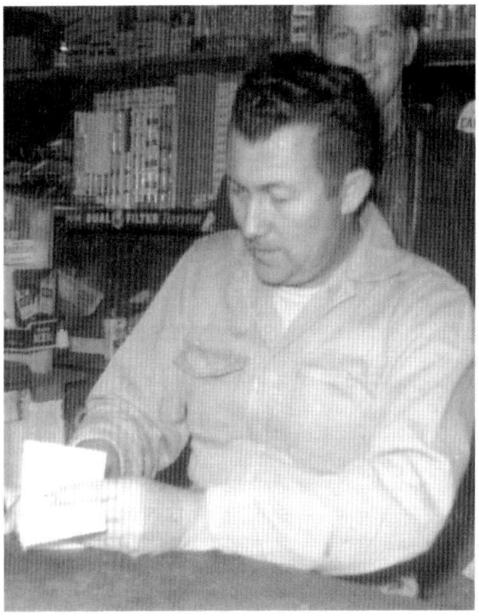

Foil Carriker

A century-old Cabarrus institution ended in 1997 when Foil Carriker, grandson of Midland's first businessman, John Washington Carriker, retired and closed Carriker's Service & Produce Store (below). It was the latest, and last, permutation of an establishment that began as a simple shed built by Foil's grandfather. Foil's father, Arthur Oscar Carriker, continued the store in a different location, one that was destroyed by fire in 1956. Carriker's was a family-owned convenience market, offering a little bit of everything, including a hangout for locals who were lovingly and laughingly known as "loafers." Foil and his wife, Kat, were joined behind the counter by their children, who became the last generation to work there before its closing. Shown at left in 1960 are Foil (foreground) and Buford Barnhardt. (Both, courtesy of Town of Midland.)

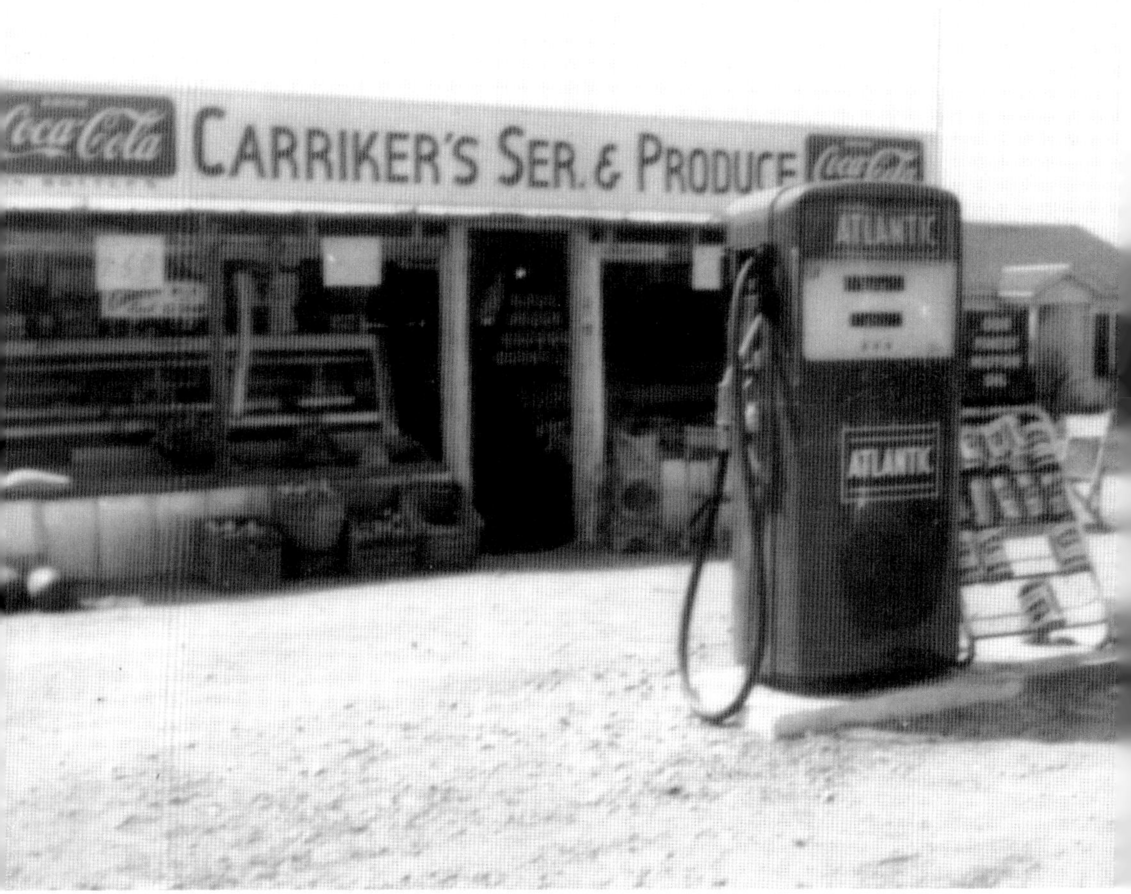

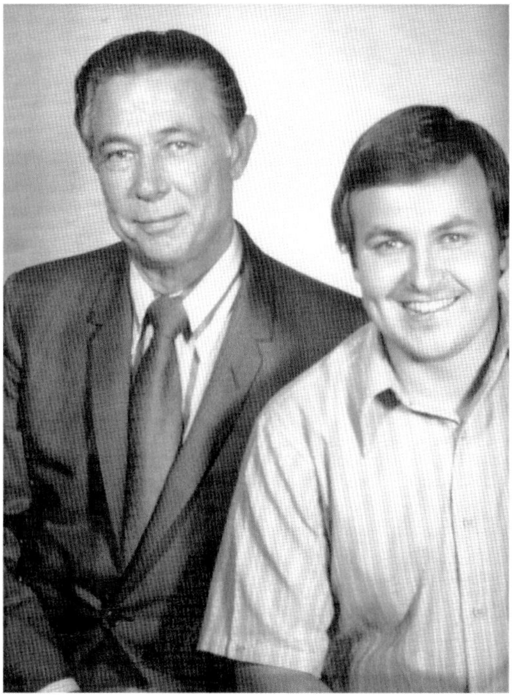

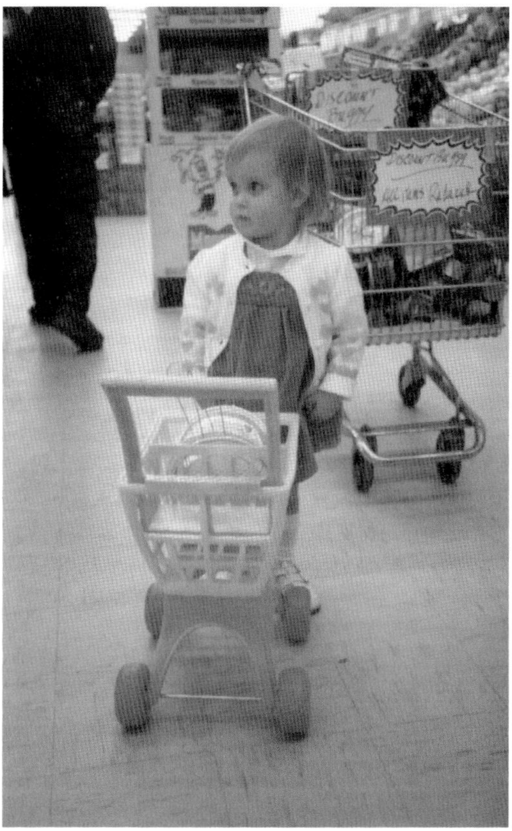

Dover Family
In 2009, Elizabeth Ann Dover (below, as a toddler) convinced her parents to develop her late grandparents' four-acre spread on Highway 29 between Concord and Charlotte into a vineyard specializing in North Carolina wines. Her family has been in the food business since 1913, when Aud Dover started his independently owned Dover's Supermarket in Concord's Brown Mill community, an enterprise later operated by his son Leonard (above, left) and grandson Audy (above, right). Audy has developed other businesses in the area, including Our Town Cinemas in nearby Davidson, a movie theater that serves food and beverages. (Both, courtesy of Elizabeth Ann Dover.)

Bernard Davis Jr.

Davis has tirelessly devoted himself to capturing the community's black history, writing and publishing the 2010 book *Portraits of the African-American Experience in Concord-Cabarrus, North Carolina: 1860–2008*. The majority of the images featured in his book were taken by Davis, who operated a downtown Concord photography studio from 1982 through 2005. (Courtesy of Bernard Davis Jr.)

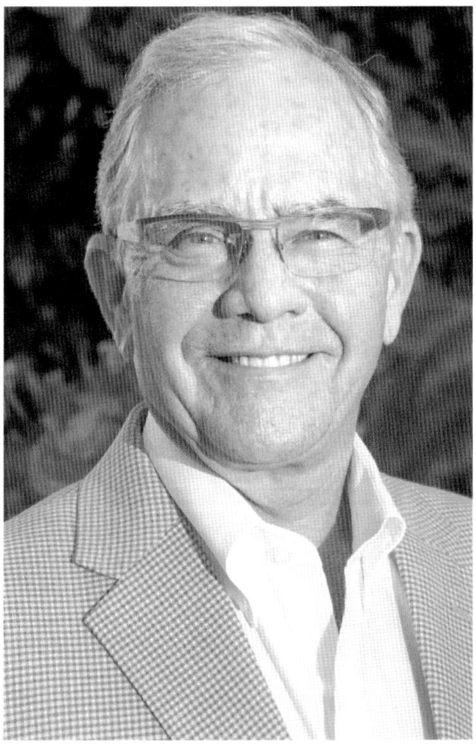

Francis P. Koster

Issues such as the ecosystem, energy sources, and health care may intimidate most people, but not "America's Optimistic Futurist." This nationally known author and lecturer puts a hopeful spin on bleak issues, directing others toward solutions. Dr. Koster is the author of the book *Discovering the New America: Where Local Communities Are Solving National Problems*, which offers plans to combat a range of concerns from birth defects to homelessness. (Courtesy of Fran Koster.)

CHAPTER FIVE

Shapers of Young Minds

A common childhood experience links each generation: the teacher, mentor, or coach who first piqued an intellectual curiosity, imparted an unshakable life lesson, or provided guidance at an impressionable time. Each educator who has ever etched chalk onto a blackboard is legendary in at least one student's mind. Yet some have left marks so indelible, their instructions cannot be erased from memory.

Martin Henderson Winecoff so strongly believed in the value of education that he orchestrated the building of a school for rural children who otherwise would have been deprived of the opportunity to learn. A tragedy detoured Lorraine Gray from the altar, yet she found a lifelong love in teaching. Before integration brought black and white students into the same classrooms, the dedicated faculties of George Washington Carver and Logan High Schools educated generations of African American teens.

As a Concord Spider, Charles E. Rimer was a star athlete. He returned to his alma mater to build new legacies as a coach and principal. Fran Black Holland challenged her students to imagine their destinies, while Dwight and Ruby Blackwelder employed firsthand experiences as an educational tool. Bob Mauldin, Arden Ray, and Aldon Levon Coefield were more than coaches—they were counselors whose exemplary conduct forever altered lives.

Some Cabarrus County citizens profiled here earned respect for gestures outside of the classroom, like Jay M. Robinson, whose impact was felt across the entire state of North Carolina. The "dancing mother" to many, Peggè Lee Sapp Haywood used not a schoolroom but a studio to tap her students' creative spirits.

The shapers of young minds celebrated in this chapter represent the hundreds of others who have so unforgettably charted futures for thousands of Cabarrus County students.

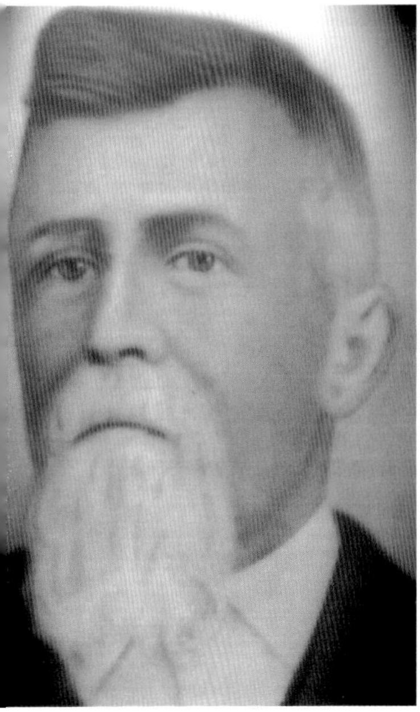

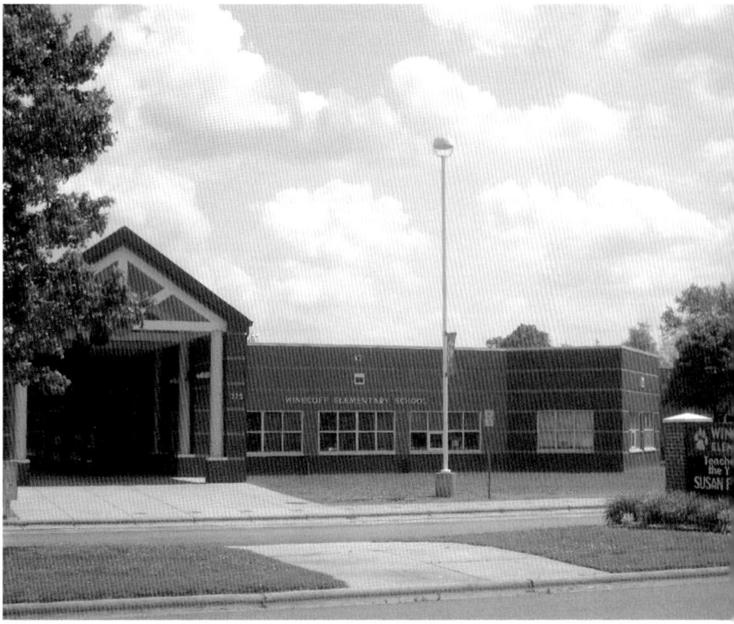

Martin Henderson Winecoff

The elementary school (right) that today bears his name dates to 1877, when Winecoff, a Confederate veteran, donated the land and provided the lumber to construct a school for children in then-rural northern Cabarrus County. Originally a small structure with wooden plank benches, the school later expanded into a high school. After integration, it ultimately returned to its elementary school roots. (Left, courtesy of Harriet Hunter and Winecoff Elementary School; right, photograph by the author.)

Paul B. Barringer (OPPOSITE PAGE)

This eminent Davidson College and University of Virginia professor influenced the lives of many turn-of-the-century collegians, but genealogists also owe him a debt of gratitude. At age 74, Barringer penned his memoirs, *The Natural Bent*, its title taken from a line in Plato's *Republic*. In it, Barringer related with incisive clarity his illustrious lineage, a family rife with captains of battle and industry. The book was published posthumously in 1949. (Courtesy of ECHS.)

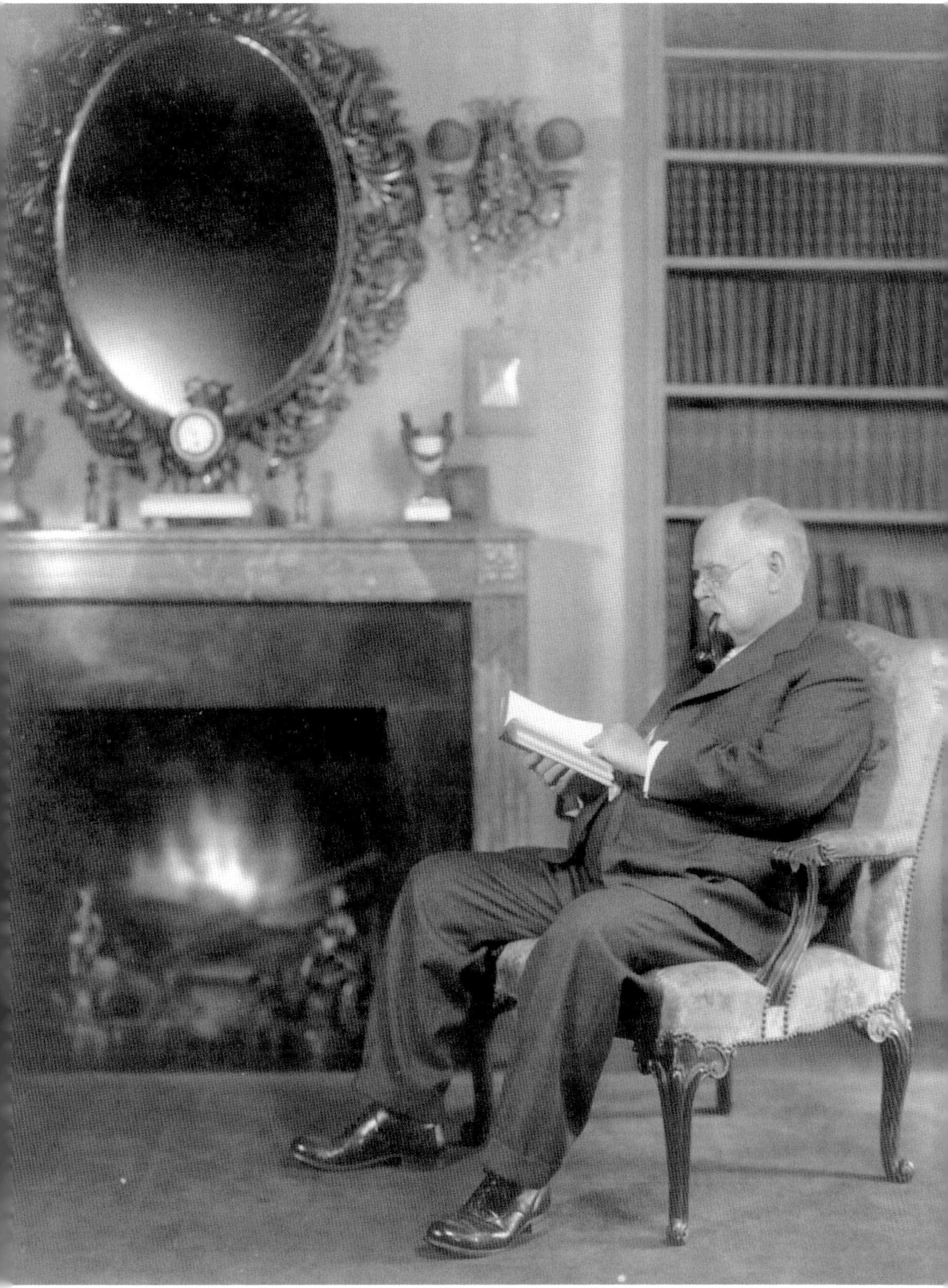

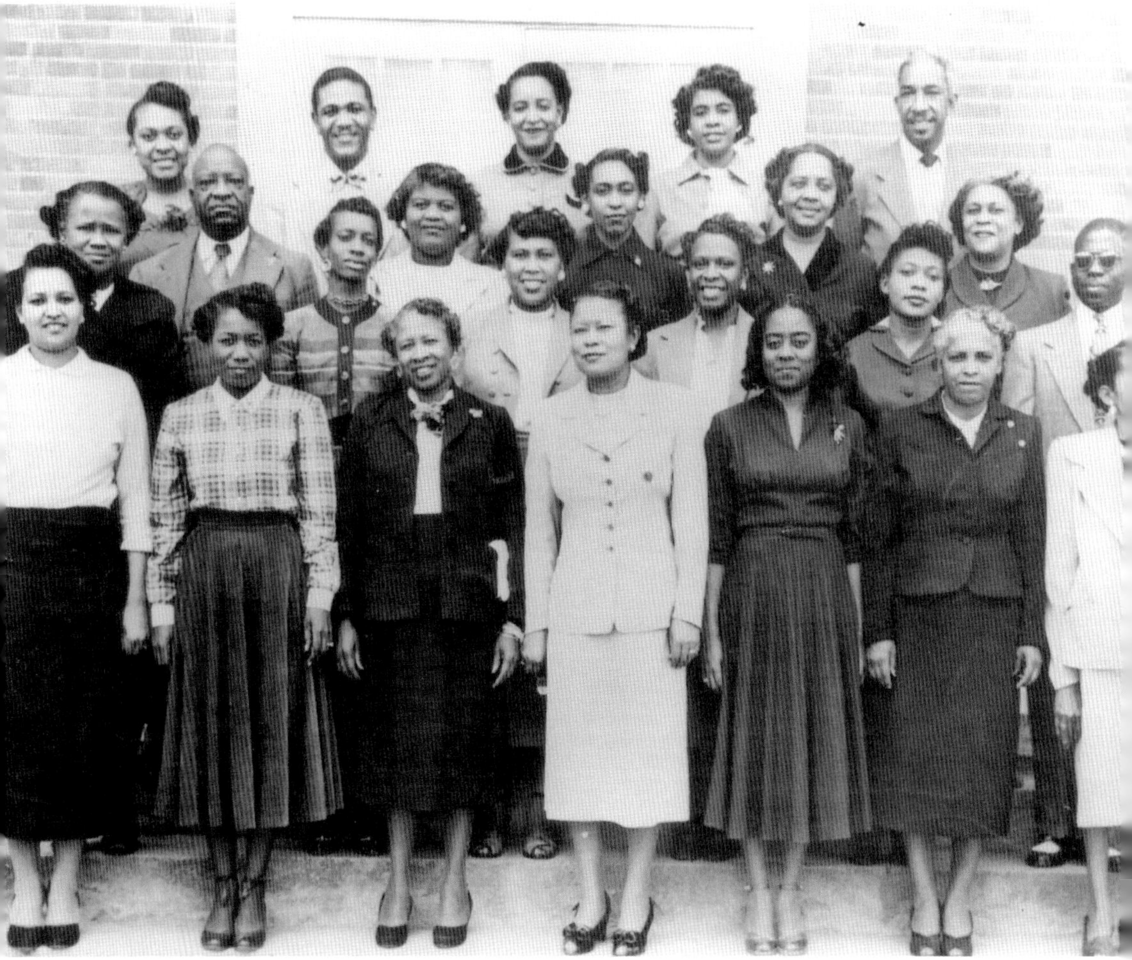

George Washington Carver High School

Kannapolis's esteemed high school for students of color closed its doors in 1967 with the advent of desegregation, with most of its students resuming their education at A.L. Brown High School. Many of its teachers, including Hannah Reid (front row, center), continued shaping young minds at other Cabarrus County schools that formerly accommodated white students only. The faculty of George Washington Carver High School assembled for this group photograph around 1953. Shown are, from left to right, (first row) Virginia Taylor, Catherine Litaker, Mary Johnson, Hannah Reid, Maggie Bryant, Ora Wesley, and Effie Brown; (second row) Margaret Willie, Gwendolyn Smith, Effie Cochran, Mary Hughes, Nancy Miller, and Van Foster; (third row) William L. Reid (principal), Lena Kirk, Vernice Dungee, Gladys Kino, and unidentified; (fourth row) Rosa Sellers, Ira Brewer, Betty McConnehey, Dorothy Whitmire, and Earl Whitmire. (Courtesy of KHA.)

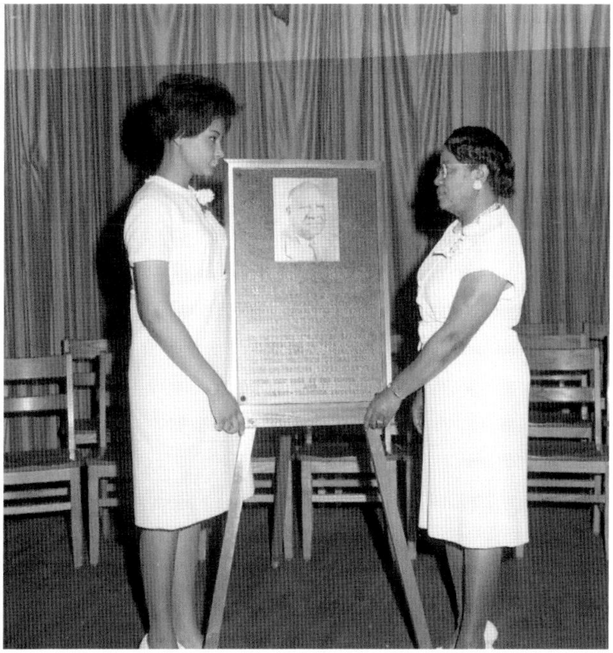

William L. Reid

From 1933 to 1963, Reid, an educator and principal, devoted himself to George Washington Carver High School, the pre-integration high school for Kannapolis's African American students. This photograph from May 29, 1966, shows Carver senior Deborah Johnson (left) presenting to the school a plaque commemorating Reid's service. At right is Reid's widow, Hannah. (Courtesy of KHA.)

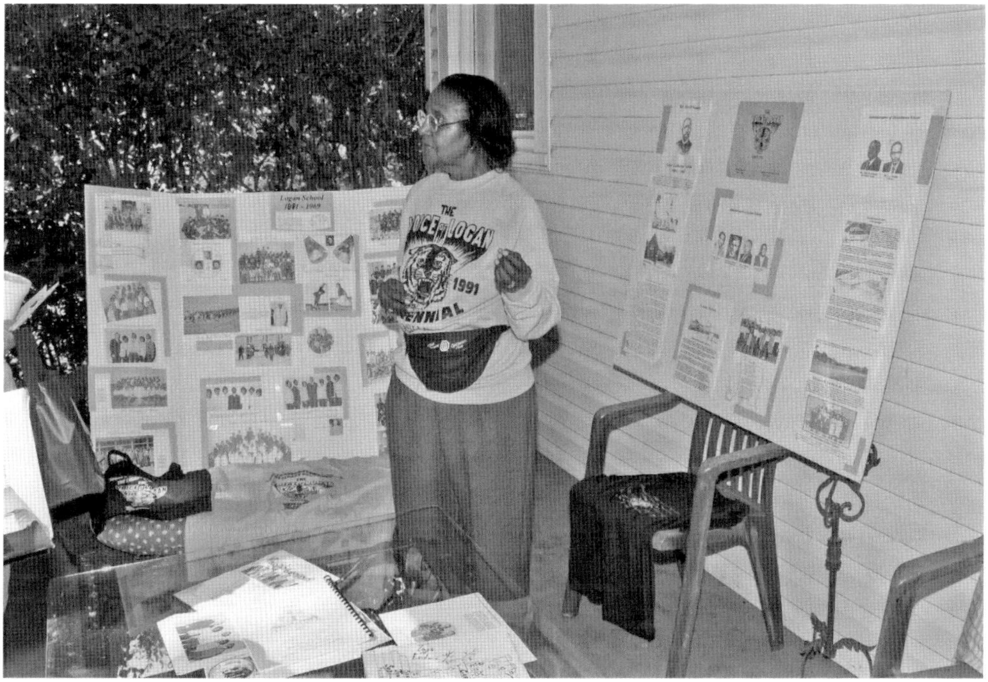

Logan High School

When Concord initiated public schools in 1891, the Concord Colored School opened. In 1924, it was renamed after its administrator, Frank T. Logan. It offered primary and secondary education. Logan closed after desegregation in the late 1960s, but its surviving educators and alumni preserve its history. In this photograph from the 2010 Concord History Walk, former Logan teacher Vernie King shares stories about the school's heritage. (Photograph by the author.)

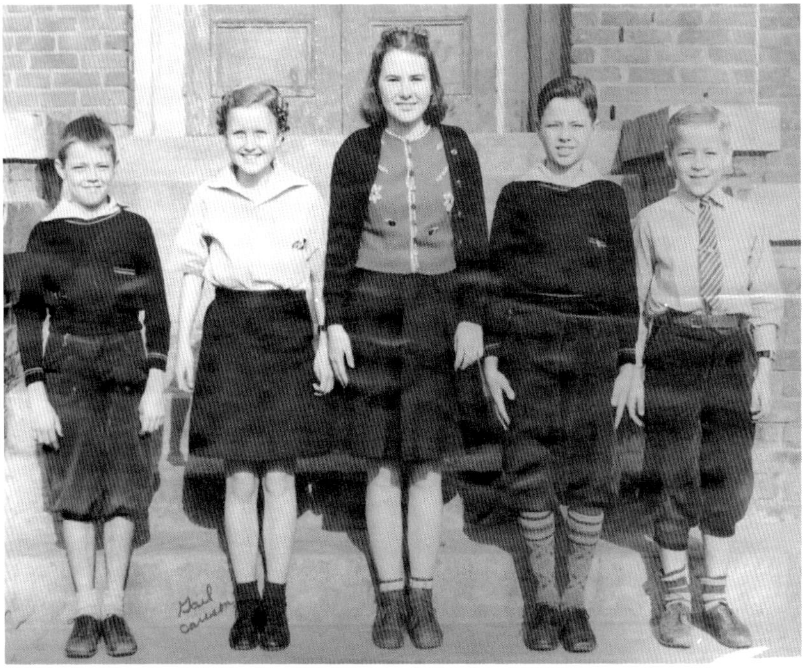

Charles E. Rimer (ABOVE AND OPPOSITE PAGE)

"Next to my family, Concord High School (CHS) is the most important thing in my life," Rimer often said. Yet the Concord Spiders were also his family. This included the football players who were his teammates, the ones he later coached, and the students who listened to his morning loudspeaker announcements as their principal. For his wife, Carleen, and daughters Terri and Vanessa, autumn Friday evenings were football nights. Rimer's pigskin passion and love of Concord's black and gold was a family affair.

As a National Honor Society student at CHS in the mid-1940s, Charlie Rimer lettered in baseball and football, but the latter was his passport to a brighter future. He was the Spiders' 1945 team captain and refused to be sidelined by a broken leg bone: "nevertheless he was one of the most dependable ground gainers in the circuit, an ace blocking back and tops on defense," an area sportswriter reported at the time. Another sports injury—a broken shoulder, in 1949—netted Rimer an unexpected fringe benefit while at Davidson College, where he attended on a full athletic scholarship: he was cared for by a nursing student who was destined to become his wife. He served in the Army after college and earned the Korean Service Award in 1952. Rimer's three-decade career in the Concord/Cabarrus County school system began in 1955; in that period, he was, among other positions, a history teacher, CHS's head football and baseball coach, principal at Clara Harris School, principal at Concord Junior High, and, lastly, CHS principal beginning in 1969, where he remained for 17 years. Many of his students were unaware that Rimer was also the commanding officer of the North Carolina National Guard's Concord unit, helping maintain peace during racial unrest in the early 1970s. An inaugural inductee of the Cabarrus County Sports Hall of Fame, Rimer passed away in 2013. His impeccable character was presaged in this 1952 yearbook dedication to the young educator at his first, pre-Concord teaching job at Badin (North Carolina) High School: "This dedication is evidence of our admiration for his knowledge as an instructor, our appreciation of his skill and understanding as a coach, and our high regard for him as a Christian gentleman."

These photographs show Rimer at three stages of his life. At top, Rimer (far right) poses with Long School Junior Red Cross members, from left to right, Glen Burris, Nadene Carson, Iris Lee Bost, and Bill Burris. Above on the opposite page, Rimer is seen as the CHS football captain. On the opposite page, below, Rimer is CHS principal in the mid-1970s. (All, courtesy of Vanessa Rimer Lynch.)

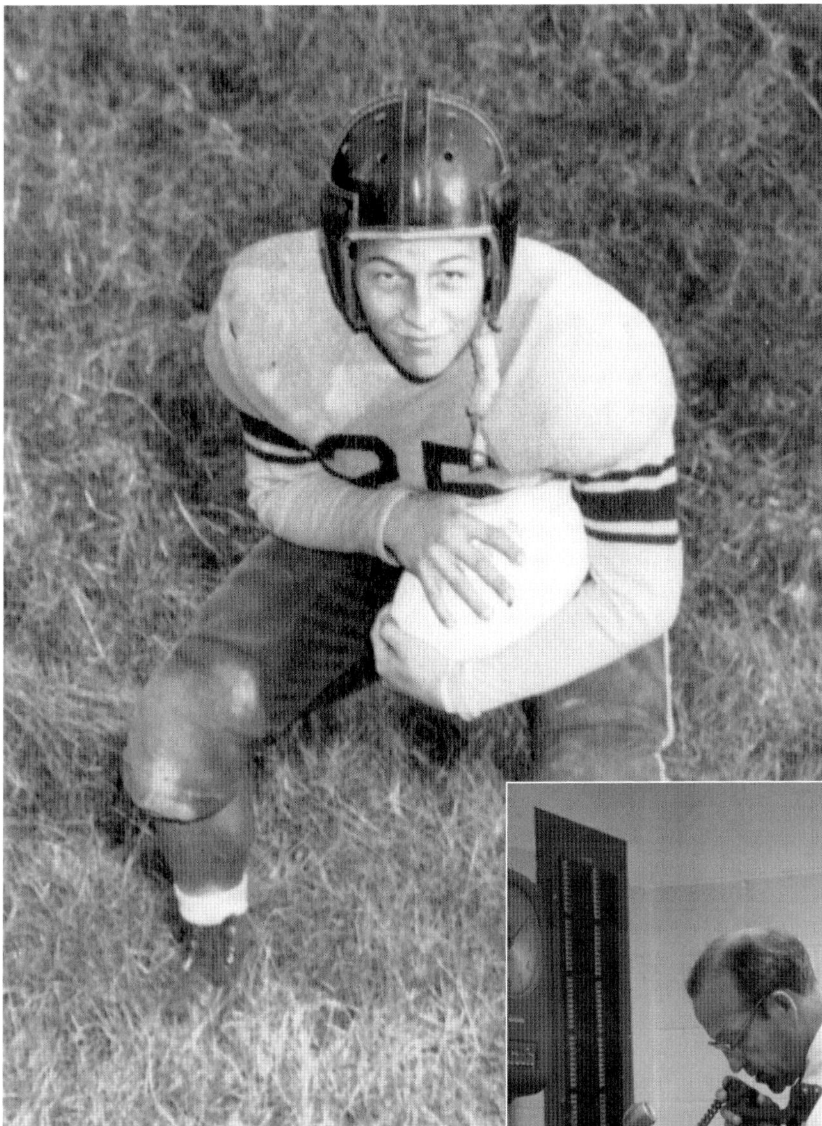

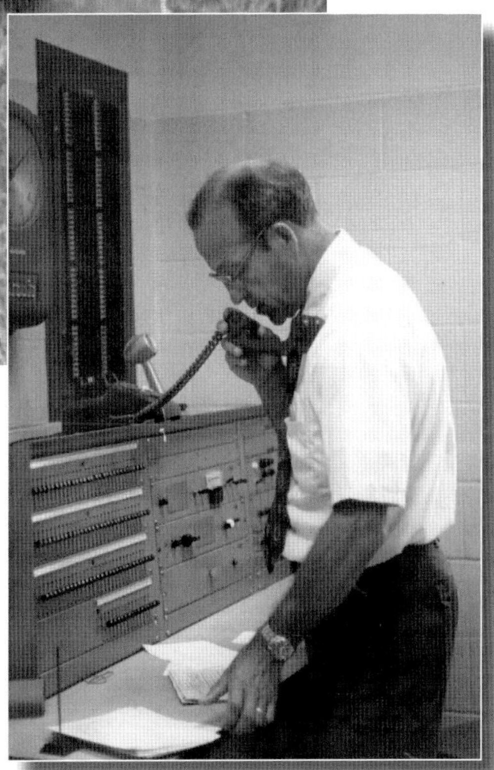

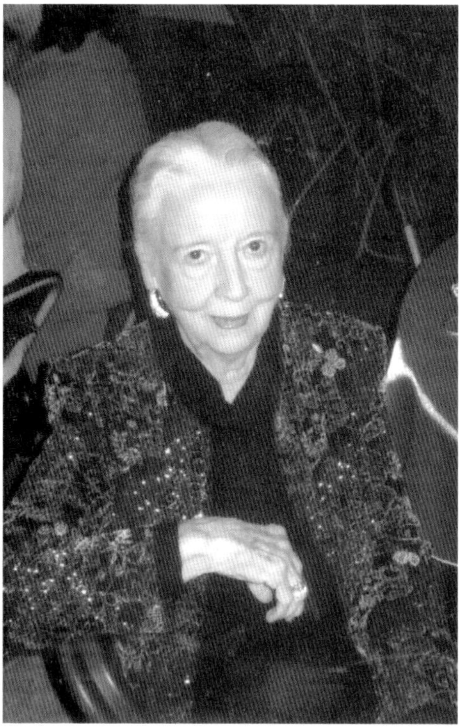

Fran Black Holland (ABOVE AND OPPOSITE PAGE)

This elegant icon of education is best known for teaching English and Bible, but Fran Black Holland instructed some of her first Concord High School students in a subject some might find uncomfortable: death. She assigned roughly 100 students in a humanities class the task of writing their own funeral eulogies. Such an assignment might seem the fictional domain of Mark Twain, but, through this class exercise, impressionable intellects were challenged to imagine the life they had yet to live. Charting futures became her hallmark, as the grammatical and spiritual foundations Holland imparted during her 32 years before a chalkboard guided a legion of adolescents toward new horizons.

Holland had spent two years teaching high school Bible in Selma, North Carolina, when she was hired in 1951 by Kannapolis superintendent W.J. Bullock as a Bible instructor at A.L. Brown High School. She began teaching ninth-grade English two years later, staying on staff at Brown until 1959, when Concord principal Ralph Glenn recruited her to teach ninth grade and senior English at Concord High School. She remained at CHS until her retirement in 1983, also serving as senior class advisor for seven years.

Holland's community résumé includes membership in the Concord Rotary Club, the Concord Business and Professional Women, the Sidney Lanier Book Club, and the Cabarrus Senior Democrats, as well as teaching Sunday school for nearly five decades. She is a 2007 recipient of the Order of the Long Leaf Pine, North Carolina's highest civilian honor. She hosts an annual Christmas celebration in loving memory of her first husband, Kannapolis pharmacist Baxter F. Black Jr., and her second husband, Cannon Mills scientist Victor B. Holland Jr.

"I hope I made a difference in their lives, educationally and in every way," she admits when reflecting upon the hundreds of students that passed through her classrooms over the decades. As evidenced by the successes of many who studied under her and the personal visits and letters she receives from her former pupils, Holland's mission was accomplished.

In the 1959 photograph at opposite left, Fran and husband Baxter F. Black Jr. hold their daughter, legendary local Janet Ward Black; their other child is 1st Lt. Frank Black. She addresses the BPW in the 1971 photograph at opposite right. (Above and opposite left, courtesy of Fran Black Holland; opposite right, courtesy of Debbie Morse.)

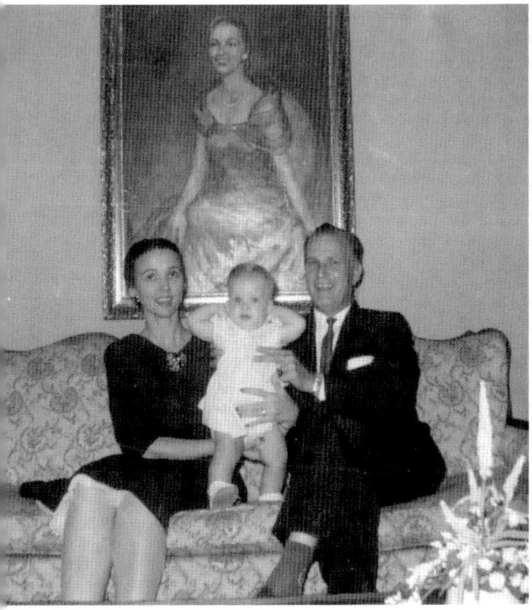

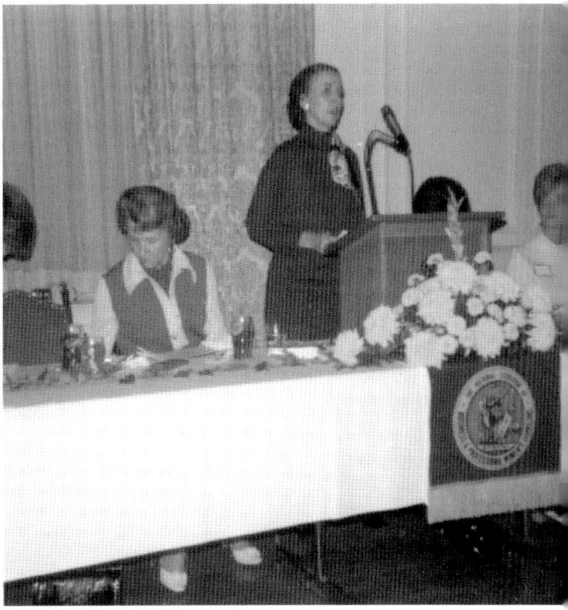

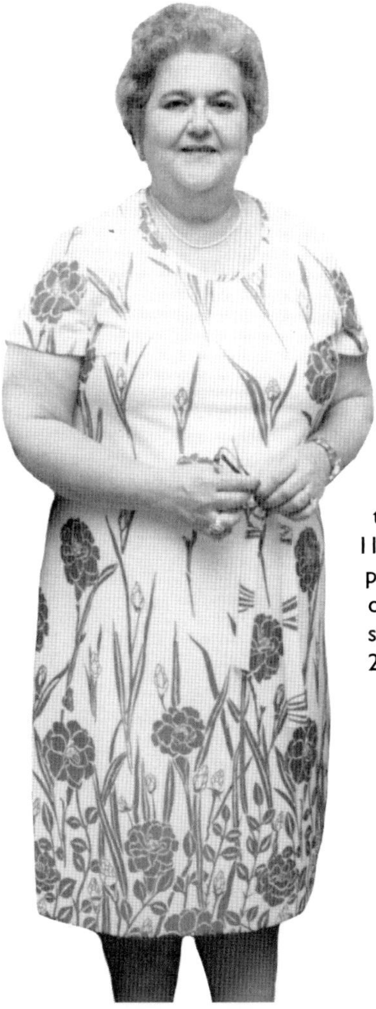

Evelyn S. Campbell

The daughter of Concord legendary local Oliver A. Swaringen, Campbell spent a quarter century as an English teacher, preparing a new generation as the sponsor of Concord High School's Future Teachers Club. Her extracurricular passion was the Concord Business and Professional Women club, which named her its 1974 Woman of the Year; she also served as club president. Campbell retired in 1980 and died in 2013. (Courtesy of Debbie Morse.)

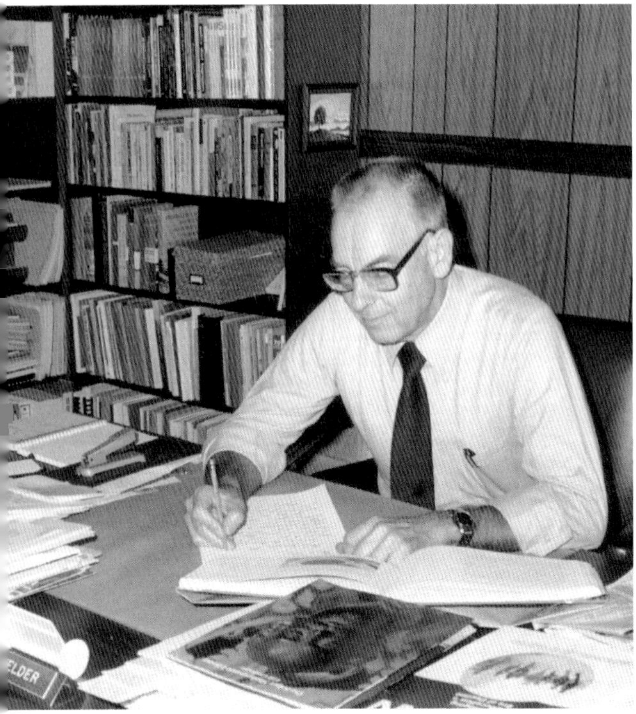

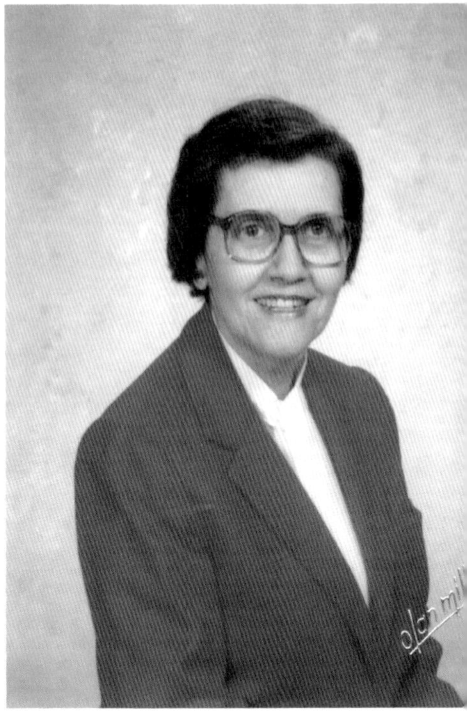

Dwight and Ruby Blackwelder

"Dedicated to a man and a woman who together give us a glimpse of how the future will treat us . . . who consider us a maturing youth instead of a child who must be reprimanded before he starts any mischief . . . who teach us to learn for ourselves by not pampering or consoling us." Thus began the Concord High School Class of 1956's dedication of its *Spider Web* yearbook to this couple, known for their application of experiential learning methods and their appreciation for literature and fine arts. Their journey as educators began as English teachers, with Ruby also sponsoring a forensic club, grooming debating champions such as Jim Richards and Ann Ridenhour. During their decades of devotion to Concord's hallowed halls of learning, Dwight and Ruby were steered into new directions, with Dwight stepping into administration as the Concord City Schools' director of secondary education and Ruby taking charge of the Concord Junior High (Middle) School library as its media specialist. Among their shared accomplishments were the 1971 acquisition of a Project Media grant, which enriched the junior high library's audio-visual resources, and their 1973 chaperoning of a group of high school students on a tour of Europe—both of which exemplified the Blackwelders' commitment to encouraging students' educational self-exploration. In a 1979 *Daily Independent* interview, Dwight Blackwelder summarized this educational philosophy by evoking the words of Oscar Wilde: "Education is a wonderful thing from time to time, but nothing worth knowing has ever been taught." (Both, courtesy of Ruby Blackwelder.)

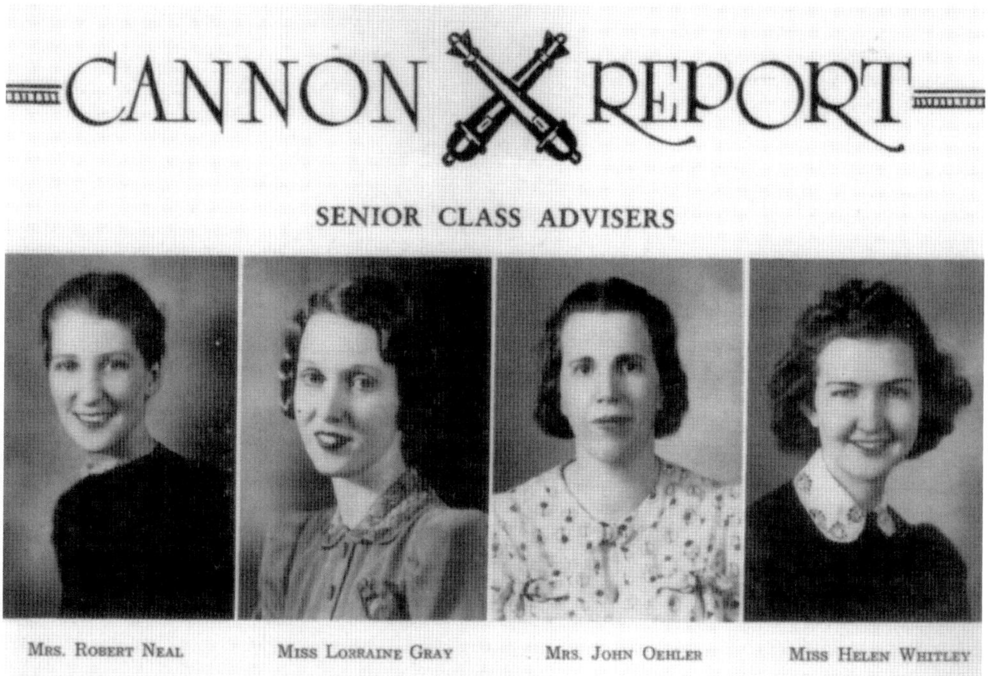

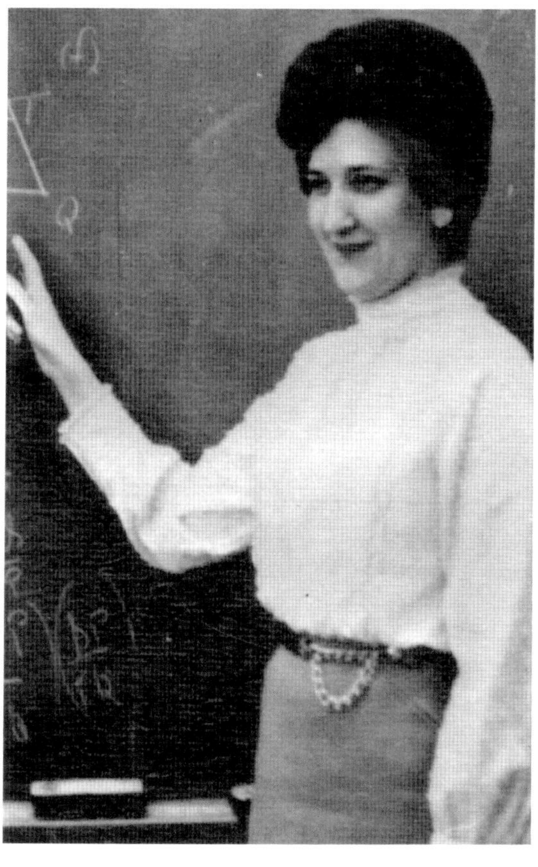

Lorraine Gray
Robbed of her fiancé in a heartbreaking automobile accident, this demure English teacher instead devoted herself to a life of education at J.W. Cannon High and A.L. Brown High, instructing several generations beginning in the 1930s. Gray, also a senior class and National Honor Society advisor, is one of four teachers shown in this excerpt from Cannon High's 1939 yearbook, *The Cannon Report*. (Courtesy of KHA.)

Frances Bounds
Amazonian in stature and appearance, Bounds taught geometry and mathematics and was student government advisor at A.L. Brown from the 1950s through the 1970s. Many of her female students were dazzled by her array of fashionable scarves. According to one alumnus, "she just adored her students," a fact commemorated by the 2006 establishment of the Sara Frances Bounds Memorial Scholarship Fund, providing financial aid to Brown graduates. (Courtesy of KHA.)

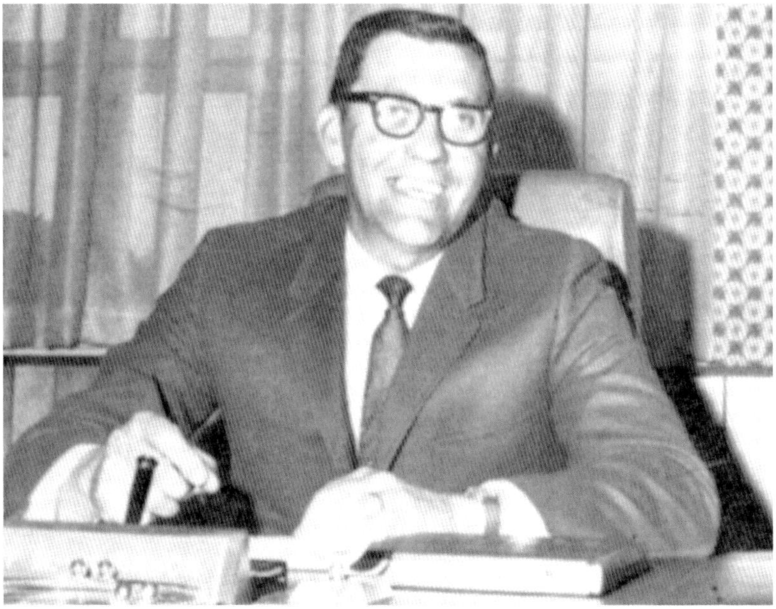

Jay M. Robinson

Dr. Robinson's folksy and practical leadership as Cabarrus County Schools superintendent (1965–1977) tethered the educational system during the transitions of desegregation. He later served as Charlotte-Mecklenburg superintendent, vice president of the University of North Carolina, and chairman of the state board of education. Concord's Jay M. Robinson High School and Charlotte's Jay M. Robinson Middle School stand in tribute to the man that North Carolina governor Jim Hunt once called "a giant of American education."

The above photograph originally appeared in the Central Cabarrus High School 1967 yearbook. The below photograph, taken in 1968 by John Kennedy for the *Concord Tribune*, shows Robinson as a member of the Cabarrus County Board of Health. Shown are, from left to right, Al Klimas, Robinson, Dr. Edwin W. Lipe, and Concord mayor S. Les Myers. (Both, courtesy of Concord Public Library.)

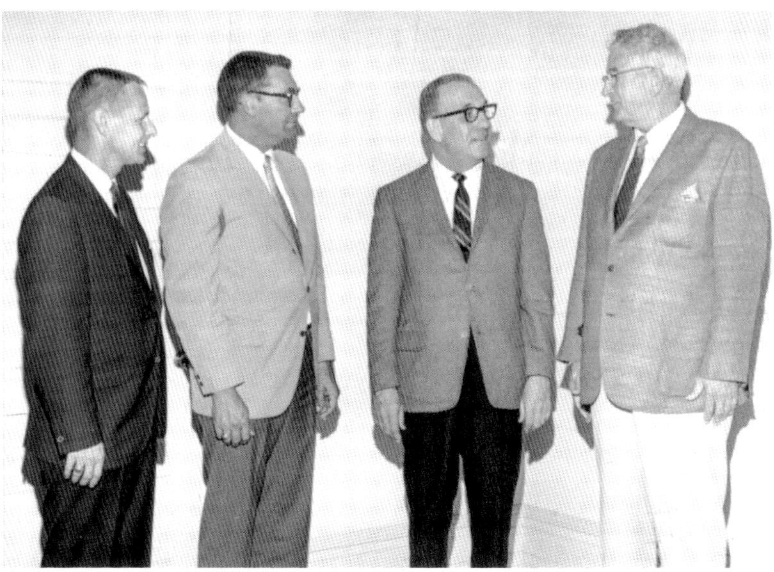

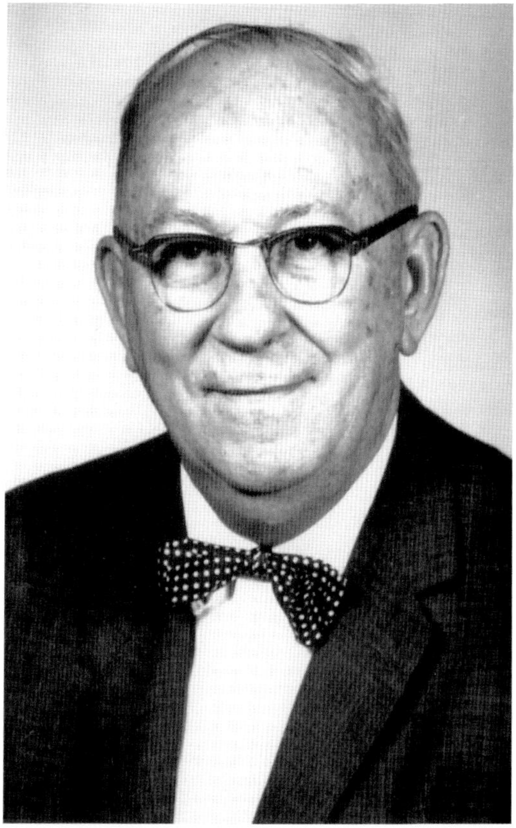

W.J. Bullock

The longtime superintendent of Kannapolis City Schools took that post in 1936 and occupied it for three decades. In 1966, he became the first North Carolinian to serve on the national council of the YMCA, as its elected vice president. A.L. Brown High School's physical education building bears Bullock's name. (Courtesy of KHA.)

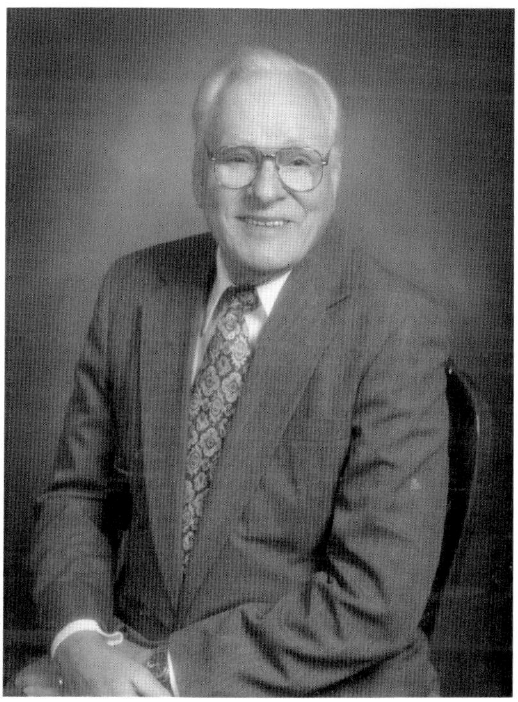

William M. Irvin

A Cabarrus County native, Korean War veteran, and educator, Dr. Irvin is best remembered by midcentury students as the principal of R. Brown McAllister Elementary and, later, the superintendent of the Concord City Schools. An elementary school in Concord was named in his honor two years before his 2002 death. (Courtesy of Frank Irvin.)

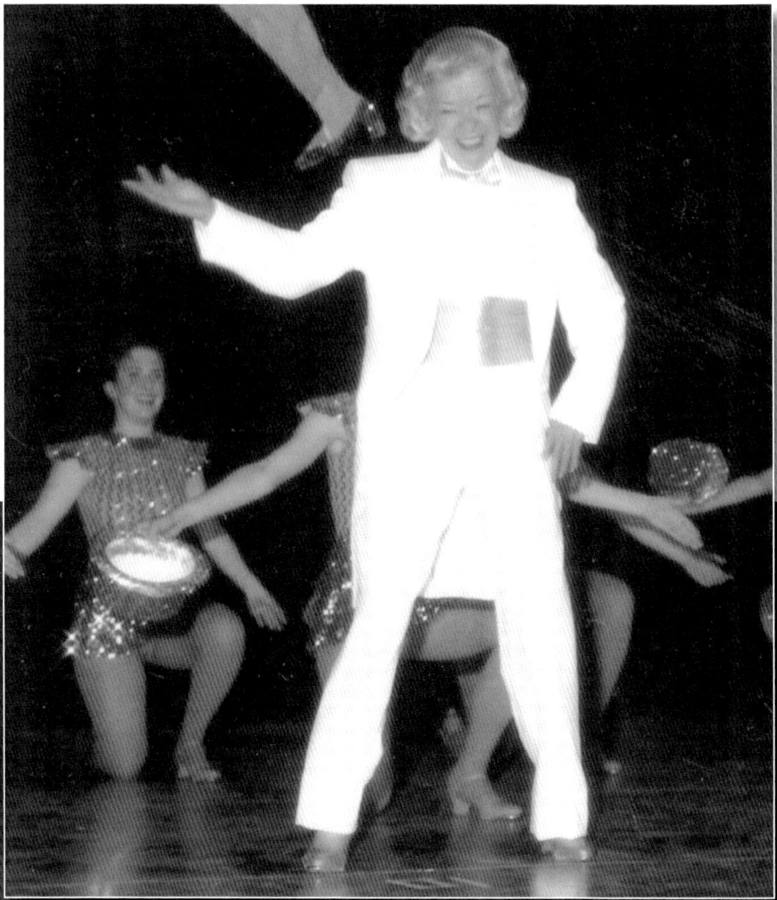

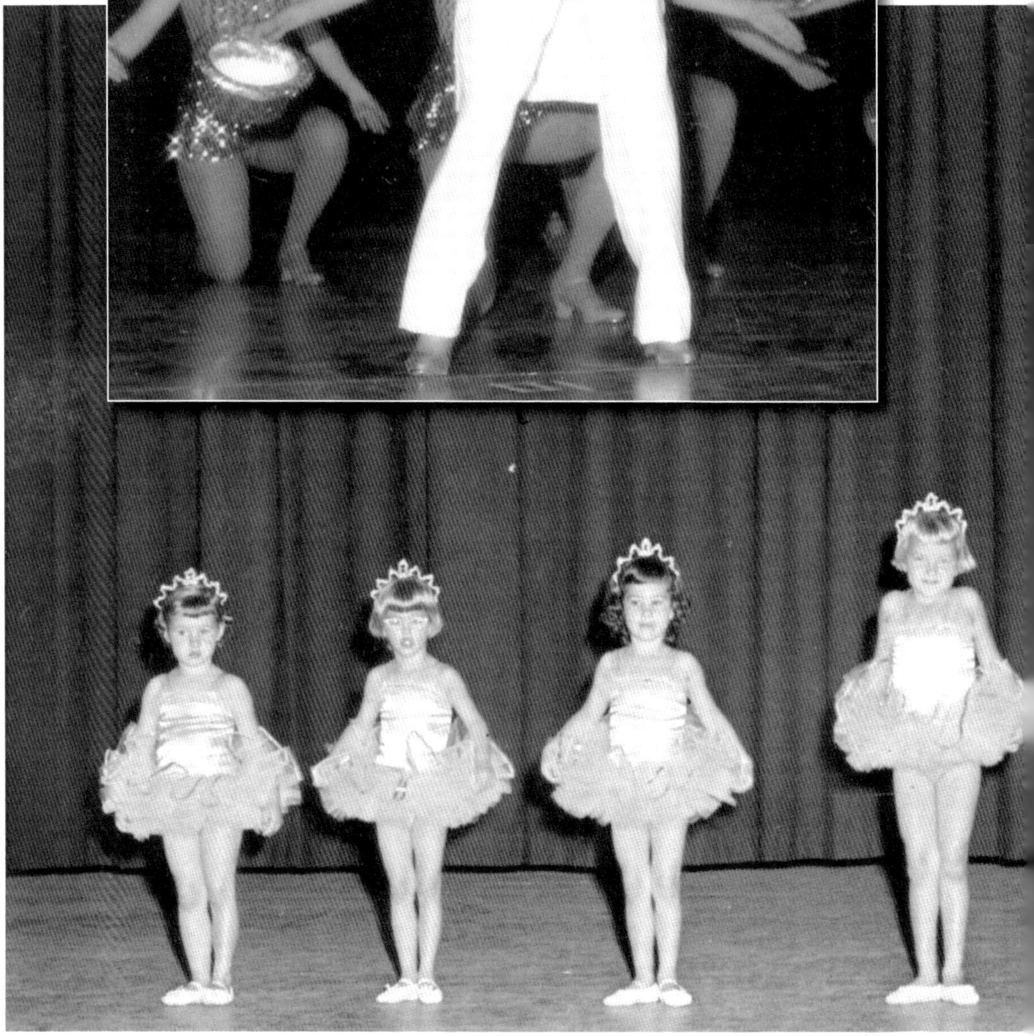

Peggè Lee Sapp Haywood (BELOW AND OPPOSITE PAGE)
Countless "dancing daughters" (and sons) mourned the 2005 passing of this delightful artiste who ran the Peggè Lee School of Dance for 40 years, operating it from the basement of her home before relocating into a larger studio. "Miss Peggè" was also involved with Carolina Dance Masters, Dance Masters of America, and the Cabarrus Arts Council. Beauty pageants were another of her passions; she cofounded the Miss Dance of America Pageant, directed the Miss Concord and Miss Cabarrus County competitions, and was an in-demand judge for pageants in other communities and states. Outside of the arts, she was committed to the Republican Party on the local, state, and national levels. Haywood sold her school to a former student, Tammy Frye Jordan, who maintained the school's name before redubbing it Cabarrus Dance Academy. In the photograph on the opposite page, the students' beloved "dancing mother" takes center stage, accompanied by the Lee-ettes. Below are some of her youngest students in a 1962 dance recital. Shown are, from left to right, Pam Porter, Dawn Ridenhour, Tammy Frye, Elizabeth Wilson, Jimmy Summers, ? Sutherland, Rosa Davis, and Elizabeth Lahr. (Both, courtesy of Tammy Frye Jordan.)

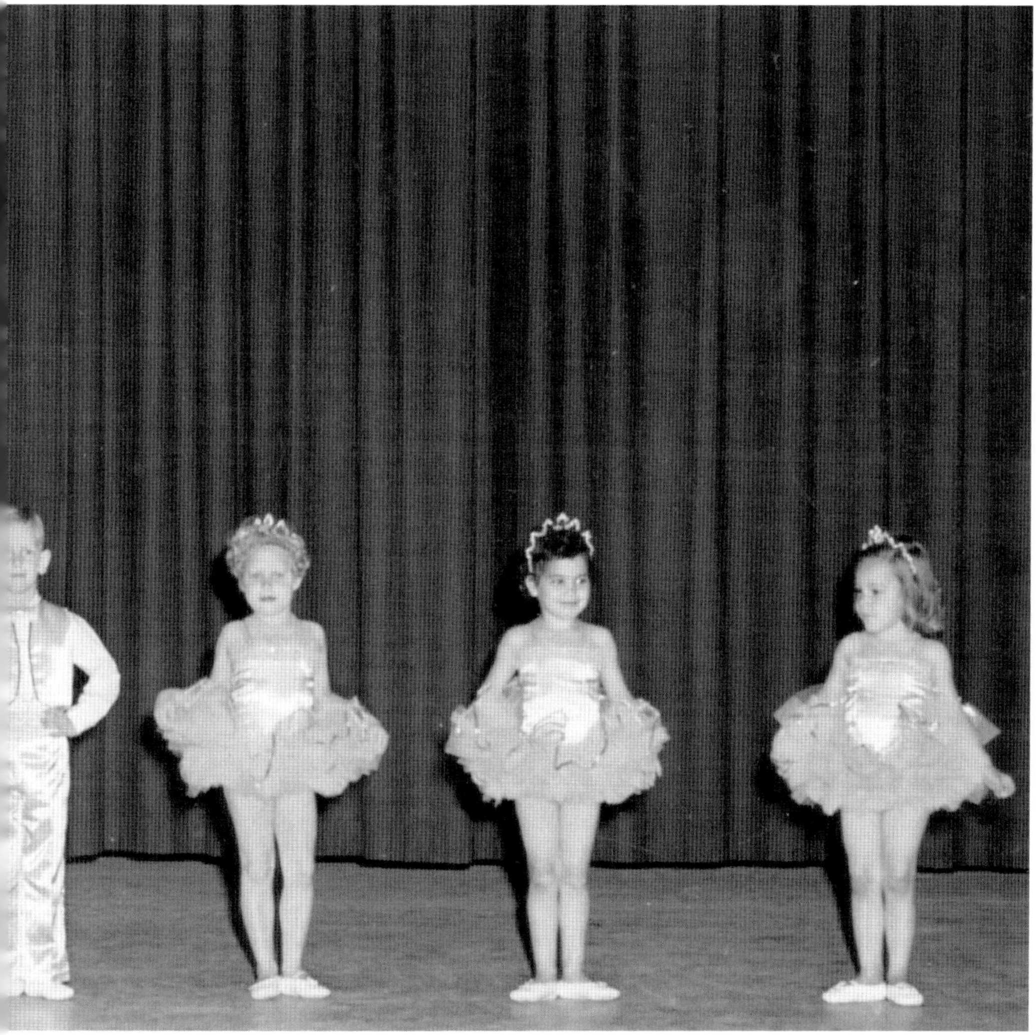

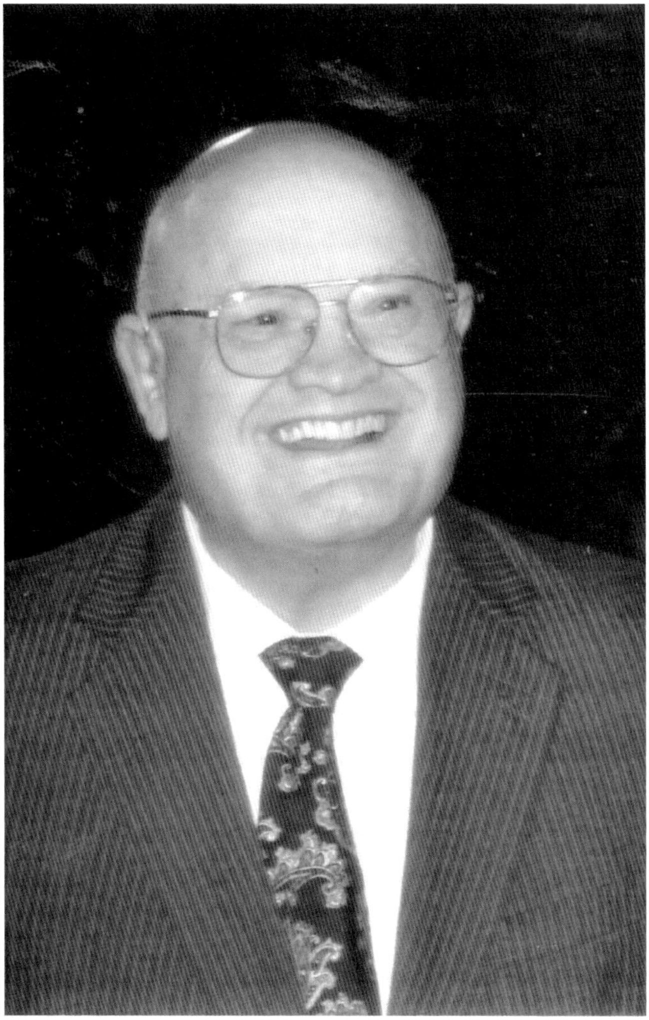

Arden Ray
While many Cabarrus County baby boomers have him to thank for their driver's education, Ray's championship seasons as a football guard and coach made him an unforgettable figure. He was drafted into the Korean War between his sophomore and junior years at Lenoir-Rhyne College, where he was nicknamed "Baby" because of his cherubic face. Upon his return in 1955, this collegiate powerhouse rallied Lenoir-Rhyne to a 9-0-1 season, followed by an undefeated season the following year, when he won MVP and All-American honors. No one dared call him "Baby," however, when he became the firm but reasonable head football coach at Mount Pleasant High School beginning in 1957. Under his leadership, the Tigers won four conference titles and the 1964 state championship, in a game many locals are still talking about. From the late 1960s through the early 1980s, Ray coached football and taught at several area high schools, including A.L. Brown, Northwest Cabarrus (where he enjoyed three championship seasons), and Central Cabarrus. Off the gridiron, Ray was renowned for his enthusiasm for vocal music. He boasted an uncanny knowledge of operatic tenors and an impressive record collection, and he frequently harmonized at local functions and as a member of the Singing Saints chorus. A 1978 inductee of the Lenoir-Rhyne College Sports Hall of Fame and a 2013 inductee of the Cabarrus County Sports Hall of Fame, Ray died in 2013. (Courtesy of Gene Furr and the Cabarrus County Sports Hall of Fame.)

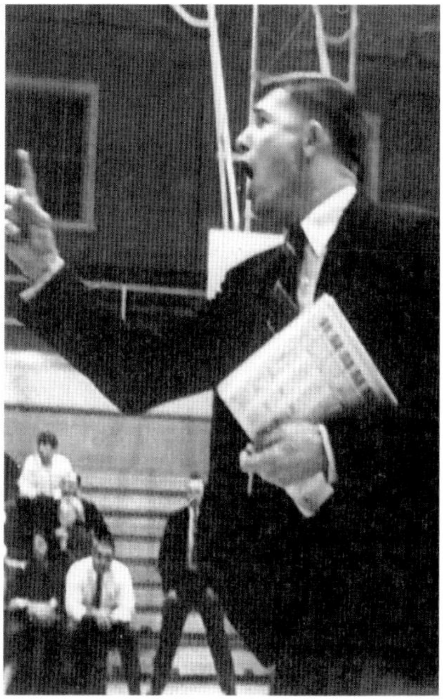

Bob Mauldin

Mauldin spent his later professional years in school administration, but it was as A.L. Brown High School's head wrestling coach from 1961 to 1969 that he became a near-mythic figure. Mauldin wondrously inspired "his boys" to rise to their full potential, prompting one former student to eulogize him thusly in 2015: "Coach Mauldin took a bunch of mill-hill boys and made them champions." (Courtesy of Kannapolis Public Library.)

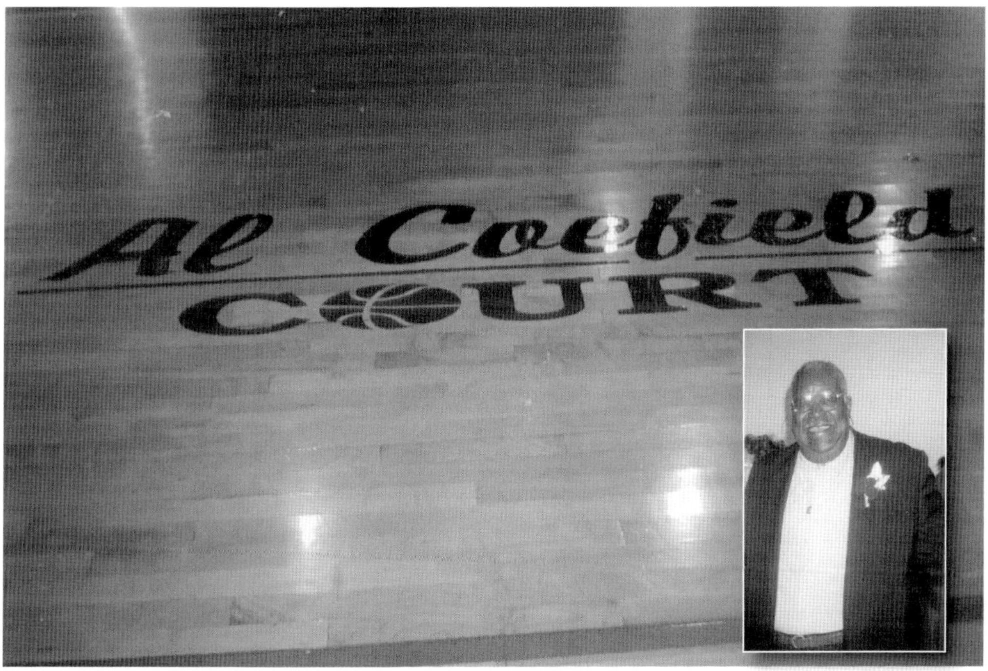

Aldon Levon Coefield

Barber-Scotia College's 2002 renaming of its basketball court for Aldon Coefield was an honor well deserved. From the mid-1960s through the mid-1970s, Coefield coached the Sabers through their glory days, garnering national sports headlines. Previously, he coached high school sports at Logan (pre-integration) and Concord (post-integration). Coefield has been inducted into the sports fall of fame at Barber-Scotia and, as a football player, the hall of fame of his alma mater, North Carolina A&T. (Both, courtesy of Al Coefield.)

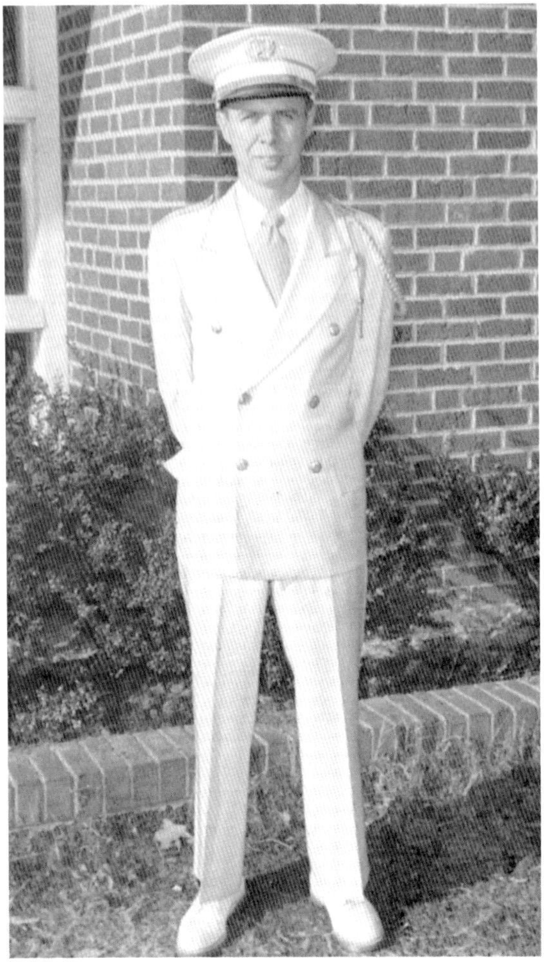

Cy Mauldin

For over half a century, Mauldin has been Cabarrus County's favorite music man. In the mid-20th century, he was the beloved band director at Winecoff High School, whose senior class dedicated its 1955 yearbook to him. This photograph appeared in the 1955 yearbook. For over 20 years, Mauldin, now well into his golden years, has served as director for the Singing Saints chorus. (Courtesy of Concord Public Library.)

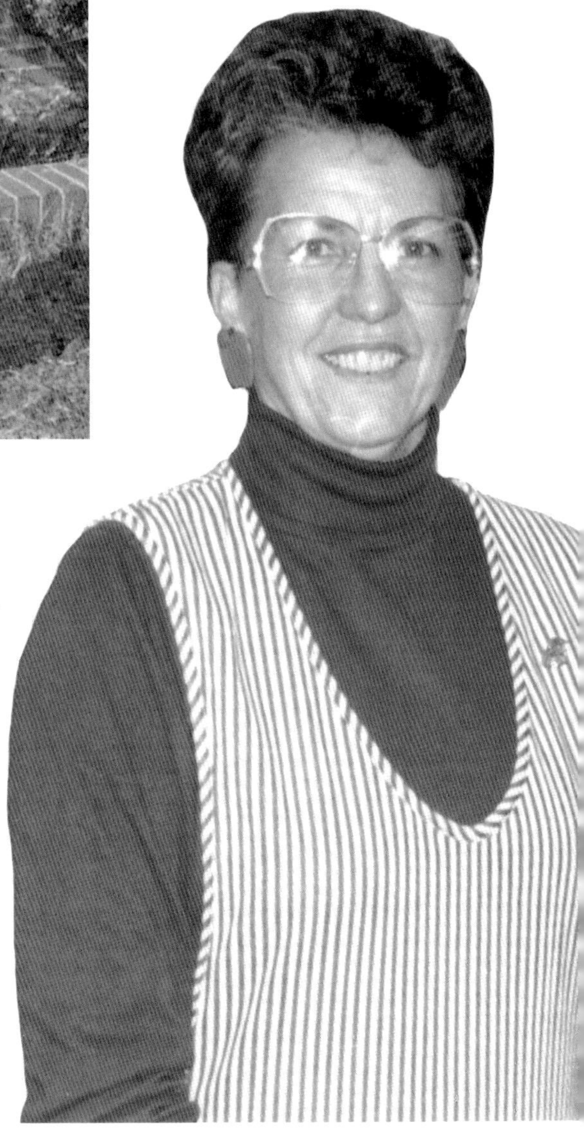

Jessie Blackwelder

Blackwelder had been known as a go-getter since her basketball days at Mount Pleasant High School. But when she retired in 2000 after a lionized career as a teacher and administrator, her plans to become a landscaper were quickly abandoned. Since then, Blackwelder has been a teen court advocate as the executive director of the Conflict Resolution Center of Cabarrus County, which also offers mediation services. (Courtesy of Concord Public Library.)

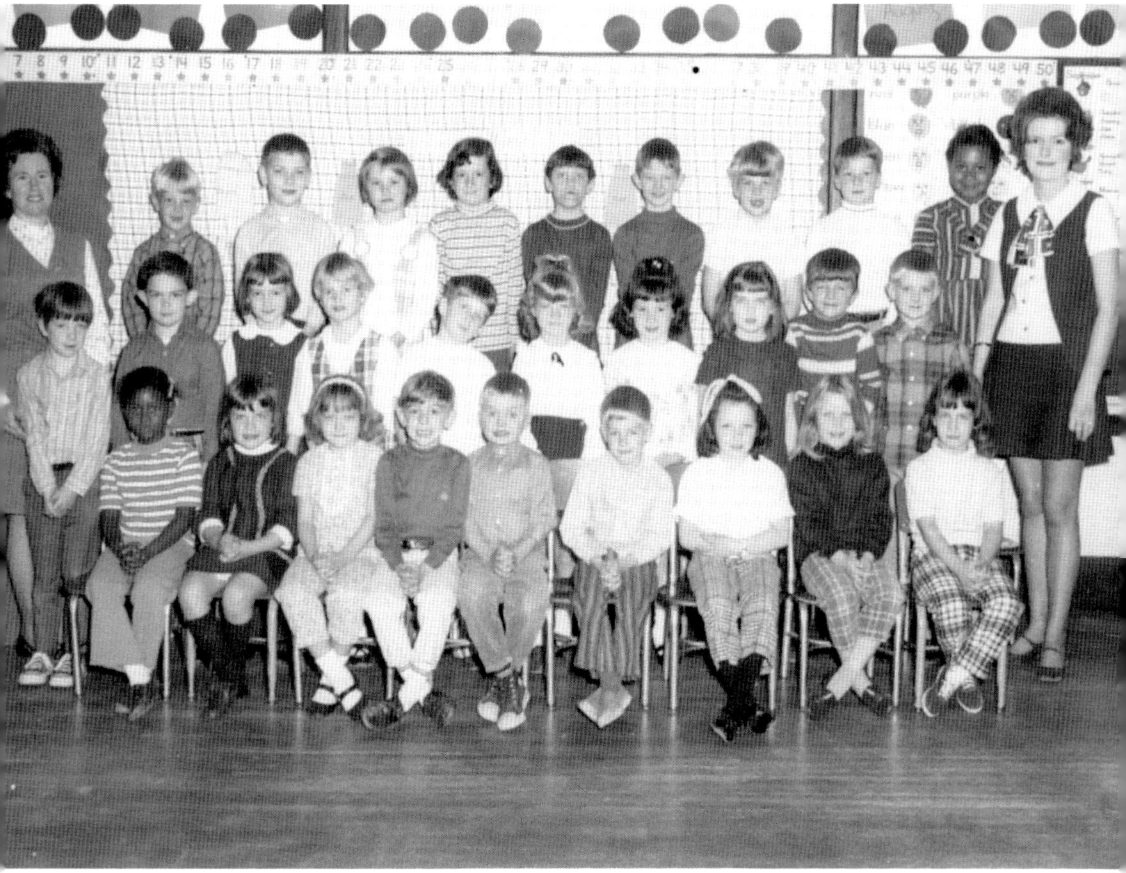

Vicki Bost Isenhour

Some children dread the annual back-to-school ritual, but not young Vicki Bost: "I adored going to school as a child and decided during the first month of school that I wanted to be a teacher when I grew up. I wanted to write on the chalkboard and be able to drink tea at lunch!" For four decades, she sustained that gusto as an elementary school teacher in Mount Pleasant, beginning in 1970 with first and fourth graders. She later taught academically gifted students after lobbying administrators for the implementation of such a program. Isenhour became enchanted with Mount Pleasant while working on the county library system's bookmobile during her college summers, regarding it as "a quintessential small Southern town," and spent the entirety of her teaching career there. Today, as a retiree, she continues to support education and public libraries as a volunteer and advocate.

In this photograph, "Miss Bost" (far right) proudly poses with her first-grade class during her first year as a teacher, 1970–1971. Gathered for the class photograph are, from left to right, (first row) Sabrina Miller, Laura Barnhardt, Patty Shoe, Timmy Kimray, Ray Garmon, Jimmy ?, Shelia Baldwin, Elizabeth McAllister, and Patricia Safrit; (second row) Phillip Barnhardt, Chip Lay, Susan Epps, Rainey Crainford, Tim Hahn, Lisa ?, Loretta Hurlocker, Annette Stallings, Todd Hopkins, and Max Kirk; (third row) Abby Layton (teacher's assistant), Carl Fox, Mitchell Nance, Melinda Huffman, Kim Lentz, Joe Moose, Zeb Bost, Todd Plott, Michael Boger, Ella Jane Bost, and Vicki Bost (Isenhour). (Courtesy of Patricia Chandler.)

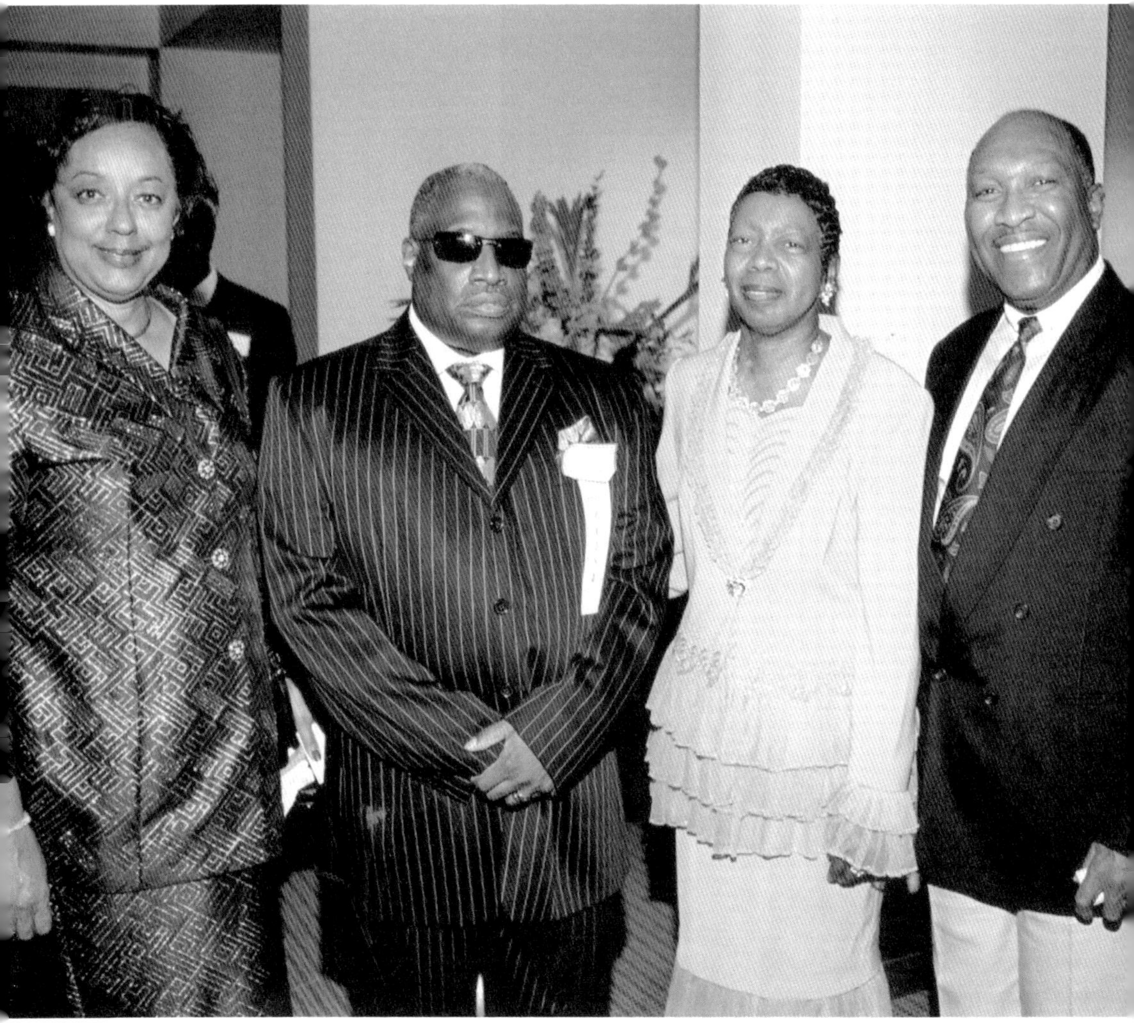

Gregory Davis

The captivating pastor of Harrisburg's Bellefonte Presbyterian Church, Gregory Davis overcame obstacles related to his blindness to become an inspirational educator, disproving the naysayers of his youth who undervalued him because of his disability. After receiving a religious studies degree from UNC-Charlotte, he earned his master of divinity degree from Duke University and his doctor of philosophy degree in religious studies from the Union Institute in Cincinnati, Ohio. Dr. Davis's academic credentials include lecturing at UNC-Charlotte's Department of Afro-American Studies and advising low-income and disabled students. The university offers a scholarship in his name. Shown here celebrating Davis's 2012 UNCC Distinguished Alumnus Award are, from left to right, Dr. Caroline Lattimore, the Reverend Dr. Davis, Mrs. Ernestine C. Davis, and Dr. Vergel Lattimore. (Courtesy of Ernestine C. Davis.)

CHAPTER SIX

The Famous, the Familiar, and the Infamous

They are the headline makers and the recognizable faces of Cabarrus County.

There is the rocket-fast running back who kept Wonders boosters on the edge of their seats and the girl with the wild imagination who held her playmates spellbound with the stories she invented. We beamed with pride when we later spied Haskel Stanback on football cards and Nancy B. Brewer on bestseller lists.

Some we may not know personally, but feel as if we do. We have seen them on television or in the newspapers. They afford us bragging rights since we hail from the same county. Some Cabarrus-born musicians moved away for fame and fortune, like R&B's George Clinton and Marshall Sehorn, while homegrown record producer Dolphus Ramseur has packaged the unique sounds of this region for a wider audience—without leaving his hometown.

Some of them are our personal friends, and our hearts swell with the successes they have achieved. Powerboat racer Carl A. Widenhouse, a Concord businessman, snared enough trophies to fill a garage, while his daughter, Margaret Hagerty, proved that you are never too old to run a marathon.

Some were raised elsewhere but settled in Cabarrus County, and we welcome them as our neighbors. Eddie Ray was a top record executive before landing in Kannapolis to direct the North Carolina Music Hall of Fame. Nikita Koloff may have flattened opponents as a "villain" in professional wrestling, but in reality he is a preacher whose heart is as big as his biceps.

This chapter examines the famous, the familiar, and the infamous of Cabarrus County.

Jim Wade J.E. Smokey

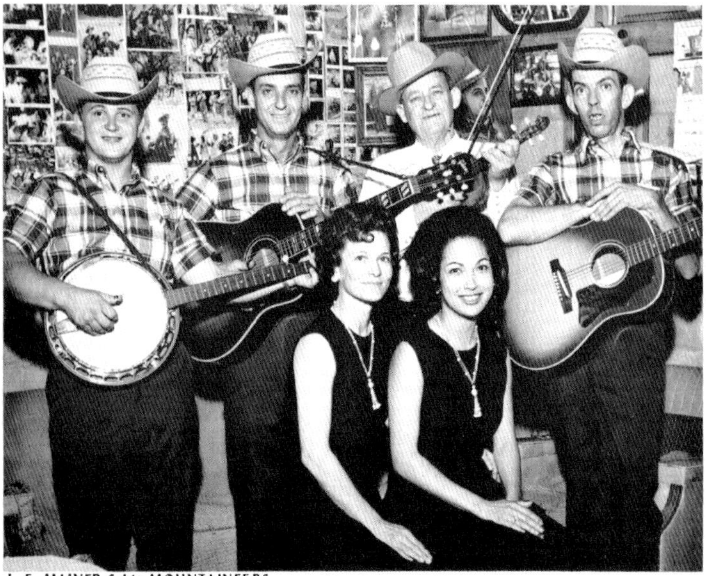

J. E. MAINER & his MOUNTAINEERS Margie Marie

J.E. Mainer and His Mountaineers

Mainer, born in 1898 and raised in the North Carolina mountains, fled the hills for the mills, settling in Concord in the early 1920s for a steady job at Gibson Mill. He brought along his nimble fiddle fingers and his love for the bluegrass music of Appalachia. He also brought his banjo-playing brother Wade, and the siblings put together a band and performed at area dances. Mainer's band was signed as regulars on WBT radio in 1934; from there, record deals followed. The band's personnel changed frequently (the photograph above shows just one permutation), as did its name—at one time, they were the "Crazy Mountaineers." Mainer's children became part of the act. Mainer eventually returned to the mountains. He died in 1971. (Both, courtesy of North Carolina Music Hall of Fame.)

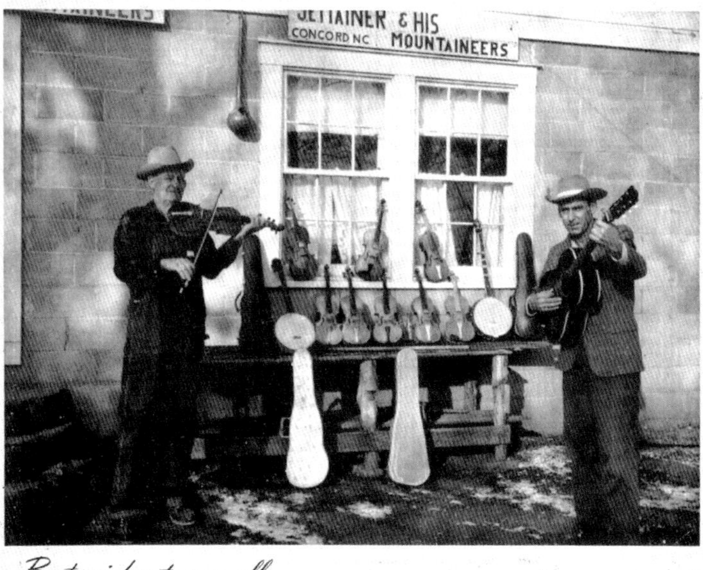

Best wishes to you all J. E. MAINER AND J. E. MAINER Jr.

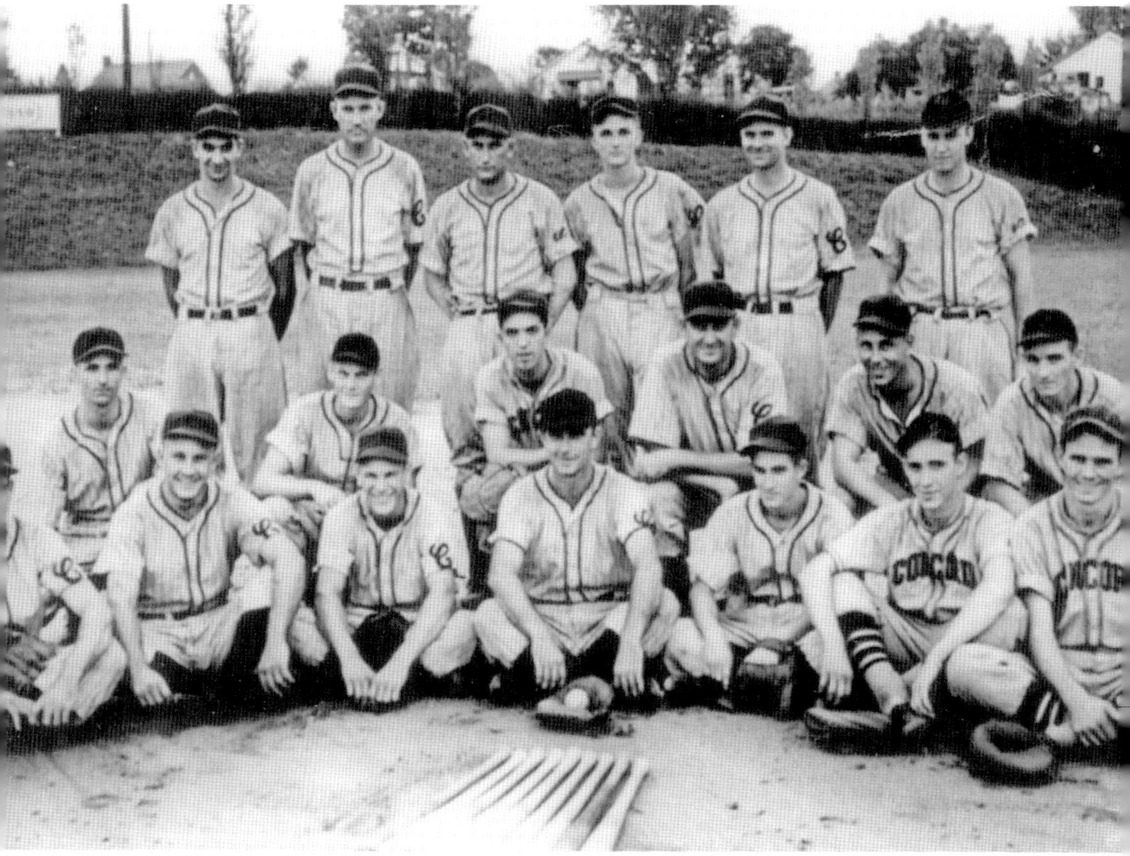

Herman H. Watts

For the mill villages of Cabarrus County, minor-league baseball teams sprouted as abundantly as cotton, providing an afternoon's escape from a world that demanded much and offered little. Among the semiprofessional teams of the Great Depression were archrivals the Concord Weavers and the Kannapolis Towelers. At one time or another, "Ginger" Watts, a catcher with a lifetime batting average of .280, was associated with both clubs (and other North Carolina teams) as a player, manager, and coach. Growing up in the bucolic Watts Crossroads of eastern Cabarrus County, Ginger was not the only member of the Watts household to swing a bat. Brother Marvin, a third baseman, was one of the greatest sluggers to emerge from the area. In 1952, after hanging up his cleats, Ginger and his associate Marvin Kirk purchased the long-standing Heilig's Store in Mount Pleasant and operated it until he retired. Watts's love for America's pastime was clear to anyone who happened by his house on West Franklin Street—its fence was constructed of baseball bats. He died in 1978.

Ginger managed the 1943 Victory League champion Concord Weavers (pictured). Shown are, from left to right, (first row) Richard Mauney, Bob Boger, Billy Goodman, Ginger Watts, Harold McNaulty, Ralph Ritchie, and Johnny Tallent; (second row) Chaver Alred, Troy Furr, Boots Fletcher, Archie White, Bill Kluttz, and Leroy Stewart; (third row) Toots Rogers, Slim Ingram, Virgil "Coddle Creek" Taylor, Don Harwood, Marvin Watts, and Shade Honeycutt. Goodman was a legendary local of Concord who went on to a successful major-league career with the Boston Red Sox. (Courtesy of Wimp Kindley and the *Independent Tribune*.)

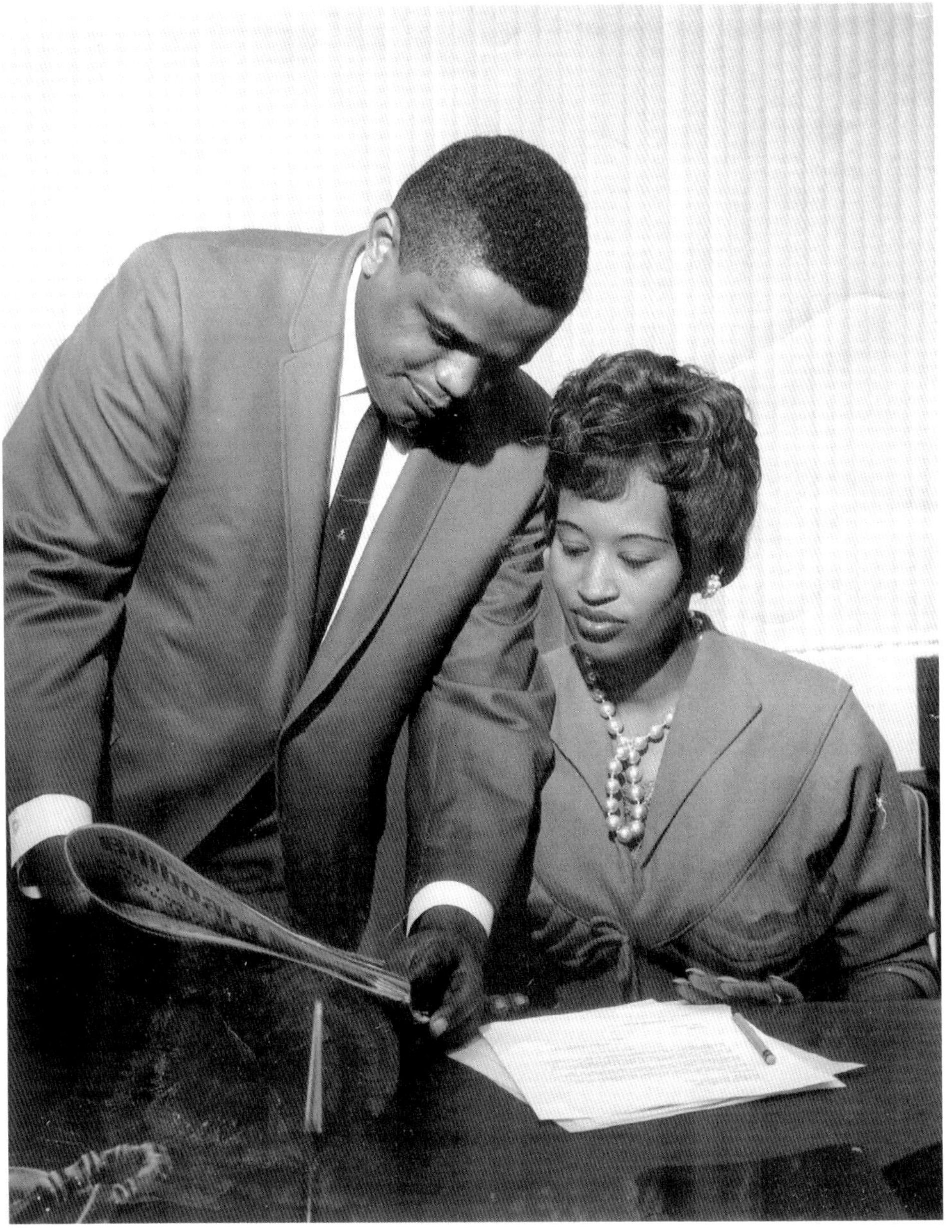

Eddie Ray (ABOVE AND OPPOSITE PAGE)
He once assisted the careers of Fats Domino, Ricky Nelson, and Pink Floyd. Today, Eddie Ray watches over museum exhibits of Nina Simone, James Taylor, and Fantasia. Currently the operation director of Kannapolis's North Carolina Music Hall of Fame, Ray climbed the music-business ladder, beginning as a Decca Records stock boy and eventually becoming the first black executive at a major record label. The cowriter of the 1950s hit "Hearts of Stone," he chronicled his career in the 2012 book *Against All Odds: The Remarkable Life of Eddie Ray*. The above photograph, taken around 1965, shows Ray and an unidentified clerk at the Hollywood office of Capital-Tower Records. The 2014 photograph on the opposite page shows Ray at the North Carolina Music Hall of Fame. (Above, courtesy of North Carolina Music Hall of Fame; opposite, photograph by James Nix, courtesy of the *Independent Tribune*.)

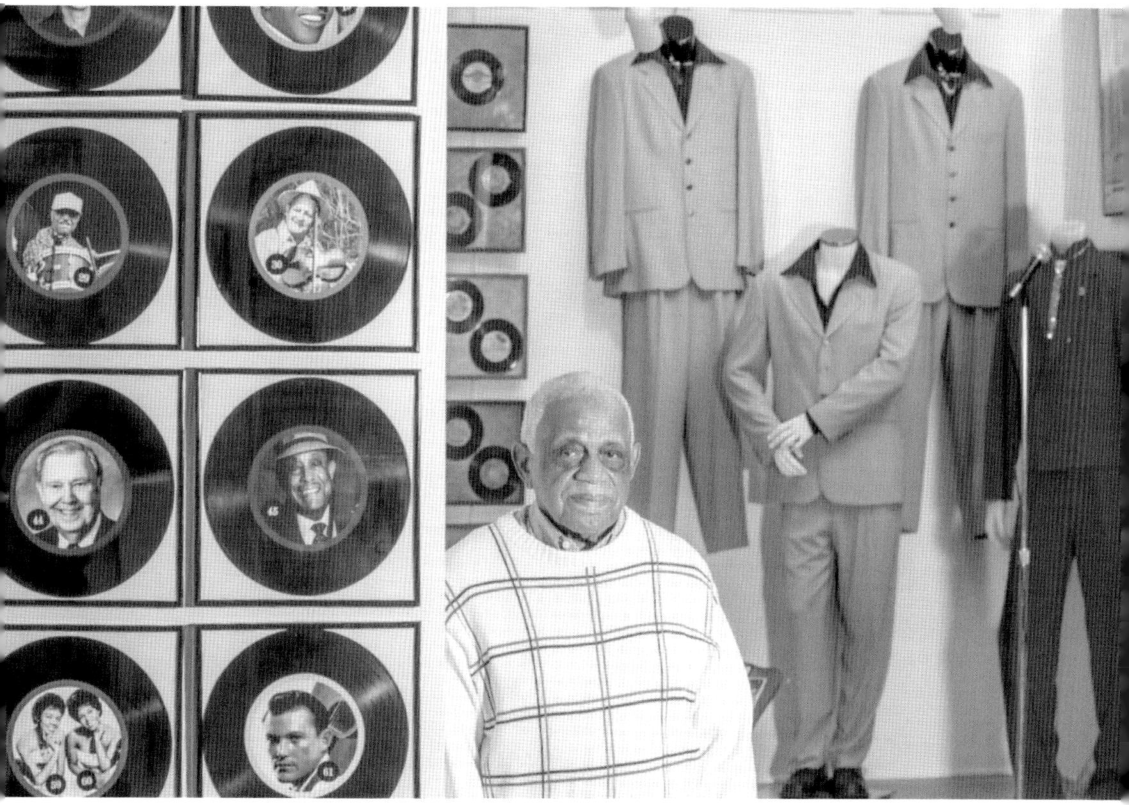

George Clinton

A family relocation, not the "Mothership Connection," transported Clinton from his hometown of Kannapolis to New Jersey, where he was raised. In 1955, he formed his first band, the Parliaments, rehearsing in the back room of a barbershop. In the 1970s, his soul-funk fusion group Funkadelic dominated the rhythm-and-blues charts. Clinton has been inducted into the North Carolina Music Hall of Fame. (No photograph available.)

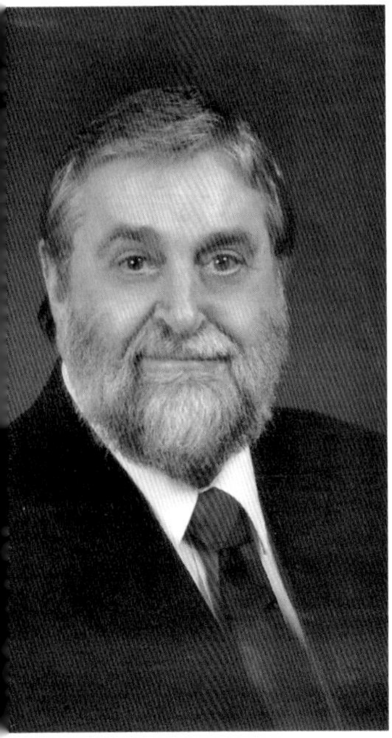

Marshall Sehorn

The Concord of his youth might have been segregated, but this hit-maker judged people by their musicianship, not their skin color. After gigging with local bands, Sehorn, a 1953 Winecoff High School graduate, headed to Harlem in the late 1950s to become a rhythm-and-blues record promoter and talent scout. Big, bearded, and boisterous, he trolled Southern nightclubs and dives, his uncanny ear for raw talent leading him to discover Charlotte singer Wilbert Harrison, whom he signed to a record deal for his chart-topper, "Kansas City." Another discovery was former boxer Lee Dorsey, introduced to Sehorn by New Orleans pianist Allen Toussaint. As a producer/composer team, Sehorn and Toussaint were behind a string of New Orleans–based hits, including Dorsey's "Ya-Ya" and "Working in the Coal Mine." The liner notes on the back side of the Dorsey album (below) recount the artist's meeting with his producer. Sehorn's success helped him launch the fabled Sea-Saint Studios, where acts as varied as Dr. John and Paul McCartney and Wings recorded. At Sea-Saint, he was also the producer behind the disco smash by LaBelle, "Lady Marmalade." Despite his success, Sehorn never forgot his roots, visiting Concord annually and even stopping by Troutman's Barbecue for a true taste of home. He died in New Orleans in 2006. (Left, courtesy of Charlie Sehorn; below, courtesy of Heritage Auctions.)

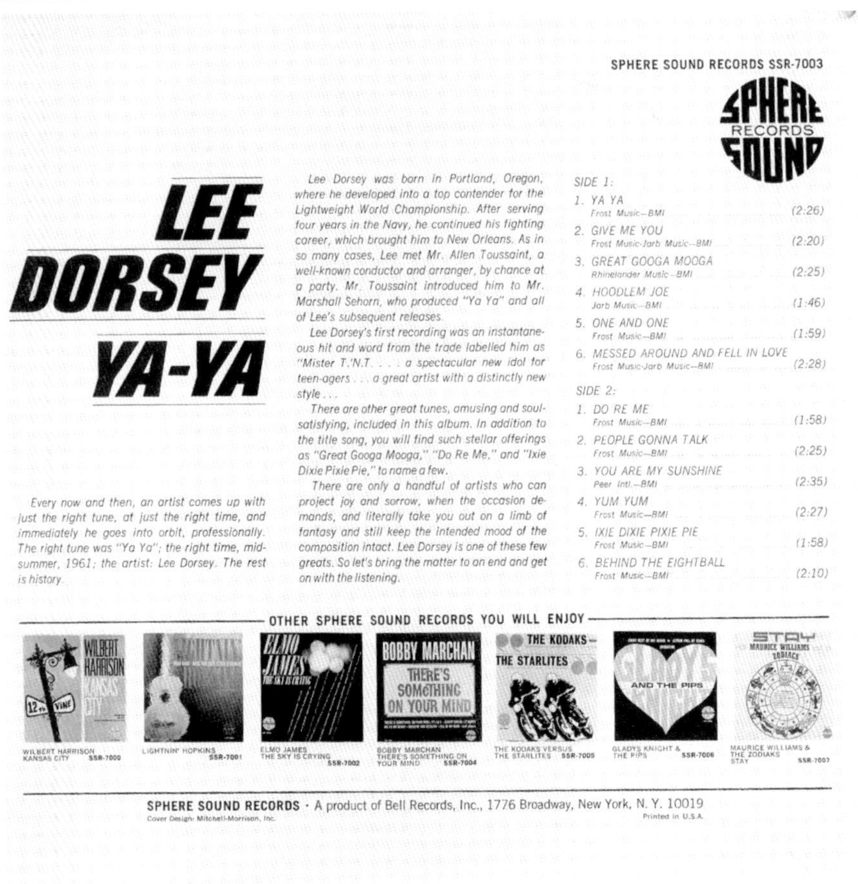

SPHERE SOUND RECORDS SSR-7003

SPHERE RECORDS SOUND

LEE DORSEY YA-YA

Every now and then, an artist comes up with just the right tune, at just the right time, and immediately he goes into orbit, professionally. The right tune was "Ya Ya"; the right time, mid-summer, 1961; the artist: Lee Dorsey. The rest is history.

Lee Dorsey was born in Portland, Oregon, where he developed into a top contender for the Lightweight World Championship. After serving four years in the Navy, he continued his fighting career, which brought him to New Orleans. As in so many cases, Lee met Mr. Allen Toussaint, a well-known conductor and arranger, by chance at a party. Mr. Toussaint introduced him to Mr. Marshall Sehorn, who produced "Ya Ya" and all of Lee's subsequent releases.

Lee Dorsey's first recording was an instantaneous hit and word from the trade labelled him as "Mister T.'N.T. . . . a spectacular new idol for teen-agers . . . a great artist with a distinctly new style . . .

There are other great tunes, amusing and soul-satisfying, included in this album. In addition to the title song, you will find such stellar offerings as "Great Googa Mooga," "Do Re Me," and "Ixie Dixie Pixie Pie," to name a few.

There are only a handful of artists who can project joy and sorrow, when the occasion demands, and literally take you out on a limb of fantasy and still keep the intended mood of the composition intact. Lee Dorsey is one of these few greats. So let's bring the matter to an end and get on with the listening.

SIDE 1:

1. YA YA — Frost Music—BMI (2:26)
2. GIVE ME YOU — Frost Music-Jarb Music—BMI (2:20)
3. GREAT GOOGA MOOGA — Rhinelander Music—BMI (2:25)
4. HOODLEM JOE — Jarb Music—BMI (1:46)
5. ONE AND ONE — Frost Music—BMI (1:59)
6. MESSED AROUND AND FELL IN LOVE — Frost Music-Jarb Music—BMI (2:28)

SIDE 2:

1. DO RE ME — Frost Music—BMI (1:58)
2. PEOPLE GONNA TALK — Frost Music—BMI (2:25)
3. YOU ARE MY SUNSHINE — Peer Intl.—BMI (2:35)
4. YUM YUM — Frost Music—BMI (2:27)
5. IXIE DIXIE PIXIE PIE — Frost Music—BMI (1:58)
6. BEHIND THE EIGHTBALL — Frost Music—BMI (2:10)

OTHER SPHERE SOUND RECORDS YOU WILL ENJOY

WILBERT HARRISON KANSAS CITY SSR-7000
LIGHTNIN' HOPKINS SSR-7001
ELMO JAMES THE SKY IS CRYING SSR-7002
BOBBY MARCHAN THERE'S SOMETHING ON YOUR MIND SSR-7004
THE KODAKS VERSUS THE STARLITES SSR-7005
GLADYS KNIGHT & THE PIPS SSR-7006
MAURICE WILLIAMS & THE ZODIAKS STAY SSR-7007

SPHERE SOUND RECORDS · A product of Bell Records, Inc., 1776 Broadway, New York, N. Y. 10019
Cover Design: Mitchell-Morrison, Inc.
Printed in U.S.A.

Dolphus Ramseur

His hand-me-down clock radio would not keep time, but its scratchy speaker filled this Concord kid's ears with the sounds of the 1970s and set his sights on a vocation outside of the textile mills. Ramseur's record label and music management company, Ramseur Records, has packaged the authentic sounds of Cabarrus County for a broader audience. Ramseur's (foreground center) clients include Bombadil, Samantha Crain, and the Avett Brothers (pictured). (Photograph by Steve Exum.)

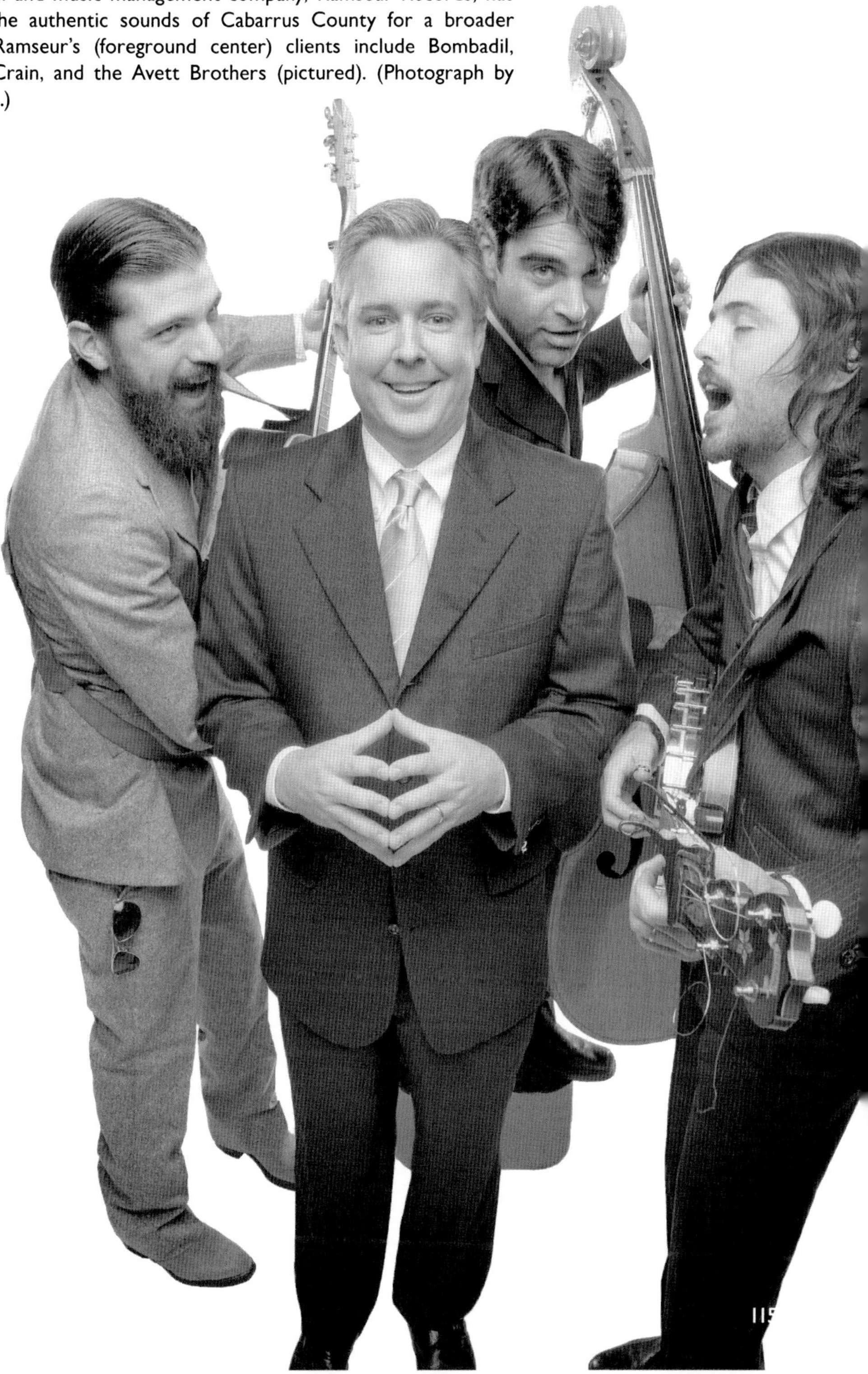

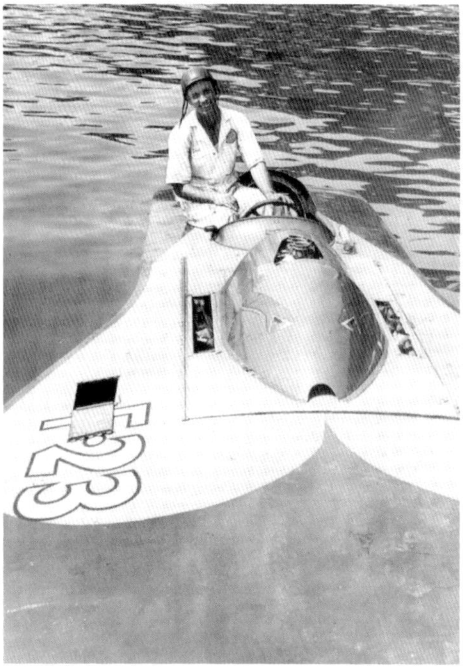

Carl A. Widenhouse

Widenhouse, a considerate sportsman, once said, "Motor boat racing is still the cleanest sport in the world because racers look after their competitors." Known for his Concord concrete company, Widenhouse netted an astounding 105 racing awards beginning in 1949. He no doubt would have won more, had he not lost his life in a speedboat accident at a 1961 racing regatta in Roanoke Rapids, North Carolina. (Courtesy of Margaret Hagerty.)

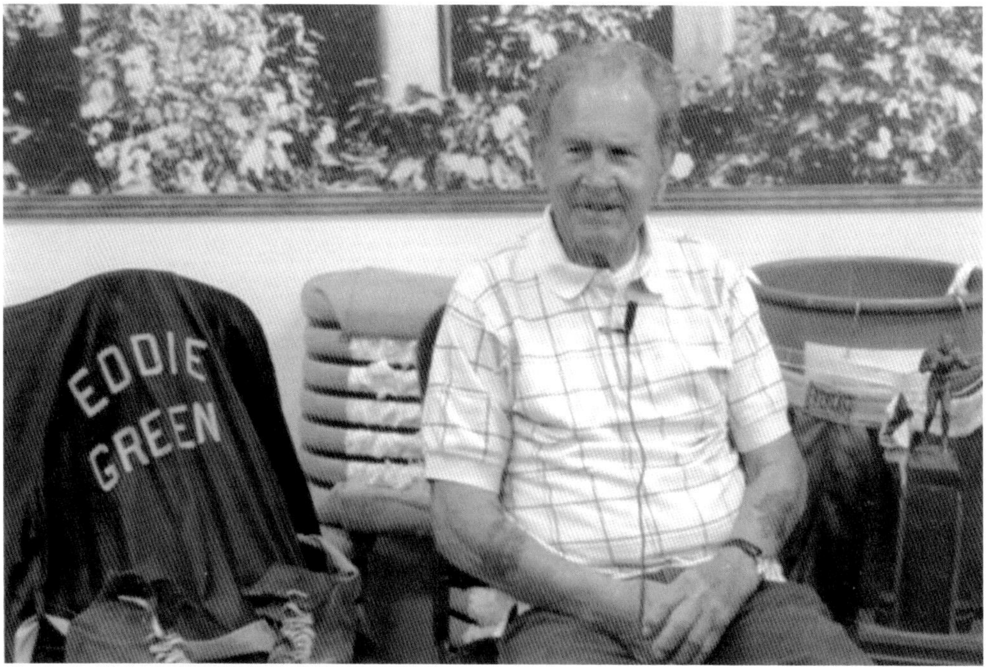

Eddie Green

His bruised opponents groused about his "atomic fists," but to this middleweight's daughters, Green was a gentle father. Going professional in 1939, "the Kannapolis Flash" won 56 of 63 fights before hanging up his gloves in 1957 to devote more time to his family. Green enjoyed reminiscing about his boxing career, as shown at this 2012 Kannapolis History Associates event. He died in 2013. (Courtesy of Gene Furr.)

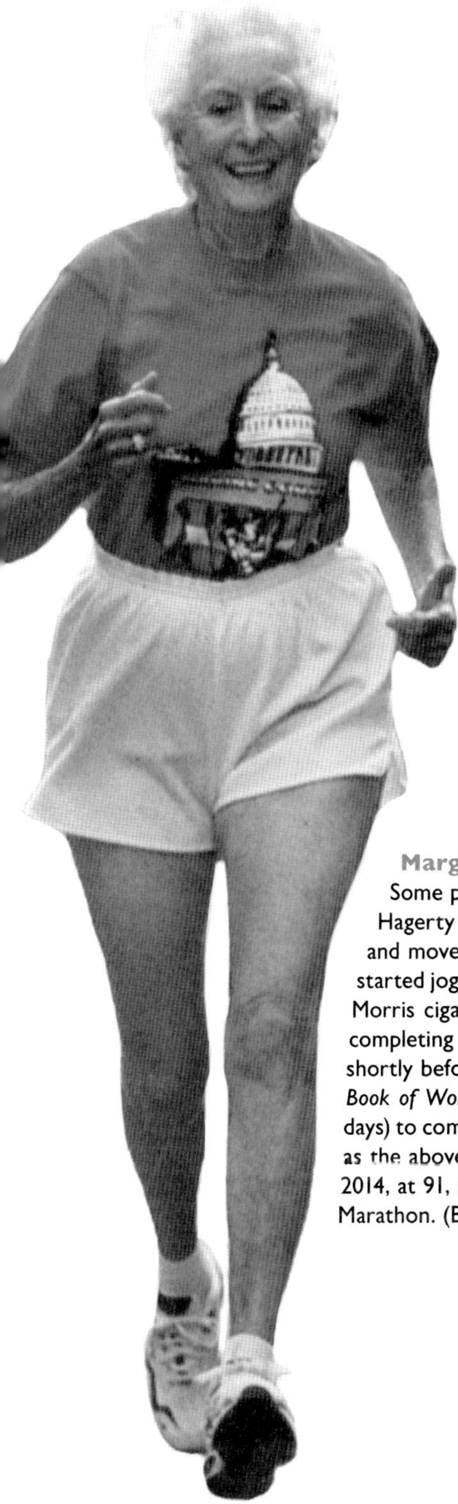

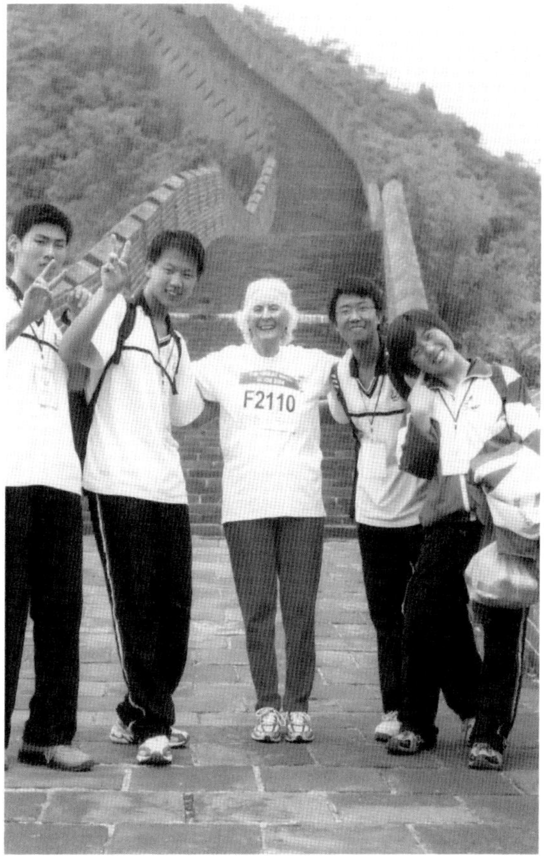

Margaret Hagerty

Some people will go to great lengths to stop smoking—Concord's Hagerty went around the world. At 64, she was advised to "get outside and move" to kick her habit, so she laced up her running shoes and started jogging. Her first competition was a 10K at, ironically, the Philip Morris cigarette plant. Hagerty began to push her limits, successfully completing her first full marathon at 66. She continued to run until shortly before her August 2015 death. In 2004, she made the *Guinness Book of World Records* for becoming the oldest person (81 years, 101 days) to complete a marathon on each of the seven continents, including, as the above photograph shows, a race at the Great Wall of China. In 2014, at 91, she became the oldest person to finish the New York City Marathon. (Both, courtesy of Margaret Hagerty.)

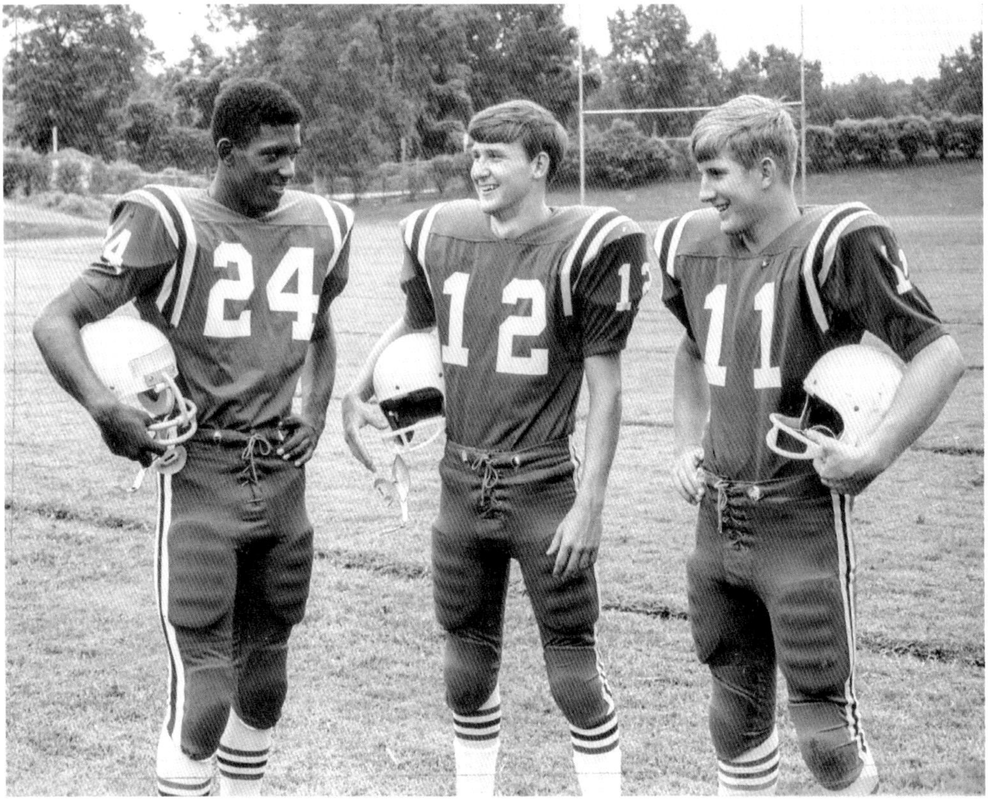

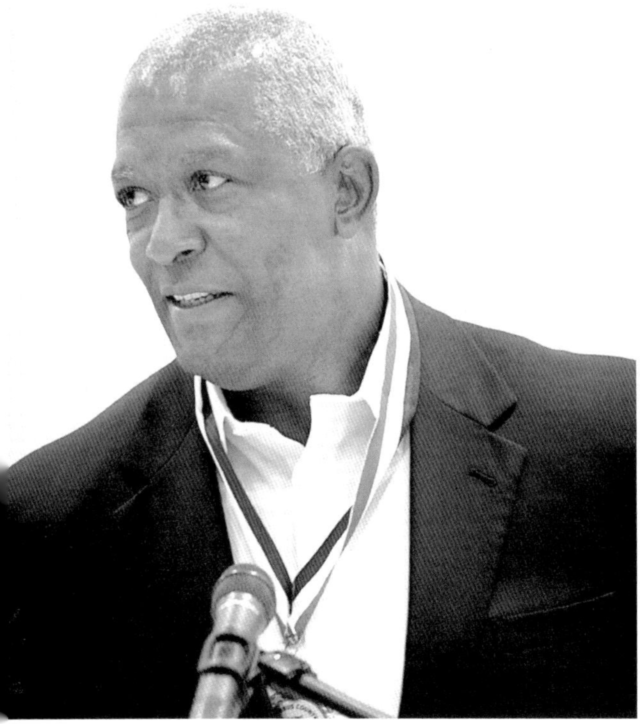

Haskel Stanback

Kannapolis football fans knew that Stanback was one to watch, beginning in 1966, when the fleet-footed freshman rallied George Washington Carver High School to the state championship. His sophomore, junior, and senior years were spent as the superstar running back at A.L. Brown High, where his big regret, according to K-town football expert Scott Boggs, was the "crushing blow" of losing the Bell to Concord. Shown above in 1969 are A.L. Brown's Stanback (left), Mark Russell (center), and Randall Perkins.

College recruiters swarmed around Stanback, who entered the University of Tennessee in 1970. In 1974, he was drafted in the fifth round by the Cincinnati Bengals and then played for the Atlanta Falcons for seven seasons. Stanback was inducted into the Cabarrus Sports Hall of Fame in 2013 (left). (Above, courtesy of Scott Boggs; left, photograph by and courtesy of Gene Furr.)

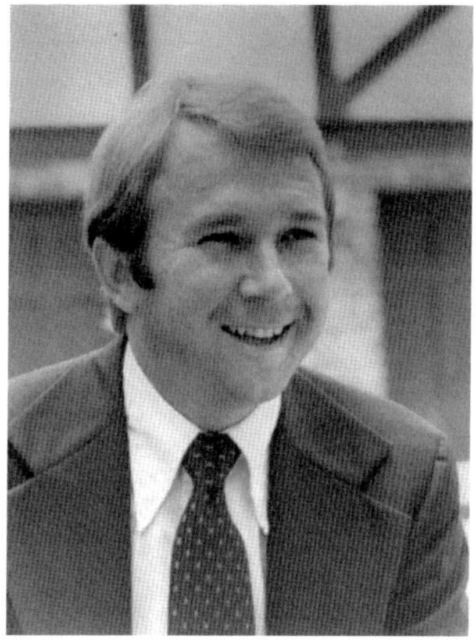

George Shinn

Adversity has long courted this Kannapolis native. A former millworker, Shinn built a personal fortune by acquiring trade schools and sports franchises. In 1988, he became a media darling by bringing the NBA to basketball-frenzied North Carolina via the Charlotte Hornets. But 22 seasons later, he sold the team after provocative relocations and personnel challenges. Through the George Shinn Foundation, he engages in Christian-based charity work. (Courtesy of KHA.)

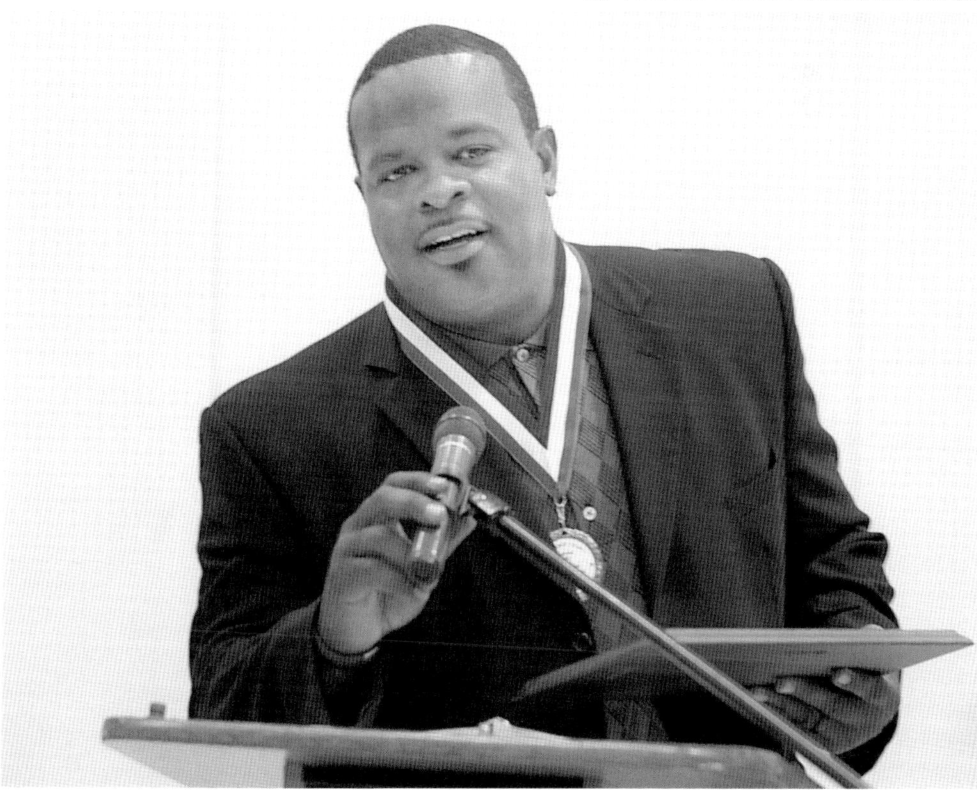

Natrone Means

"Natrone Means Business," an ESPN commentator famously said of this Harrisburg-born running back's 1994 season with San Diego, where he helped zoom the Chargers to the Super Bowl. He later played for the Jacksonville Jaguars and Carolina Panthers before retiring from the NFL in 2000. As shown here, Means was inducted into the Cabarrus Sports Hall of Fame in 2013. (Photograph by and courtesy of Gene Furr.)

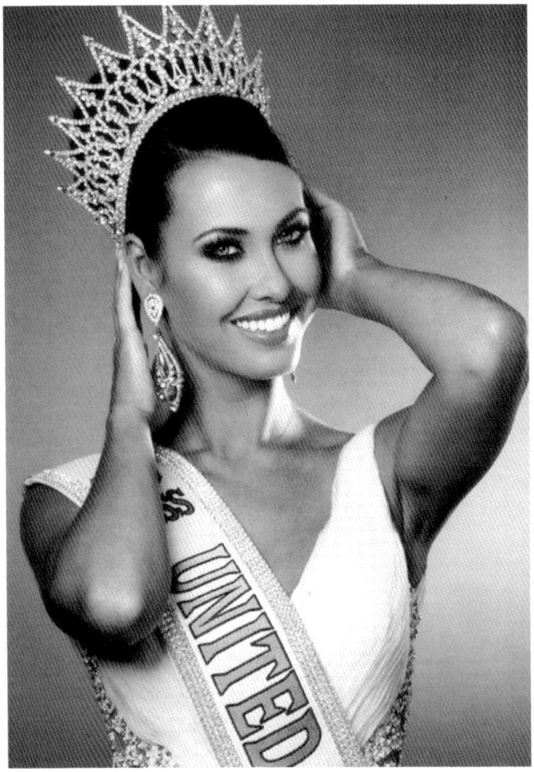

Elizabeth Safrit

This 2010 graduate of A.L. Brown High School brought global attention to the Towel City after being crowned the 2014 Miss United States, then ranked third in the Miss World competition. The daughter of Kannapolis's Wally and Lynne Scott Safrit, Elizabeth has used her celebrity to champion youth- and child-related programs, including Rock the Vote and Save the Children. (Courtesy of the *Independent Tribune.*)

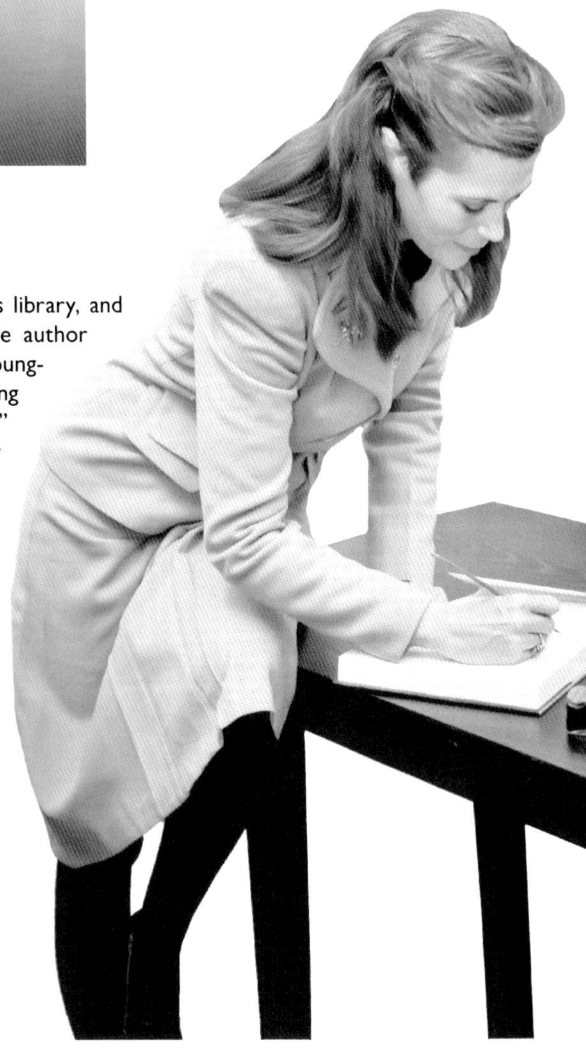

The Lady Soliloque

Her favorite childhood haunt was Concord's library, and today, she contributes to its shelves as the author of the universe of Enoch the Traveler, a young-adult science-fiction series of novels being developed as a television miniseries. "Lady S" is not anchored to fantasy. In 2015, she drew upon her North Carolina heritage to pen the nonfiction book *Dear Yankee: Letters from a Southern Lady.* (Courtesy of Lady Soliloque.)

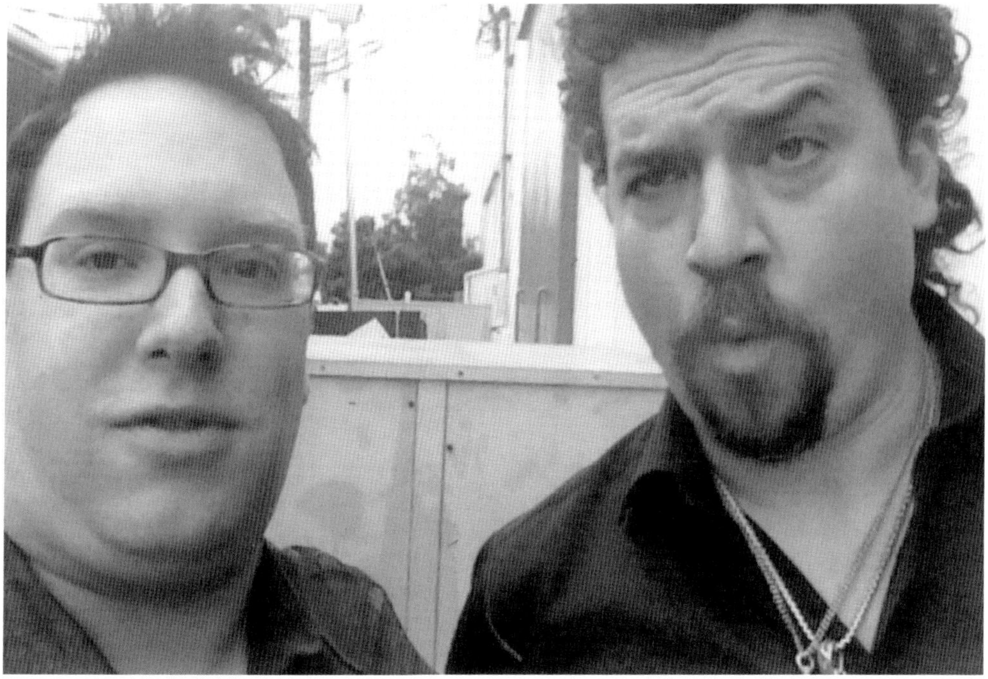

Jonathan M. Ewart
This Concord thespian first appeared onstage in 1982 with Ralph Covington's Cabarrus Youth Theatre. Ewart's deep involvement with Old Courthouse Theatre includes numerous roles onstage and backstage, including directing its Living Room Reading Series. His screen appearances include the HBO television series *Eastbound and Down*, the brainchild of his high school classmate Jody Hill. Ewart (left) is seen here with *Eastbound*'s Danny McBride. (Courtesy of Jonathan M. Ewart.)

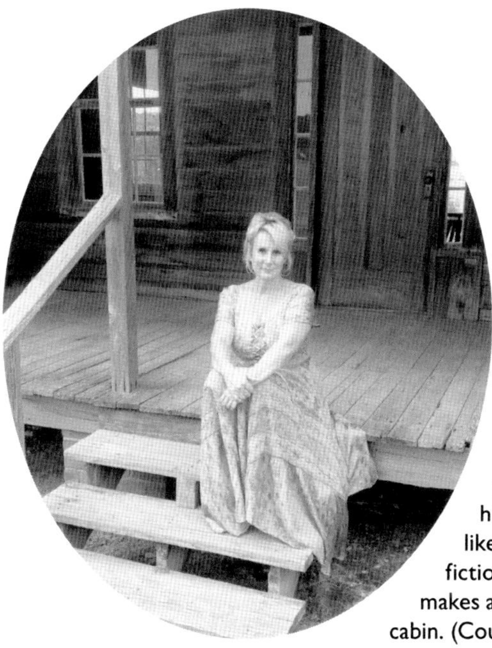

Nancy B. Brewer
To her Concord childhood playmates mesmerized by her inventive storytelling, Brewer's success as a bestselling author comes as no surprise. Her passion for Southern lore led her to a hobby of historical reenactments, which in turn blossomed like a sweet magnolia into a series of novels mixing fictional characters with American history. She often makes appearances in period clothing and writes from a log cabin. (Courtesy of Nancy B. Brewer.)

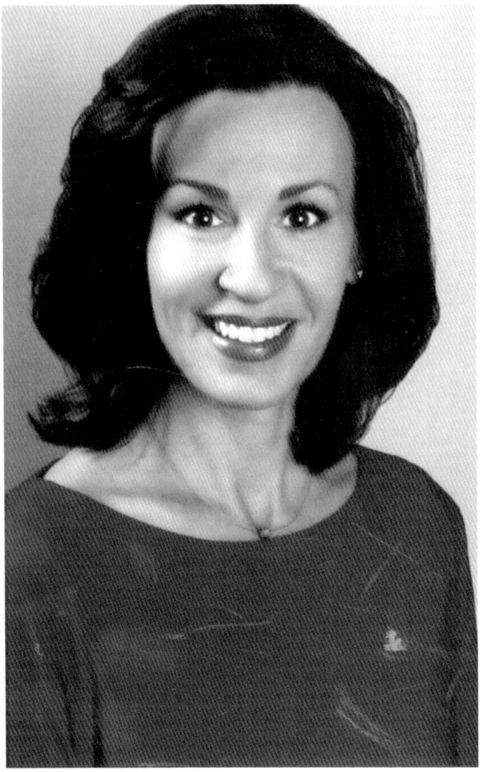

Claudine Chalfant

Those who remember this Concord native's community service with the Boys and Girls Club's Keystone Club proudly smile as they tune in to Chalfant as weekday evening anchor for Time Warner Cable News. Before landing at the Charlotte-based network, Chalfant reported at three different North Carolina television markets, where she received an Emmy nomination and an Associated Press Award for hurricane coverage. (Courtesy of Time Warner Cable News.)

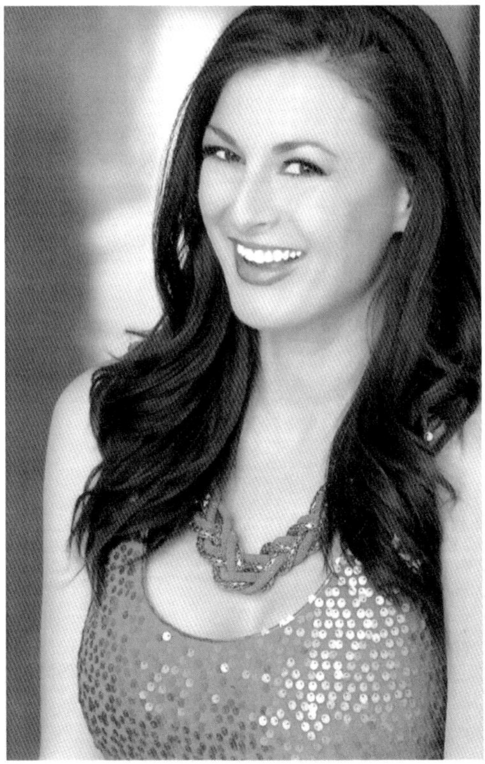

Rachel Reilly

While some of her fellow 2002 Northwest Cabarrus High School graduates met their future mates online, Reilly met hers on television, as a cast member of *Big Brother.* Since her 2010 debut on that series, this charismatic redhead has become one of reality television's most popular stars. Reilly's credits include *The Amazing Race*, the soap opera *The Bold and the Beautiful*, and Fox's *Hollywood Today Live*. (Courtesy of Noreen Reilly.)

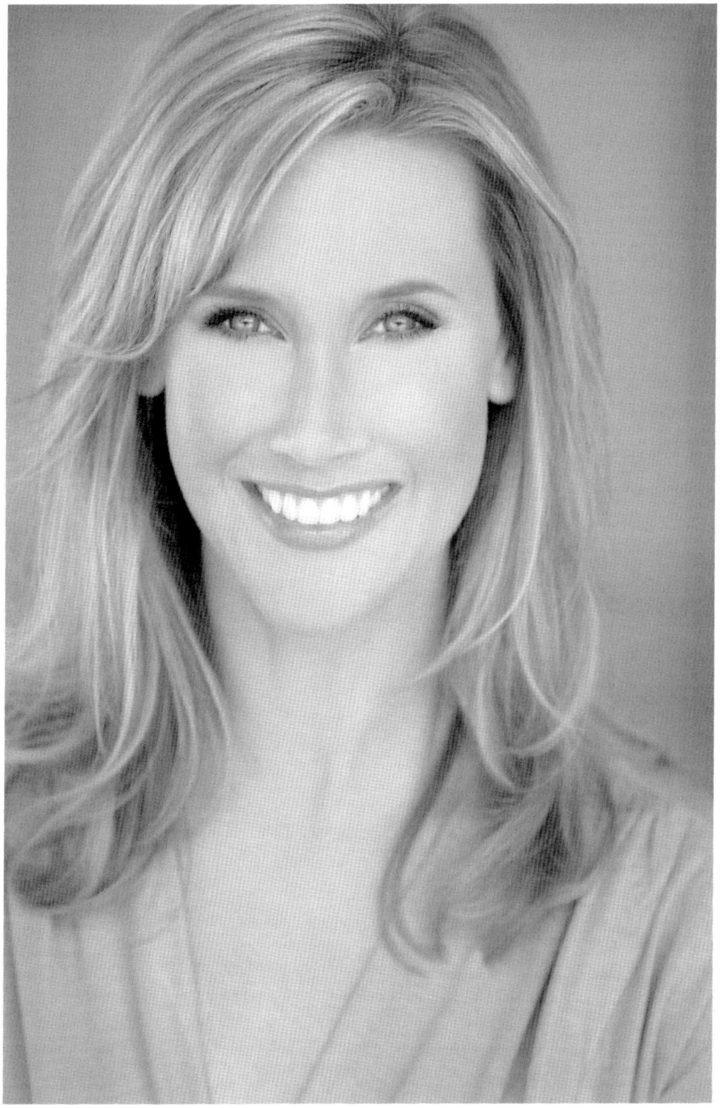

Beth Troutman

Currently the coanchor of WCNC/Channel 36's 6:00 p.m. and 11:00 p.m. broadcasts in Charlotte, as a youth, Beth began performing in a musical duo with her brother Brandon. For decades, the von Trapp–like singing Troutman family serenaded Cabarrus County families at Christmastime. The granddaughter of legendary local of Concord Raiford Troutman, she made a 2004 congressional run for the US House of Representatives for the Eighth District against the incumbent congressman, Republican Robin Hayes. As reported by the *Washington Post*, Troutman, a Democrat, was spurred into action after witnessing how so many of her North Carolina friends and neighbors had "[lost] hope for the future and faith in their leaders." Several heavy hitters threw their weight behind her campaign, including actor Martin Sheen, who knew Troutman from her previous job in production on the television political drama *The West Wing*. Hayes was reelected in a 55.5 percent–to–44.5 percent vote. Troutman has since left the political arena, but she continues to champion for a variety of causes as a media personality. Recently, she has been the lead host of the nationally syndicated television program *RightThisMinute* and a social media expert on NBC's *Today Show*. (Courtesy of Beth Troutman.)

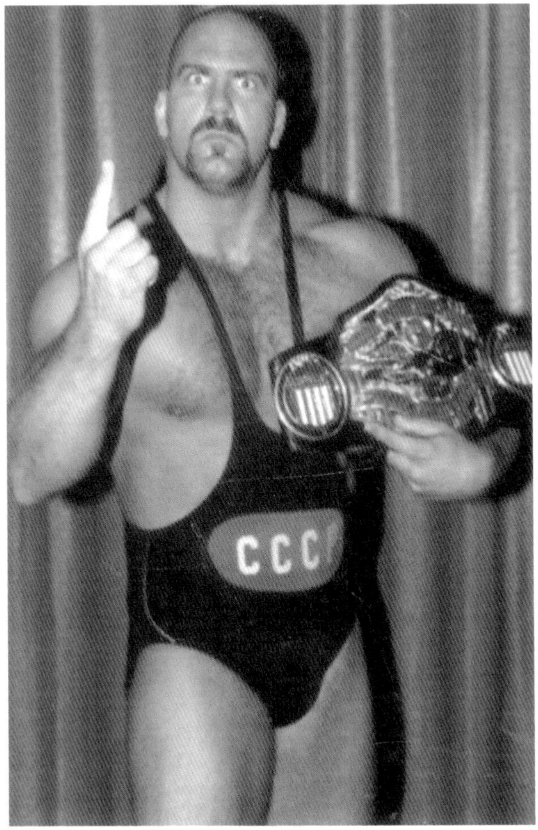

Nikita Koloff
Today, he might be spied power walking on Union Street or at the Research Campus or seen on television with daughter Kolby on Lifetime's *Preachers' Daughters*. But, during the Cold War's final years, Koloff, professional wrestling's "Russian Nightmare," played his "evil" part with such bone-crunching panache that he was the sport's most-hated villain in the 1980s. Conversely, in real life, he is a friendly, inspirational figure and evangelical minister. (Courtesy of Nikita Koloff.)

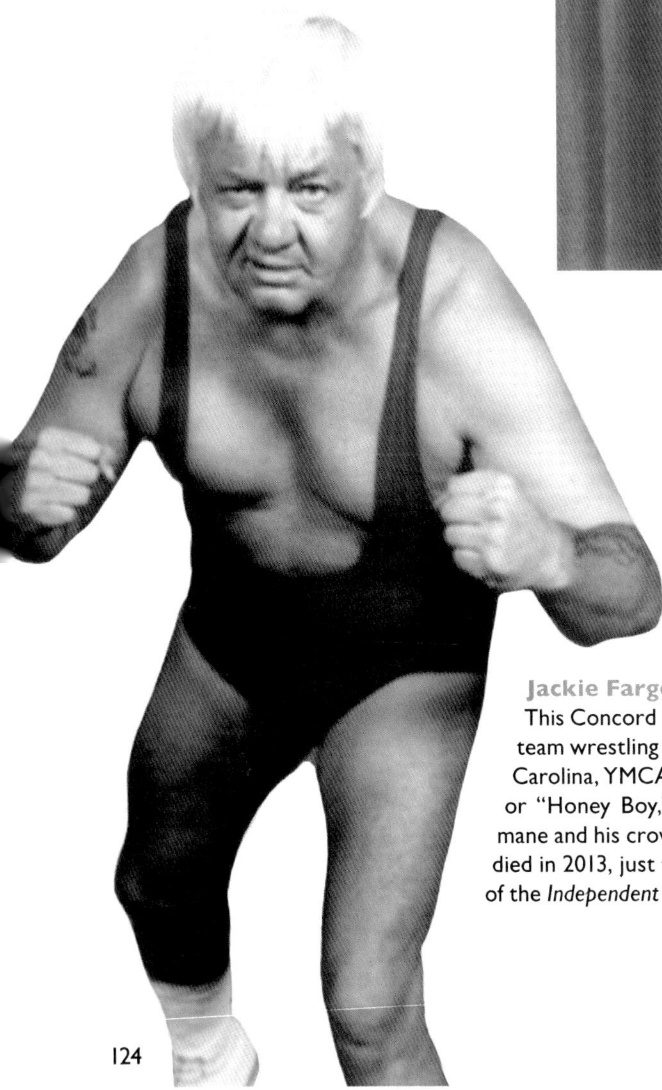

Jackie Fargo
This Concord native, born Henry Faggart, launched his tag-team wrestling career in the 1950s at the Goldsboro, North Carolina, YMCA. Sometimes known in the ring as "Wildman" or "Honey Boy," Fargo's trademarks were his white-blond mane and his crowd-pleasing gait, called the "Fargo Strut." He died in 2013, just two days shy of his 83rd birthday. (Courtesy of the *Independent Tribune*.)

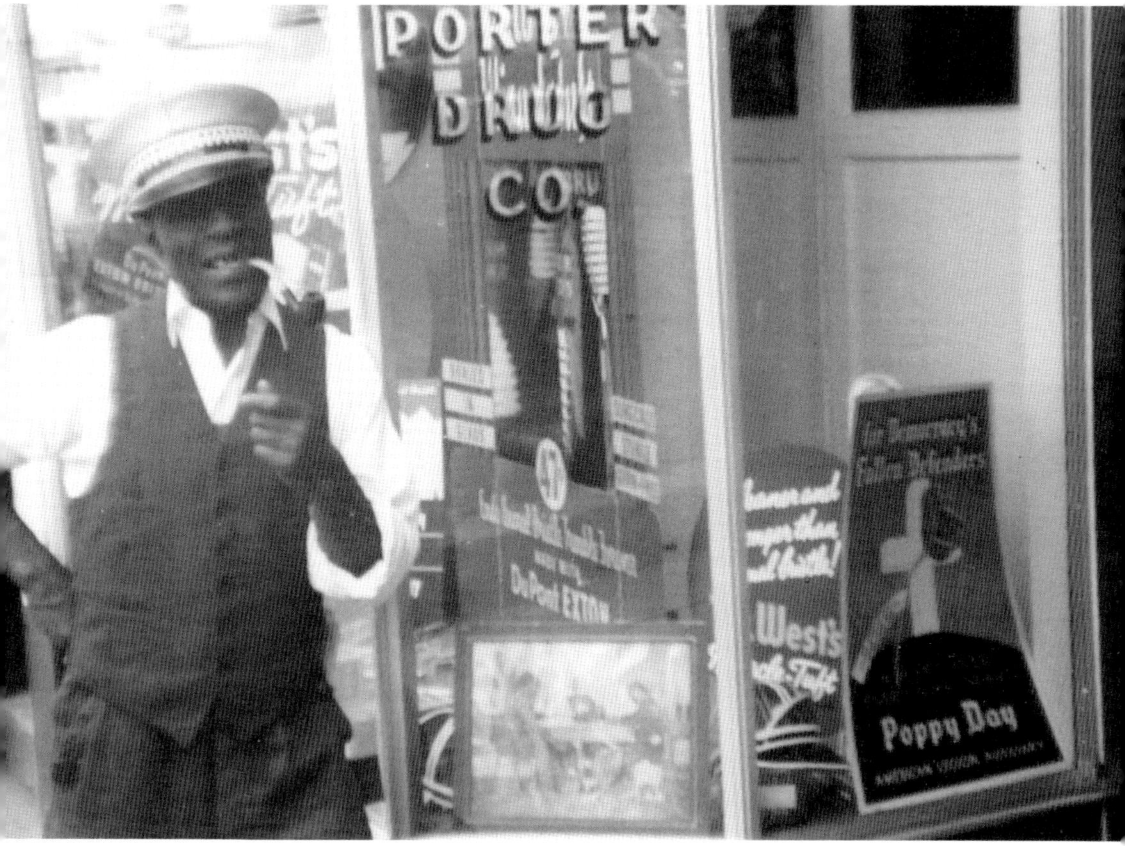

William Mason

His death notice in the January 13, 1975, *Concord Tribune* referred to Mason, who was born in 1882, as a "widely known Concord eccentric." Others might call him a "card" or a "character." Whatever the descriptor, this midcentury frequenter of downtown Concord businesses was best known as the city's unofficial "traffic cop," pretending to direct vehicles at the town square of Union Street and Depot Street (now Cabarrus Avenue).

An oft-told story attributed to Mason is said to have occurred one day when he was on his traffic "beat." An out-of-town motorist asked him, "Could you tell me how to get to the Concord Church of God?" Scratching his chin while briefly pondering the query, Mason, pointing up North Union Street toward its three churches, is said to have replied, "Well, I know Mr. Burrage has got a church up the street. And I know Mr. Cannon's got a church. And so does Mr. Coltrane." And, after a dramatic pause, he pronounced, "But I don't think God has got a church in Concord!"

It is not known whether this anecdote actually happened or is merely an urban legend. Yet this tale takes locals back to a gentler time, when a man of simple means was offered a "job" and was appreciated by his community. (Courtesy of Rosemary Goodman.)

INDEX

INDEX